The questions were highly situational which forced me to perform some level of analysis in trying to determine the most appropriate answer. The questions were also structured in a way that allows one to use common sense to rule out incorrect choices but at the same time did not explicitly present the correct answer. The answers that were provided in the package did not simply state the correct letter but fully explained why the answer was correct and why the other choices were incorrect. This methodology was very helpful during my exam study preparation because I was able to effectively connect the *PMBOK® Guide* concepts with the specific situations and why the actions taken were appropriate or inappropriate.

—Barry Mascoe

Sample Exam Questions™:
PMI® Project Management Professional (PMP®)

Sixth Edition

John A. Estrella, PhD, CMC, PMP
Charles Duncan, PhD, PMP
Sami Zahran, PhD, PMP
Rossetta Sornabala, MBA, PMP, PMI-ACP
Jamal El Ali, MBA, PMP, CSM

ISBN: 978-0-9784354-8-6
ISBN (eBook): 978-0-9784354-9-3

Agilitek Corporation
PO Box 77045
6579 Highway 7
Markham, ON L3P 0C8
Canada

agilitek.com

About the Authors

John A. Estrella, *PhD, CMC, PMP,* is the Co-Founder and President of Agilitek Corporation and Brain Sensei Inc.; Academic Coordinator and Course Instructor at The G. Raymond Chang School of Continuing Education at Ryerson University; and a Member of the Board of Governors and National Commissioner at Scouts Canada.

Charles Duncan, *PhD, PMP, APM Practitioner Qualification*, and recent board level appointment in Cloud Security, manages a consulting group that specializes in software contract development, technical project trouble shooting, and management training.

Sami Zahran, *PhD, PMP*, has over three decades of experience in the software industry assuming senior positions with large organizations including ICL, the United Nations, DEC, and currently with IBM. Sami regularly teaches courses on his areas of expertise, and frequently speaks at numerous international conferences and workshops.

Rossetta Sornabala, MBA, PMP, PMI-ACP, has provided thought leadership for IT infrastructure projects including large-scale transformation, migrations, implementations, change management and process realignment initiatives associated with M&A activities in Fortune 500 companies.

Jamal El Ali, MBA, PMP, CSM, developed Jamal's Four-Step Process to help organizations recover their troubled and failing projects and keep them on track. He is an author, a consultant and a lecturer at The G. Raymond Chang School of Continuing Education at Ryerson University.

Contact Information

Agilitek Corporation
PO Box 77045
6579 Highway 7
Markham, ON L3P 0C8
Canada

agilitek.com

Preface to the Sixth Edition

With the release of the *A Guide to the Project Management Body of Knowledge (PMBOK® Guide)* Sixth Edition, the Project Management Institute (PMI) changed the names of some knowledge areas, and added and updated processes across process groups. PMI also released the *Agile Practice Guide* along with the *PMBOK® Guide.* Both of these guides were incorporated into this edition.

Preface

This book was designed to help you prepare, in a time-efficient manner, for PMI's PMP exam. The distilled format of this book will provide you with the fundamental knowledge in project management as an aid to passing the exam with the minimum amount of effort.

We wrote this book with four categories of readers in mind: planners, crammers, refreshers, and teachers.

Planners. Planners are very deliberate in their approach to taking the exam. They thoroughly research the topic and allocate sufficient time to prepare for the exam. These types of readers can quickly dive right into Chapter 3, "Practice Test A," Chapter 5, "Practice Test B," Chapter 7, "Practice Test C," and Chapter 9, "Practice Test D," to try the four sets of sample exam questions. If you feel confident about taking the actual exam after answering the practice questions, you may skip the solutions in Chapter 4, "Answers to Practice Test A," Chapter 6, "Answers to Practice Test B,", Chapter 8, "Answers to Practice Test C,", and Chapter 10, "Answers to Practice Test D."

Crammers. Crammers should make sure to carefully read the information in this Preface before attempting the sample exam questions in Chapters 3, 5, 7, and 9. If you did not score well on the practice questions, carefully read the solutions in Chapters 4, 6, 8, and 10.

Refreshers. If you previously failed the exam or have taken an exam preparation course but would like to further boost your confidence, we consider you to be part of the refreshers group. Try the sample exam questions to determine your areas of strength and weakness. Read the corresponding sections in the Project Management Body of Knowledge (*PMBOK® Guide*) for your weak areas and focus on the same topics in the solution chapters.

Teachers. Teachers may use the book as a valuable course supplement. They can measure students' understanding of each knowledge area by focusing on specific questions from Chapter 4, Chapter 6, Chapter 8, and Chapter 10.

Chapter 1, "Quick Review Questions," and Chapter 2, "Quick Review Solutions," are meant to be a quick review before you try the practice questions. Make sure that you can confidently answer all the questions in Chapter 1 and that you have reviewed the correct answers in Chapter 2 before moving on to the remaining chapters.

The PMP exam is scored immediately, so you will know whether you've passed at the conclusion of the test. You're given four hours to complete the exam, which consists of 200 randomly generated questions. Only 175 of the 200 questions are scored. Twenty-five of the 200 questions are *pretest* questions that will appear randomly throughout the exam. These 25 questions are used by PMI to capture statistical information and to determine whether they can or should be used on future exams.

The following table shows the breakdown of the actual exam questions by domain.

Domain	Percent of Questions	Number of Questions
1. Initiating the project	13%	26
2. Planning the project	24%	48
3. Executing the project	31%	62
4. Monitoring and controlling the project	25%	50
5. Closing the project	7%	14
Total	100%	200

If you are unsure how to answer a question, use the process of elimination. Eliminate one choice that you know is incorrect. This simple trick will increase your likelihood of guessing the correct answer from 25% to 33%. For the remaining choices, determine which one seems *correct* but is not appropriate or relevant for the question. After you do this, you will be left with two choices, thus giving you a 50% chance of answering the question correctly. If the two remaining choices appear to be both correct, make an educated guess and pick the answer that is *more correct* than the other. In contrast, you can also select an answer that is *least incorrect* compared to the other remaining choice.

As you go through each question, make sure to pace yourself properly. If you find yourself spending too much time on a question, just mark it and proceed to the next question. You can always go back later. Lastly, before you start the exam, write down all formulas, acronyms, and other terms on a blank piece of paper that will be provided to you. It is best to do this when your mind is still fresh. This technique will enable you to easily recall important information later on.

Disclaimer

Although every effort was made to ensure the accuracy of the contents of this book, we cannot guarantee 100% correctness of the information contained herein. Likewise, we cannot guarantee with 100% certainty that reading this book will result in you passing the exam.

If you find any factual anomalies, spelling mistakes, or grammatical errors in the book, kindly send your discoveries, comments, and suggestions to contact@agilitek.com.

Good luck on the exam!

Acknowledgment

This book would not have been possible without the dedicated effort of numerous individuals, including the founders, supporters, and volunteers of the Project Management Institute (PMI).

We also would like to thank Luisito Pangilinan, A. J. Sobczak, Roserene Balana, Norma Nieves, Raymond Chung, Rhea Bautista, and Barry Mascoe for their assistance with this book.

Vanina Mangano and Dan Gindin served as technical editors when we aligned this book to the *PMBOK® Guide* Fourth Edition.

Luisito and Roserene helped us again when we updated this book for the *PMBOK® Guide* Fifth Edition. Shari Brand provided valuable comments to the questions and explanations.

When we updated this book to align with the *PMBOK® Guide* Sixth Edition, Luisito redesigned the cover page. Shari served as the technical editor.

Table of Contents

Chapter 1: Quick Review Questions

The following questions are categorized by the knowledge areas of *A Guide to the Project Management Body of Knowledge, Sixth Edition (PMBOK® Guide)*. Take note that some questions came from the Appendix. There are also questions from the Project Management Institute's (PMI) *Code of Ethics and Professional Conduct*. Before you sit for the Project Management Professional (PMP)® exam, you should be familiar with these publications and what is covered in them. The following questions are designed to test your familiarity with them, as well as your understanding and knowledge of general project management terms and concepts.

A Guide to the Project Management Body of Knowledge, Sixth Edition

General Knowledge of *PMBOK® Guide*

1. At a minimum, you need to be familiar with at least four PMI publications before taking the PMP exam. List them in the space provided below.

   a. _____

   b. _____

   c. _____

   d. _____

2. List the five process groups in the order that they appear in the *PMBOK® Guide*.

   a. INITIATION

   b. PLANNING

   c. EXECUTION

   d. MONITORING

   e. Closing

3. List the ten Knowledge Areas in the order that they appear in the *PMBOK® Guide*.

   a. _____

   b. _____

   c. _____

   d. _____

   e. _____

   f. _____

   g. _____

   h. _____

   i. _____

   j. _____

4. List the three key components of a process as outlined in the *PMBOK® Guide*.

   a. _____

   b. _____

   c. _____

5. Organizational structure is an enterprise environmental factor that influences a project. List the ten common organizational structure types.

   a. _____

   b. _____

   c. _____

   d. _____

   e. _____

   f. _____

   g. _____

   h. _____

   i. _____

   j. _____

6. List the two processes that should be performed when starting a project.

   a. _____

   b. _____

7. List the one process that should be performed when closing a project.

   a. _____

8. The *PMBOK® Guide* consistently uses the verb-noun format to describe each process. If you carefully examine the verb portion of the process name, it should give you an indication that a given process belongs to a certain process group. The noun portion of the process name should also give you a hint of the expected deliverable for that process. For example, the Develop Project Management Plan process indicates that you need to "develop" something after you have started your project—with the "Project Management Plan" as the expected deliverable. List the 10 common verbs that are used to name the processes within the Planning process group.

a. _____

b. _____

c. _____

d. _____

e. _____

f. _____

g. _____

h. _____

i. _____

j. _____

9. List the six common verbs that are used to name the processes within the Executing process group.

a. _____

b. _____

c. _____

d. _____

e. _____

f. _____

10. List the four common verbs that are used to name the processes within the Monitoring and Controlling process group.

    a. _____

    b. _____

    c. _____

    d. _____

Chapter 4: Project Integration Management

11. List the 10 subsidiary plans of the project management plan.

    a. _____

    b. _____

    c. _____

    d. _____

    e. _____

    f. _____

    g. _____

    h. _____

    i. _____

    j. _____

Chapter 5: Project Scope Management

12. List the eight tools and techniques that a project manager can use when collecting requirements.

    a. _____

    b. _____

    c. _____

    d. _____

    e. _____

    f. _____

    g. _____

    h. _____

13. List the three common methods for creating a work breakdown structure (WBS)?

    a. _____

    b. _____

    c. _____

Chapter 6: Project Schedule Management

14. What are the four types of activity dependencies or logical relationships?

    a. _____

    b. _____

    c. _____

    d. _____

15. List eight activity durations estimating tools and techniques.

    a. _____

    b. _____

    c. _____

    d. _____

    e. _____

    f. _____

    g. _____

    h. _____

16. What are the two common formulas for three-point estimating?

    a. _____

    b. _____

Chapter 7: Project Cost Management

Define the following Earned Value Management (EVM) acronyms.

17. What is PV? _____

18. What is EV? _____

19. What is AC? _____

20. What is SV? _____

21. What is CV? _____

22. What is SPI? _____

23. What is CPI? _____

24. What is EAC? _____

25. What is ETC? _____

26. What is TCPI? _____

27. What is VAC? _____

28. List the two EVM performance index formulas.

    a. _____

    b. _____

29. List the four EVM forecasting formulas for EAC.

    a. _____

    b. _____

    c. _____

    d. _____

30. List the two to-complete performance index formulas.

    a. _____

    b. _____

31. List the two estimate to complete equations.

    a. _____

    b. _____

32. List the three EVM variance analysis measurements.

    a. _____

    b. _____

    c. _____

Chapter 8: Project Quality Management

Define the following quality-specific acronyms.

33. What is PDCA? _____

34. What is TQM? _____

35. What is ISO? _____

36. What is COQ? _____

37. Name the two costs of quality.

    a. _____

    b. _____

38. What are the two categories of the cost of quality for avoiding failures?

    a. _____

    b. _____

39. What are the two categories of the cost of quality where money must be spent because of failures?

    a. _____

    b. _____

40. List the five components of a SIPOC value chain.

    a. _____

    b. _____

    c. _____

    d. _____

    e. _____

Chapter 9: Project Resource Management

41. List in order the five stages of developing a team.

    a. _____

    b. _____

    c. _____

    d. _____

    e. _____

42. What are the five general techniques for resolving conflict?

    a. _____

    b. _____

    c. _____

    d. _____

    e. _____

Chapter 10: Project Communications Management

43. List the sequence of steps in a basic communication model.

    a. _____

    b. _____

    c. _____

    d. _____

    e. _____

44. List the three broad classifications of communication methods.

    a. _____

    b. _____

    c. _____

Chapter 11: Project Risk Management

45. List five strategies for negative risks or threats.

    a. _____

    b. _____

    c. _____

    d. _____

    e. _____

46. List five strategies for positive risks or opportunities.

   a. _____

   b. _____

   c. _____

   d. _____

   e. _____

Chapter 12: Project Procurement Management

47. What are the three major types of contracts?

   a. _____

   b. _____

   c. _____

There are six potential variations of the major types of contracts.

48. What is FFP?   _____

49. What is FPIF?   _____

50. What is FP-EPA?   _____

51. What is CPFF?   _____

52. What is CPIF?   _____

53. What is CPAF?   _____

Chapter 13: Project Stakeholder Management

54. List the five data representation models that can used for stakeholder identification.

    a. _____

    b. _____

    c. _____

    d. _____

    e. _____

55. List the five levels of stakeholder engagement.

    a. _____

    b. _____

    c. _____

    d. _____

    e. _____

56. How can feedback be collected?

    a. _____

    b. _____

    c. _____

    d. _____

    e. _____

57. List three team data analysis techniques for monitoring stakeholders.

    a. _____

    b. _____

    c. _____

58. What are the two decision making techniques used when monitoring stakeholders?

   a. _____

   b. _____

59. What communication techniques are used for monitoring stakeholders?

   a. _____

   b. _____

60. List five interpersonal and team skills for monitoring stakeholder engagement.

   a. _____

   b. _____

   c. _____

   d. _____

   e. _____

Glossary – Common Acronyms

Define the following acronyms.

61. What is CCB? _____

62. What is CPM? _____

63. What is EF? _____

64. What is EVM? _____

65. What is ES? _____

66. What is FPEPA? _____

67. What is IFB? _____

68. What is LF? _____

69. What is LOE? _____

70. What is OBS? _____

71. What is PDM? _____

72. What is PMBOK? _____

73. What is QFD? _____

74. What is RACI? _____

75. What is RAM? _____

76. What is RBS? _____

77. What is RFI? _____

78. What is RFP? _____

79. What is RFQ? _____

80. What is SOW? _____

81. What is SWOT? _____

PMI's Code of Ethics and Professional Conducts

82. The *PMI Code of Ethics and Professional Conduct* applies to which individuals?

    a. _____

    b. _____

    c. _____

    d. _____

83. What two types of responsibility, fairness and honesty standards were mentioned in the *PMI Code of Ethics and Professional Conduct*?

    a. _____

    b. _____

Key Concepts and Process Groups

This section presents questions based on key project management concepts (e.g., projects, programs, portfolios, project management skills, etc.) and various processes from initiating to closing projects.

Fill in the blanks or answer the following questions.

84. _____ are temporary initiatives with defined start and end dates.

85. The concept of incrementally and continually refining the characteristics of a product, service or result as the project progresses is known as _____.

86. Unlike projects, _____ are ongoing initiatives that generate repetitive results.

87. _____ are individuals, groups or organizations with a vested interest in the execution and/or the outcome of the project.

88. The _____ is usually an executive within the organization who has authority over the project from providing funding to influencing stakeholders.

89. The _____ focuses on specified project objectives, controls assigned project resources, and manages the constraints of individual projects.

90. _____ are groups of related projects.

91. _____ include projects, programs and subportfolios.

92. The _____ serves as a central oversight in the management of projects and programs within an organization.

93. What is a key disadvantage for a project manager when working in a functional organization? _____

94. _____ are considered the opposite of functional organizations.

95. _____, _____, and _____ are the three common types of matrix structures.

96. The two categories of organizational process assets are _____, and _____.

97. _____ refer to conditions which are beyond the control of the project team but can influence the project outcome.

98. Project sponsor, project team, functional managers, customers/users, and program manager are examples of _____.

99. Project management administrative staff can be _____ and/or

_____.

Initiating the Project

Determine if each of the following statements is true or false. If the statement is false, provide the correct answer to the underlined term(s) to make the statement true.

100. The <u>Initiating Process Group</u> includes processes to obtain formal authorization to start a project or phase.

   _____

101. Processes in the Initiating Process Group help select the <u>project sponsor</u>.

   _____

102. <u>Project boundaries</u> define the point in time when a decision is made for the project to proceed to its completion.

   _____

103. The key purpose of the Initiating Process Group is to <u>develop the project charter and to plan stakeholder management</u>.

   _____

104. Large complex projects should be <u>managed as a program</u>.

   _____

105. A decision can be made to continue, delay, or discontinue a project at <u>the beginning of each phase</u>.

   _____

106. Project charter is an output of the <u>Identify Stakeholders</u> process.

   _____

107. A business case may be created as a result of <u>market demand, organizational need, customer request, technological advance, legal requirement, ecological impacts, and/or social need</u>.

   _____

108. Examples of agreements include <u>contracts, letters of intent, and email</u>.

    _____

109. Interpersonal and team skills include <u>conflict management, facilitation, and meeting management</u>.

    _____

110. The <u>project charter</u> documents the business needs, assumptions and constraints, and high-level requirements.

    _____

111. The <u>Develop Project Charter</u> process identifies the individuals, groups, or organizations that could impact or be impacted by the project.

    _____

112. The <u>stakeholder management plan</u> is an output of the Identify Stakeholders process.

    _____

113. Stakeholders can be classified based on their <u>level of authority and level of concern</u> regarding the project outcomes.

    _____

Planning the Project

Match the following Planning Process Group outputs to the correct knowledge area.

114. Basis of estimates   _____

115. Communications management plan   _____

116. Team charter   _____

117. Schedule management plan   _____

118. Quality metrics   _____

119. Project management plan   _____

120. Requirements traceability matrix   _____

121. Risk register   _____

122. Source selection criteria   _____

123. Stakeholder management plan   _____

Knowledge Areas

A. Project Integration Management
B. Project Scope Management
C. Project Schedule Management
D. Project Cost Management
E. Project Quality Management
F. Project Resource Management
G. Project Communications Management
H. Project Risk Management
I. Project Procurement Management
J. Project Stakeholder Management

Determine if each of the following statements is true or false. If the statement is false, provide the correct answer to the underlined term(s) to make the statement true.

124. Focus groups comprise of cross-functional stakeholders.

   _____

125. The requirements traceability matrix enables the organization to link each requirement to business and project objective.

   _____

126. The project scope management plan documents how the project team will define the project scope, develop the work breakdown structure, and control the changes.

   _____

127. The Create WBS process enables the project team to subdivide the project into smaller and more manageable components.

   _____

128. Regression analysis can be used if it is not yet possible to decompose a deliverable or subcomponent into the level of detail where a WBS can be developed.

   _____

129. The scope baseline includes the <u>description of work, the WBS, and the project schedule.</u>

_____

130. The lowest level of WBS components is called a <u>work package.</u>

_____

Fill in the following blanks.

131. _____ and _____ are examples of scheduling methods.

132. The _____ can establish the unit of measure, level of accuracy and control thresholds.

133. The horizontal value chain of a SIPOC model can be used to draw a
_____.

134. RACI chart is an example of a _____.

135. In the communication channels formula _____, n represents the number of stakeholders.

136. _____ and _____ distributions are commonly used in quantitative risk analysis.

137. _____ can be used to show the probability of all the possible project completion dates.

Executing the Project

Match the following Executing Process Group outputs to the correct process. An output may belong to more than one process.

138. Agreements   _____

139. Change requests   _____

140. Deliverables   _____

141. Issue log   _____

142. Lessons learned register   _____

143. Project communications   _____

144. Resource calendars   _____

145. Selected sellers   _____

146. Team performance assessments   _____

147. Work performance data   _____

Processes

A. Direct and Manage Project Work
B. Manage Project Knowledge
C. Manage Quality
D. Acquire Resources
E. Develop Team
F. Manage Team
G. Manage Communications
H. Implement Risk Responses
I. Conduct Procurements
J. Manage Stakeholder Engagement

Determine if each of the following statements is true or false. If the statement is false, provide the correct answer to the underlined term(s) to make the statement true.

148. The Direct and Manage Project Work process requires the implementation of approved changes such as corrective action, preventive action, and defect repair.

     _____

149. Root cause analysis (RCA) is one of the data analysis tools used when managing quality in a project.

     _____

150. Virtual teams rely heavily on e-mails, conference calls and web-based collaboration tools to fulfill their roles.

     _____

151. Negotiation is an example of interpersonal and team skills.

     _____

152. In the Tuckman ladder, forming occurs after storming.

     _____

153. Examples of <u>interpersonal skills</u> that a project manager may use include conflict management, influencing, and motivation.

_____

154. <u>Proposal evaluation techniques</u> are meetings between the buyer and all prospective sellers.

_____

155. "Most <u>government jurisdictions</u> require public advertising or online posting of pending government contracts".

_____

156. "<u>An issue log</u> is used to document changes that occur during a project."

_____

157. <u>Escalation process</u> can be found in the communications management plan.

_____

Fill in the following blanks.

158. Approved change requests are reviewed and approved for implementation by the

_____.

159. _____ may include corrective action, preventive action, defect repair, and updates.

160. Project team members are considered _____ if they are selected in advance.

161. When a team functions as a well-organized unit, they have achieved the

_____ stage of the Tuckman ladder.

162. _____ is a general conflict resolution technique where parties focus on areas of agreement rather than areas of difference.

163. Nodding, paraphrasing and maintaining eye contact are examples of

_____ techniques.

164. The language of the _____ should reflect all agreements reached.

165. "A _____ is a mutually binding legal agreement that obligates the seller to provide the specified products, services, or results; and obligates the buyer to compensate the seller".

166. The _____ process "allows the project manager to increase support and minimize resistance from stakeholders."

167. Project issues are tracked (added, updated, and closed) using an

_____.

Monitoring and Controlling the Project

Match the following Monitoring and Controlling Process Group outputs to the correct process. An output may belong to more than one process.

168. Work performance reports   _____

169. Approved change requests   _____

170. Work performance information   _____

171. Accepted deliverables   _____

172. Schedule forecasts   _____

173. Cost forecasts   _____

174. Quality control measurements _____

175. Closed procurements   _____

176. Validated deliverables   _____

Processes

A. Monitor and Control Project Work
B. Perform Integrated Change Control
C. Validate Scope
D. Control Scope
E. Control Schedule
F. Control Costs

G. Control Quality
H. Control Resources
I. Monitor Communications
J. Monitor Risks
K. Control Procurements
L. Monitor Stakeholder Engagement

Determine if each of the following statements is true or false. If the statement is false, provide the correct answer to the underlined term(s) to make the statement true.

177. Schedule variance (SV) and schedule performance index (SPI) are typically used for <u>schedule forecasting</u>.

   _____

178. The <u>estimate to complete (ETC)</u> can be compared to the budget at completion (BAC) to determine if the project is still within acceptable tolerance ranges.

   _____

179. Change management plan and configuration management plan are used as inputs to the <u>Validate Scope</u> process.

   _____

180. To bring the project back on track, a project manager may apply <u>schedule compression techniques</u> such as fast tracking or crashing the schedule.

   _____

181. Schedule variance = SV = <u>EV − PV</u>.

   _____

182. Cost variance = CV = <u>PV − AC</u>.

   _____

183. Use the equation AC + [(BAC − EV) / (CPI x SPI)] for <u>EAC forecast for ETC work performed at present CPI</u>.

   _____

184. The equation for <u>TCPI based on BAC</u> is (BAC − EV) / (BAC − AC).

   _____

Fill in the following blanks.

185. Examples of _____ include alternatives analysis, trend analysis, and variance analysis.

186. "The _____ helps to detect the impact of any change or deviation from the scope baseline on the project objectives".

187. The three key dimensions of EVM are _____,

    _____, and _____.

188. Lessons learned register, quality metrics, and test and evaluation documents are used as

    inputs in the _____ process.

189. "_____ are the documented results of Control Quality
    activities."

190. Monitoring residual risk is part of the _____ process.

191. To get paid, vendors issue _____.

192. ADR stands for _____.

Closing the Project

Determine if each of the following statements is true or false. If the statement is false, provide the correct answer to the underlined term(s) to make the statement true.

193. The three tools and techniques of the Close Project or Phase process are expert judgment, data analysis, and meetings.

    _____

194. Dealing with excess project material is an activity associated with the Close Project or Phase process.

    _____

195. As part of the Close Project or Phase process, the project team measures stakeholder satisfaction.

    _____

196. The Close Project or Phase process "is performed once or at predetermined points in the project.

    _____

197. A key output of the Close Project or Phase is when the project team transitions the final product, service, or result.

    _____

198. Formal procurement closure, including terms and conditions of the contract, can be found in the <u>business case</u>.

_____

199. "The <u>final report</u> provides a summary of the project performance."

_____

200. <u>Document analysis, regression analysis, and trend analysis</u> are typically included in the final report summary.

_____

Bonus Questions

Determine if each of the following statements is true or false. If the statement is false, provide the correct answer to the underlined term(s) to make the statement true.

201. <u>Backward pass</u> is a CPM technique for calculating the late start and finish dates.

_____

202. <u>WBS ID</u> is a "numbering system used to uniquely identify each component of the work breakdown structure (WBS)".

_____

203. <u>Summary activity</u> is a "group of related schedule activities aggregated and displayed as a single activity".

_____

204. <u>Hard logic</u> is synonymous with mandatory dependency.

_____

205. <u>Gantt chart</u> is a "special type of bar chart used in sensitivity analysis for comparing the relative importance of the variables."

_____

Chapter 2: Quick Review Solutions

The following questions are categorized by the knowledge areas of *A Guide to the Project Management Body of Knowledge, Sixth Edition (PMBOK® Guide)*. Take note that some questions came from the Appendix. There are also questions from the Project Management Institute's (PMI) *Code of Ethics and Professional Conduct*. Before you sit for the Project Management Professional (PMP)® exam, you should be familiar with these publications and what is covered in them. The following questions are designed to test your familiarity with them, as well as your understanding and knowledge of general project management terms and concepts.

A Guide to the Project Management Body of Knowledge, Sixth Edition Answers

The page numbers refer to the page number of the corresponding text in the *PMBOK® Guide, Sixth Edition.*

General Knowledge of *PMBOK® Guide*

1. At a minimum, you need to be familiar with at least four PMI publications before taking the PMP exam. List them in the space provided below.

    a. *Project Management Professional (PMP®) Handbook*
    b. *PMI Code of Ethics and Professional Conduct*
    c. *A Guide to the Project Management Body of Knowledge (PMBOK® Guide)—Sixth Edition*
    d. *Project Management Professional (PMP®) Examination Content Outline*

2. List the five process groups in the order that they appear in the *PMBOK® Guide* (page 23).

    a. Initiating
    b. Planning
    c. Executing
    d. Monitoring and Controlling
    e. Closing

3. List the ten Knowledge Areas in the order that they appear in the *PMBOK® Guide* (pages 23-24).

    a. Project Integration Management
    b. Project Scope Management
    c. Project Schedule Management
    d. Project Cost Management
    e. Project Quality Management
    f. Project Resource Management
    g. Project Communications Management
    h. Project Risk Management
    i. Project Procurement Management
    j. Project Stakeholder Management

4. List the three key components of a process as outlined in the *PMBOK® Guide* (page 22).

    a. Inputs
    b. Tools and techniques
    c. Outputs

5. Organizational structure is an enterprise environmental factor that influences a project. List the six common organizational structure types (page 47).

    a. Organic or simple
    b. Functional (centralized)
    c. Multi-divisional
    d. Matrix – strong
    e. Matrix – weak
    f. Matrix – balanced
    g. Project-oriented (composite, hybrid)
    h. Virtual
    i. Hybrid
    j. PMO

6. List the two processes that should be performed when starting a project (page 25).

    a. Develop Project Charter
    b. Identify Stakeholders

7. List the one process that should be performed when closing a project (page 25).

    a. Close Project or Phase

8. The *PMBOK® Guide* consistently uses the verb-noun format to describe each process. If you carefully examine the verb portion of the process name, it should give you an indication that a given process belongs to a certain process group. The noun portion of the process name should also give you a hint of the expected deliverable for that process. For example, the Develop Project Management Plan process indicates that you need to "develop" something after you have started your project—with the "Project Management Plan" as the expected deliverable. List the 10 common verbs that are used to name the processes within the Planning process group (page 25).

    a. Collect   f. Estimate
    b. Create   g. Identify
    c. Define   h. Perform
    d. Determine   i. Plan
    e. Develop   j. Sequence

- Integration – Develop Project Management Plan
- Scope – Plan Scope Management, Collect Requirements, Define Scope, and Create WBS
- Schedule – Plan Schedule Management, Define Activities, Sequence Activities, Estimate Activity Durations, and Develop Schedule
- Cost – Plan Cost Management, Estimate Costs, and Determine Budget
- Quality – Plan Quality Management
- Resource Management – Plan Resource Management
- Communications – Plan Communications Management
- Risk Management – Plan Risk Management, Identify Risks, Perform Qualitative Risk Analysis, Perform Quantitative Risk Analysis, and Plan Risk Responses
- Procurement – Plan Procurement Management
- Stakeholder – Plan Stakeholder Management

9. List the six common verbs that are used to name the processes within the Executing process group (page 25.

   a. Acquire
   b. Conduct
   c. *Develop
   d. Direct
   e. Implement
   f. Manage

- Integration – Direct and Manage Project Work, and Manage Project Knowledge
- Quality – Manage Quality
- Resource – Acquire Resources, Develop Team, and Manage Team
- Communications – Manage Communications
- Procurement – Conduct Procurements
- Stakeholder – Manage Stakeholder Engagement

*Note that the verb "develop" is also used to describe some of the process names in the Initiating and Planning process groups.

10. List the four common verbs that are used to name the processes within the Monitoring and Controlling process group (page 25).

   a. Control
   b. Monitor
   c. *Perform
   d. Validate

- Integration – Monitor and Control Project Work, and Perform Integrated Change Control
- Scope – Validate Scope and Control Scope
- Schedule – Control Schedule
- Cost – Control Costs
- Quality – Control Quality
- Resource – Control Resources
- Communications – Control Communications
- Risk – Monitor Risks
- Procurement – Control Procurements
- Stakeholder – Monitor Stakeholder Engagement

*Note that the verb "perform" is also used to describe some of the process names in the Planning process groups.

Chapter 4: Project Integration Management

11. List the 10 subsidiary plans of the project management plan (page 87).

a. Scope management plan
b. Requirements management plan
c. Schedule management plan
d. Cost management plan
e. Quality management plan
f. Resource management plan
g. Communications management plan
h. Risk management plan
i. Procurement management plan
j. Stakeholder management plan

Chapter 5: Project Scope Management

12. List the eight tools and techniques that a project manager can use when collecting requirements (page 138).

a. Expert judgment
b. Data gathering
c. Data analysis
d. Decision making
e. Data representation
f. Interpersonal and team skills
g. Context diagram
h. Prototypes

13. List the three common methods for creating a work breakdown structure (WBS) (page 159)?

    a. Top-down approach
    b. Organization-specific guidelines
    c. WBS template

Chapter 6: Project Schedule Management

14. What are the four types of activity dependencies or logical relationships (page 190)?

    a. Finish-to-start (FS)
    b. Finish-to-finish (FF)
    c. Start-to-start (SS)
    d. Start-to-finish (SF)

15. List eight activity durations estimating tools and techniques (page 195).

    a. Expert judgment
    b. Analogous estimating
    c. Parametric estimating
    d. Three-point estimating
    e. Bottom-up estimating
    f. Data analysis
    g. Decision making
    h. Meetings

16. What are the two common formulas for three-point estimating (page 245)?

    a. Triangular distribution: $cE = (cO + cM + cP) / 3$
    b. Beta distribution (traditional): $cE = (cO + 4cM + cP) / 6$

Chapter 7: Project Cost Management

Define the following Earned Value Management (EVM) acronyms (page 267).

17. What is PV?   Planned value
18. What is EV?   Earned value
19. What is AC?   Actual cost
20. What is SV?   Schedule variance
21. What is CV?   Cost variance
22. What is SPI?   Schedule performance index
23. What is CPI?   Cost performance index
24. What is EAC?   Estimate at completion
25. What is ETC?   Estimate to complete
26. What is TCPI?   To-complete performance index
27. What is VAC?   Variance at completion

28. List the two EVM performance index formulas (page 267).

    a.   SPI = EV / PV
    b.   CPI = EV / AC

29. List the four EVM forecasting formulas for EAC (page 267).

    a.   EAC = AC + bottom-up ETC
    b.   EAC = AC + BAC − EV
    c.   EAC = BAC / CPI
    d.   EAC = AC + [(BAC − EV) / (CPI x SPI)]

30. List the two to-complete performance index formulas (page 267).

    a.   TCPI based on the BAC = (BAC − EV) / (BAC − AC)
    b.   TCPI based on the EAC = (BAC − EV) / (EAC − AC)

31. List the two estimate to complete equations (page 267).

    a.   ETC = EAC − AC
    b.   ETC = Reestimate

32. List the three EVM variance analysis measurements (page 267).

    a.   CV = EV − AC
    b.   SV = EV − PV
    c.   VAC = BAC − EAC

Chapter 8: Project Quality Management

Define the following quality-specific acronyms (pages 274-275).

33. What is PDCA?	Plan-do-check-act cycle
34. What is TQM?	Total quality management
35. What is ISO?	International Organization for Standardization
36. What is COQ?	Cost of quality

37. Name the two costs of quality (page 283).

    a.   Cost of conformance
    b.   Cost of nonconformance

38. What are the two categories of the cost of quality for avoiding failures (page 283)?

    a.   Prevention costs
    b.   Appraisal costs

39. What are the two categories of the cost of quality where money must be spent because of failures (page 283)?

    a.   Internal failure costs
    b.   External failure costs

40. List the five components of a SIPOC value chain (pages 284-285).

    a.   Supplier
    b.   Input
    c.   Process
    d.   Output
    e.   Customer

Chapter 9: Project Resource Management

41. List in order the five stages of developing a team (page 338).

    a.   Forming
    b.   Storming
    c.   Norming
    d.   Performing
    e.   Adjourning

42. What are the five general techniques for resolving conflict (page 349)?

    a.   Withdraw/avoid
    b.   Smooth/accommodate
    c.   Compromise/reconcile
    d.   Force/direct
    e.   Collaborate/problem solve

Chapter 10: Project Communications Management

43. List the sequence of steps in a basic communication model (pages 371-372).

    a.   Encode
    b.   Transmit message
    c.   Decode
    d.   Acknowledge
    e.   Feedback/response

44. List the three broad classifications of communication methods (page 374).

    a.   Interactive communication
    b.   Push communication
    c.   Pull communication

Chapter 11: Project Risk Management

45. List five strategies for negative risks or threats (pages 442-443).

    a. Escalate
    b. Avoid
    c. Transfer
    d. Mitigate
    e. Accept

46. List five strategies for positive risks or opportunities (page 444).

    a. Escalate
    b. Exploit
    c. Share
    d. Enhance
    e. Accept

Chapter 12: Project Procurement Management

47. What are the three major types of contracts (pages 471-472)?

    a. Fixed-price contracts (also known as lump sum)
    b. Cost-reimbursable contracts (also known as cost plus)
    c. Time and material contracts (T&M)

There are six potential variations of the major types of contracts (pages 471-472).

48. What is FFP?	Firm fixed price contracts
49. What is FPIF?	Fixed price incentive fee contracts
50. What is FP-EPA?	Fixed price with economic price adjustments contracts
51. What is CPFF?	Cost plus fixed fee contracts
52. What is CPIF?	Cost plus incentive fee contracts
53. What is CPAF?	Cost plus award fee contracts

Chapter 13: Project Stakeholder Management

54. List the five data representation models that can used for stakeholder identification (pages 512-513).

    a. Power/interest grid
    b. Stakeholder cube
    c. Salience model
    d. Directions of influence
    e. Prioritization

55. List the five levels of stakeholder engagement (page 521).

    a. Unaware
    b. Resistant
    c. Neutral
    d. Supportive
    e. Leading

56. How can feedback be collected (page 527)?

    a. Conversations (both formal and informal)
    b. Issue identification and discussion
    c. Meetings
    d. Progress reporting
    e. Surveys

57. List three data analysis techniques for monitoring stakeholders (page 533).

    f. Alternatives analysis
    g. Root cause analysis
    h. Stakeholder analysis

58. What are the two decision making techniques used when monitoring stakeholders (page 534)?

    a. Multicriteria decision analysis
    b. Voting

59. What communication techniques are used for monitoring stakeholders (page 534)?

    a. Feedback
    b. Presentations

60. List five interpersonal and team skills for monitoring stakeholder engagement (page 534).

    a. Active listening
    b. Cultural awareness
    c. Leadership
    d. Networking
    e. Political awareness

Glossary – Common Acronyms

Define the following acronyms (pages 696-697).

61. What is CCB?   Change control board
62. What is CPM?   Critical path methodology
63. What is EF?   Early finish date

64. What is EVM?	Earned value management
65. What is ES?	Early start date
66. What is FPEPA?	Fixed price with economic price adjustments
67. What is IFB?	Invitation for bid
68. What is LF?	Late finish date
69. What is LOE?	Level of effort
70. What is OBS?	Organizational breakdown structure
71. What is PDM?	Precedence diagramming method
72. What is PMBOK?	Project Management Body of Knowledge
73. What is QFD?	Quality function deployment
74. What is RACI?	Responsible, accountable, consult, and inform
75. What is RAM?	Responsibility assignment matrix
76. What is RBS?	Risk breakdown structure
77. What is RFI?	Request for information
78. What is RFP?	Request for proposal
79. What is RFQ?	Request for quotation
80. What is SOW?	Statement of work
81. What is SWOT?	Strengths, weaknesses, opportunities, and threats

PMI's Code of Ethics and Professional Conducts

The page numbers refer to the page number of the corresponding text in the *PMI's Code of Ethics and Professional Conduct.*

82. The *PMI Code of Ethics and Professional Conduct* applies to which individuals (page 1)?

a. All PMI members
b. Non-members who hold a PMI certification
c. Non-members who apply to commence a PMI certification process
d. Non-members who serve PMI in a volunteer capacity

83. What two types of responsibility, fairness and honesty standards were mentioned in the *PMI Code of Ethics and Professional Conduct* (page 2)?

a. Aspirational Conduct
b. Mandatory Conduct

Key Concepts and Process Groups

The page numbers refer to the page number of the corresponding text in the *PMBOK® Guide, Sixth Edition.*

This section presents questions based on key project management concepts (e.g., projects, programs, portfolios, project management skills, etc.) and various processes from initiating to closing projects.

Fill in the blanks or answer the follow questions.

84. Projects are temporary initiatives with defined start and end dates (page 4).

85. The concept of incrementally and continually refining the characteristics of a product, service or result as the project progresses is known as progressive elaboration (page 565).

86. Unlike projects, operations are ongoing initiatives that generate repetitive results (page 16).

87. Stakeholders are individuals, groups or organizations with a vested interest in the execution and/or the outcome of the project (page 550).

88. The project sponsor is usually an executive within the organization who has authority over the project from providing funding to influencing stakeholders (page 34).

89. The project manager focuses on specified project objectives, controls assigned project resources, and manages the constraints of individual projects (page 29).

90. Programs are groups of related projects (page 11).

91. Portfolios include projects, programs and subportfolios (page 11).

92. The project management office (PMO) serves as a central oversight in the management of projects and programs within an organization (page 48).

93. What is a key disadvantage for a project manager when working in a functional organization (page 47)? They have little to no formal authority.

94. Project-oriented (composite, hybrid) organizations are considered the opposite of functional organizations (page 47).

95. Weak, balanced, and strong are the three common types of matrix structures (page 47).

96. The two categories of organizational process assets are processes, policies, and procedures, and organizational knowledge bases (page 39).

97. Enterprise environmental factors refer to conditions which are beyond the control of the project team but can influence the project outcome (page 38).
98. Project sponsor, project team, functional managers, customers/users, and program manager are examples of stakeholders (page 550).

99. Project management administrative staff can be dedicated and/or part-time (page 37).

Initiating the Project

Determine if each of the following statements is true or false. If the statement is false, provide the correct answer to the underlined term(s) to make the statement true.

100. The <u>Initiating Process Group</u> includes processes to obtain formal authorization to start a project or phase (page 23).

    True

101. Processes in the Initiating Process Group help select the <u>project sponsor</u> (page 23).

    False; project manager

102. <u>Project boundaries</u> define the point in time when a decision is made for the project to proceed to its completion (page 562).

    True

103. The key purpose of the Initiating Process Group is to <u>develop the project charter and to plan stakeholder management</u> (page 561).

    False; align the stakeholders' expectations to the project's purpose

104. Large complex projects should be <u>managed as a program</u> (page 562).

    False; divided into separate phases

105. A decision can be made to continue, delay, or discontinue a project at <u>the beginning of each phase</u> (page 562). <u>True</u>.

106. Project charter is an output of the <u>Identify Stakeholders</u> process (page 71).

    False; Develop Project Charter

107. A business case may be created as a result of <u>market demand, organizational need, customer request, technological advance, legal requirement, ecological impacts, and/or social need</u> (page 78).

    True

108. Examples of agreements include <u>contracts, letters of intent, and email</u> (page 78).

    True

109. Interpersonal and team skills include <u>conflict management, facilitation, and meeting management</u> (page 71).

    True

110. The <u>project charter</u> documents the business needs, assumptions and constraints, and high-level requirements (page 81).

True

111. The <u>Develop Project Charter</u> process identifies the individuals, groups, or organizations that could impact or be impacted by the project (page 503).

False; Identify Stakeholders

112. The <u>stakeholder management plan</u> is an output of the Identify Stakeholders process (page 504).

False; stakeholder register

113. Stakeholders can be classified based on their <u>level of authority and level of concern</u> regarding the project outcomes (page 512).

True

Planning the Project

Match the following Planning Process Group outputs to the correct knowledge area (pages 567-594).

114. Basis of estimates   D
115. Communications management plan   G
116. Team charter   F
117. Schedule management plan   C
118. Quality Metrics   E
119. Project management plan   A
120. Requirements traceability matrix   B
121. Risk register   H
122. Source selection criteria   I
123. Stakeholder management plan   J

Knowledge Areas

A.   Project Integration Management
B.   Project Scope Management
C.   Project Schedule Management
D.   Project Cost Management
E.   Project Quality Management
F.   Project Resource Management
G.   Project Communications Management
H.   Project Risk Management
I.   Project Procurement Management
J.   Project Stakeholder Management

Determine if each of the following statements is true or false. If the statement is false, provide the correct answer to the underlined term(s) to make the statement true.

124. Focus groups comprise of cross-functional stakeholders (page 432).

   False; facilitated workshops

125. The requirements traceability matrix enables the organization to link each requirement to business and project objective (page 149).

   True

126. The project scope management plan documents how the project team will define the project scope, develop the work breakdown structure, and control the changes (page 137).

   True

127. The Create WBS process enables the project team to subdivide the project into smaller and more manageable components (page 156).

   True

128. Regression analysis can be used if it is not yet possible to decompose a deliverable or subcomponent into the level of detail where a WBS can be developed (page 160).

   False; rolling wave planning

129. The scope baseline includes the description of work, the WBS, and the project schedule (page 161).

   False; project scope statement, WBS, and WBS dictionary

130. The lowest level of WBS components is called a <u>work package</u> (page 157).

      True

Fill in the following blanks.

131. <u>Critical</u> path and <u>agile approach</u> are examples of scheduling methods (page 175).

132. The <u>cost management plan</u> can establish the unit of measure, level of accuracy and control thresholds (pages 238-239).

133. The horizontal value chain of a SIPOC model can be used to draw a <u>flowchart</u> (page 285).

134. RACI chart is an example of a <u>responsibility assignment matrix (RAM)</u> (page 317).

135. In the communication channels formula *[n (n -1)] / 2*, *n* represents the number of stakeholders (page 370).

136. <u>Beta</u> and <u>triangular</u> distributions are commonly used in quantitative risk analysis (page 245).

137. <u>Monte Carlo analysis</u> can be used to show the probability of all the possible project completion dates (page 433).

Executing the Project

Match the following Executing Process Group outputs to the correct process (pages 597-610). An output may belong to more than one process.

138. Agreements	<u>I</u>	
139. Change requests	<u>A, C, D, E, F, H, I, and J</u>	
140. Deliverables	<u>A</u>	
141. Issue log	<u>A</u>	
142. Lessons learned register	<u>B</u>	
143. Project communications	<u>G</u>	
144. Resource calendars	<u>D</u>	
145. Selected sellers	<u>I</u>	
146. Team performance assessments	<u>E</u>	
147. Work performance data	<u>A</u>	

Processes

A. Direct and Manage Project Work
B. Manage Project Knowledge
C. Manage Quality
D. Acquire Resources
E. Develop Team
F. Manage Team
G. Manage Communications
H. Implement Risk Responses
I. Conduct Procurements
J. Manage Stakeholder Engagement

Determine if each of the following statements is true or false. If the statement is false, provide the correct answer to the underlined term(s) to make the statement true.

148. The <u>Direct and Manage Project Work</u> process requires the implementation of approved changes such as corrective action, preventive action, and defect repair (page 96).

   True

149. <u>Root cause analysis (RCA)</u> is one of the data analysis tools used when managing quality in a project (page 292).

   True

150. <u>Virtual teams</u> rely heavily on e-mails, conference calls and web-based collaboration tools to fulfill their roles (page 311).

   True

151. <u>Negotiation</u> is an example of interpersonal and team skills (page 332).

   True

152. In the Tuckman ladder, <u>forming</u> occurs after storming (page 338).

   False; norming

153. Examples of <u>interpersonal and team skills</u> that a project manager may use include conflict management, influencing, and motivation (page 341).

   True

154. <u>Proposal evaluation techniques</u> are meetings between the buyer and all prospective sellers (page 487).

   False; bidder conferences

155. "Most <u>government jurisdictions</u> require public advertising or online posting of pending government contracts" (page 487).

   True

156. "<u>An issue log</u> is used to document changes that occur during a project" (page 525).

   False, a change log

157. <u>Escalation process</u> can be found in the communications management plan (page 377).

   True

Fill in the following blanks.

158. Approved change requests are reviewed and approved for implementation by the <u>change control board (CCB)</u> (page 93).

159. <u>Change requests</u> may include corrective action, preventive action, defect repair, and updates (page 96).

160. Project team members are considered <u>pre-assigned</u> if they are selected in advance (page 333).

161. When a team functions as a well-organized unit, they have achieved the <u>performing</u> stage of the Tuckman ladder (page 338).

162. <u>Smooth/accommodate</u> is a general conflict resolution technique where parties focus on areas of agreement rather than areas of difference (page 349).

163. Nodding, paraphrasing and maintaining eye contact are examples of <u>active listening</u> techniques (page 381).

164. The language of the <u>final contract</u> should reflect all agreements reached (page 489).

165. "A <u>contract</u> is a mutually binding legal agreement that obligates the seller to provide the specified products, services, or results; and obligates the buyer to compensate the seller" (page 489).

166. The <u>Manage Stakeholder Engagement</u> process "allows the project manager to increase support and minimize resistance from stakeholders." (page 523).

167. Project issues are tracked (added, updated, and closed) using an <u>issue log</u> (page 529).

Monitoring and Controlling the Project

Match the following Monitoring and Controlling Process Group outputs to the correct process. An output may belong to more than one process (pages 615-632).

168. Work performance reports   A
169. Approved change requests   B
170. Work performance information   C, D, E, F, G, H, I, J, K, and L
171. Accepted deliverables   C
172. Schedule forecasts   E
173. Cost forecasts   F
174. Quality control measurements   G
175. Closed procurements   K
176. Validated deliverables   G

Processes

A. Monitor and Control Project Work
B. Perform Integrated Change Control
C. Validate Scope
D. Control Scope
E. Control Schedule
F. Control Costs
G. Control Quality
H. Control Resources
I. Monitor Communications
J. Monitor Risks
K. Control Procurements
L. Monitor Stakeholder Engagement

Determine if each of the following statements is true or false. If the statement is false, provide the correct answer to the underlined term(s) to make the statement true.

177. Schedule variance (SV) and schedule performance index (SPI) are typically used for <u>schedule forecasting</u> (page 267).

    True

178. The <u>estimate to complete (ETC)</u> can be compared to the budget at completion (BAC) to determine if the project is still within acceptable tolerance ranges (page 267).

    False; estimate at complete (EAC)

179. Change management plan and configuration management plan are used as inputs to the Validate Scope process (page 116).

False, Perform Integrated Change Control

180. To bring the project back on track, a project manager may apply schedule compression techniques such as fast tracking or crashing the schedule (page 215).

True

181. Schedule variance = SV = EV − PV (page 267).

True

182. Cost variance = CV = PV − AC (page 267).

False; EV − AC

183. Use the equation AC + [(BAC − EV) / (CPI x SPI)] for EAC forecast for ETC work performed at present CPI (page 267.

False; EAC forecast for ETC work considering both SPI and CPI factors

184. The equation for TCPI based on BAC is (BAC − EV) / (BAC − AC) (page 267).

True

Fill in the following blanks.

185. Examples of data analysis include alternatives analysis, trend analysis, and variance analysis (page 1111).

186. "The requirements traceability matrix helps to detect the impact of any change or deviation from the scope baseline on the project objectives" (page 169).

187. The three key dimensions of EVM are planned value, earned value, and actual cost (page 261).

188. Lessons learned register, quality metrics, and test and evaluation documents are used as input to the Control Quality process (page 300).

189. "Quality control measurements are documented results of Control Quality activities" (page 252).

190. Monitoring residual risk is part of the Monitor Risks process (page 453).

191. To get paid, vendors issue seller invoices (page 496).

192. ADR stands for <u>alternative dispute resolution</u> (page 498).

Closing the Project

Determine if each of the following statements is true or false. If the statement is false, provide the correct answer to the underlined term(s) to make the statement true.

193. The three tools and techniques of the <u>Close Project or Phase</u> process are expert judgment, data analysis, and meetings (page 121).

   True

194. Dealing with excess project material is an activity associated with the <u>Close Project or Phase</u> process (page 123).

   True

195. As part of the Close Project or Phase process, the project team measures <u>stakeholder satisfaction</u> (page 123).

   False; procurement documents

196. The <u>Close Project or Phase</u> process "is performed once or at predetermined points in the project (page 121).

   True

197. A key output of the Close Project or Phase is when the project team transitions the <u>final product, service, or result</u> (page 121).

   True

198. Formal procurement closure, including terms and conditions of the contract, can be found in the <u>business case</u> (page 125).

   False; agreements

199. "The <u>final report</u> provides a summary of the project performance" (page 127).

   True

200. <u>Document analysis, regression analysis, and trend analysis</u> are typically included in the final report summary (page 127).

   False; summary level description, scope objectives, quality objectives, cost objectives, and summary of the validation information

Bonus Questions

Determine if each of the following statements is true or false. If the statement is false, provide the correct answer to the underlined term(s) to make the statement true.

201. <u>Backward pass</u> is a CPM technique for calculating the late start and finish dates (page 210).

True

202. <u>WBS ID</u> is a "numbering system used to uniquely identify each component of the work breakdown structure (WBS)" (page 701).

False; code of accounts

203. <u>Summary activity</u> is a "group of related schedule activities aggregated and displayed as a single activity" (page 724).

True

204. <u>Hard logic</u> is synonymous with mandatory dependency (page 191).

True

205. <u>Gantt chart</u> is a "special type of bar chart used in sensitivity analysis for comparing the relative importance of the variables" (page 725).

False; tornado diagram

Chapter 3: Practice Test A

1. Which knowledge area unifies the various processes and activities within the project management process groups?

    A. Project Integration Management
    B. Project Scope Management
    C. Project Quality Management
    D. Project Resource Management

2. Over the years of working together, a senior program manager and a project manager developed a strong professional relationship. The project manager will be starting a large project within the next few weeks, so he asked the senior program manager for advice on how to deal with a new vendor (one that the company has never used). Without hesitation, the senior program manager told the project manager to just use the same contract that the company has used for smaller vendors. What should the project manager do next?

    A. Get a copy of the contract for small vendors and then ask the new vendor to sign it
    B. Ask the new vendor for a copy of its standard contract and then sign the contract
    C. Seek advice from other project managers and then personally prepare a new contract
    D. Solicit inputs from the legal and procurement departments and then proceed accordingly

3. Which project management process should a project manager perform to get a formal authorization for a project or a project phase?

    A. Develop Project Management Plan
    B. Develop Project Charter
    C. Perform Integrated Change Control
    D. Direct and Manage Project Work

4. Project managers need to perform several project management processes as part of the Project Integration Management knowledge area. During project initiation, the project manager will need to _____.

    A. Develop the project management plan
    B. Manage stakeholder engagement
    C. Develop the project charter
    D. Perform integrated change control

5. You have been asked to manage the change control process of a very large government project. Parts of your responsibilities include reviewing, approving, and managing the changes. The operations manager prepared a list of expected deliverables from your project. She asked you to cross out deliverables that are not applicable to your role. From the list below, which deliverable should you remove?

A. Change requests
B. Project management plan updates
C. Project documents updates
D. Organizational process assets updates

6. Which of the following tools or techniques is used in all of the Project Integration Management knowledge area processes?

A. Expert judgment
B. Project management information system
C. Change control tools
D. Product analysis

7. The project management plan enables the project manager to _____.

A. Monitor and control project work
B. Develop a project scope statement
C. Direct and manage project work
D. Implement integrated change control

8. A project manager gathered the following inputs: project management plan, project documents, business documents, accepted deliverables, and organizational process assets. If the project manager will use expert judgment to transform these inputs into outputs, she is likely performing which Project Integration Management knowledge area process?

A. Direct and Manage Project Work
B. Develop Project Charter
C. Perform Integrated Change Control
D. Close Project or Phase

9. Who authorizes the project charter?

A. Project initiator or sponsor
B. Program manager and project manager
C. Functional or department manager
D. Finance managers and chartered accountants

10. Which item from the following list may be initiated prior to the development of the project charter?

A. Preliminary study and project management plan
B. Benefits management plan and business case
C. Market analysis and detailed cost estimates
D. Project scope statement and work breakdown structure

11. You are working as a project management consultant for a regional financial institution. One of your key deliverables is a project charter template for the project management office. Which information should you include, via direct or indirect references, in the project charter template?

A. Project justification, success criteria, and summary milestone schedule
B. Product objectives and product scope description
C. Project requirements and deliverables, project constraints, and project assumptions
D. Project deliverables and project exclusions

12. Your company has asked you to prepare a project charter for an external manufacturing customer. The customer expects you to deliver the installation, configuration, and testing of the new state-of-the-art assembly line that was developed by your company. What key input will you need in order to prepare the project charter?

A. Project scope statement
B. Work performance reports
C. Project management plan
D. Agreements

13. The project business case serves as one of the inputs when developing a project charter. What type of information should a project manager look for in an approved project business case?

A. Business needs, analysis of the situation, recommendation, and evaluation
B. Organizational structure, industry standards, and authorization system
C. Stakeholder risk tolerances, commercial databases, and marketplace conditions
D. Infrastructure, human resources, and organizational culture

14. In order for a project to be successful, the project manager must consider various enterprise environmental factors. Which of the lists below contain only enterprise environmental factors?

A. Processes, policies, procedures, and organizational knowledge bases
B. Infrastructure, resource availability, marketplace conditions, and legal restrictions
C. Tailoring criteria, templates, change control procedures, and project closure guidelines
D. Configuration management knowledge repositories, and project files from previous projects

15. Organizational process assets guide the way we execute a project within the organization. Submitting time reports, reviewing disbursements, assigning codes of accounts, and using contract provisions are examples of _____.

A. Project closure guidelines
B. Risk control procedures
C. Financial control procedures
D. Organizational standard processes

16. What are the two categories of organizational process assets?

A. Organization communication requirements and work authorization procedures
B. Organizational standard processes and financial control procedures
C. Issue and defect management procedures, and risk control procedures
D. Processes, policies, procedures, and organizational knowledge bases

17. You have been assigned to manage a medical information system project for a major client of your company. In the past, your company has successfully delivered several similar projects for the same client. Which of the following organizational knowledge repositories would you review prior to the preparation of the project charter?

A. Organizational standard processes, standardized guidelines, templates, project customization guidelines, project closure guidelines, and issue and defect management procedures
B. Process measurement database, historical information, Lessons Learned, issue and defect management database, financial database, and configuration management knowledge base
C. Financial control procedures, issue and defect management procedures, change control procedures, risk control procedures, and organizational processes and procedures
D. Proposal evaluation criteria, security requirements, safety and health policy, project management policy, defect identification procedures, and action item tracking

18. The project business case _____.

A. Summarizes the objectives and reasons for project initiation, and helps gauge the success against the objectives
B. Is a document that formally initiates the project and identifies the project manager
C. Is developed from the project scope baseline and defines that portion of scope to be included in the contract
D. Describes, in detail, the project's deliverables and the work required to create those deliverables

19. Which project management process is used to define and document the high-level requirements and description of the project?

A. Develop Project Charter
B. Develop Project Management Plan
C. Develop Project Scope Statement
D. Monitor and Control Project Work

20. Luigi took over a project from another project manager who abruptly left the company. No one knows the state of the project. However, Luigi found some documents that contain the project high-level description, summary milestone schedule, and name and authority of the person authorizing the project. Most likely, the document that Luigi found is the _____.

A. Project charter
B. Project management plan
C. Project statement of work
D. Project scope statement

21. To complete the project charter, a project manager will need to use information provided by the _____.

A. Project initiator or sponsor
B. Project scope department
C. Enterprise environmental factors
D. Organizational process assets

22. What inputs are needed to develop the project charter?

A. Business case, benefits management plan, agreements, enterprise environmental factors, and organizational process assets
B. Project scope statement, requirements documentation, and approved changed requests
C. Project management plan, work performance data, and rejected change requests
D. Project management processes, enterprise environmental factors, and organizational process assets

23. The project management team has selected the project management processes that will be used in an oil mining project. In which document will a project sponsor be able to find such information?

A. Project charter
B. Project scope statement
C. Project management plan
D. Project statement of work

24. Executing the planned project activities to complete project deliverables and performing the activities to achieve the project objectives are actions associated with which of the following project management processes?

A. Validate and Control Scope
B. Control Cost and Schedule
C. Direct and Manage Project Work
D. Control Procurements and Monitor Risks

25. You are managing a construction project that builds roads and bridges. In addition to tangible deliverables, what intangible deliverables can the project produce or deliver as part of project execution?

A. Public benefit
B. Highway lighting
C. Traffic signs
D. Paved roads

26. Collecting the project data and facilitating the forecasting of cost and schedule are actions performed by the project manager and the project management team during which of the following project process groups?

A. Initiation
B. Planning
C. Executing
D. Monitoring and Controlling

27. Approved _____ are documented, authorized directions required to bring expected future project performance into compliance with the project management plan.

A. Corrective actions
B. Preventive actions
C. Change requests
D. Defect repairs

28. Which input to the Direct and Manage Project Work process contains the documented and authorized changes to adjust the scope of the project?

A. Approved corrective actions
B. Approved preventive actions
C. Approved change requests
D. Approved defect repair

29. A project team can use _____ to help direct and manage the project work.

A. Deliverables
B. Work performance data
C. Issue log
D. Expert judgment

30. You are working on a secret project for the military. Because of a recent military order, the project will need to include extensive changes to the information system, internal procedures, and standardized forms. These changes were considered and accommodated during project initiation and planning. From here on, what other outputs are you expected to deliver?

A. Deliverables, corrective actions, and defect repair
B. Recommended corrective actions, forecasts, and requested changes
C. Approved change requests, rejected change requests, and deliverables
D. Contract closure procedure, along with final product, service, or result

31. Which description below *best* characterizes work performance data?

A. Enumerates changes to the project scope, lists potential changes to policies, addresses mandatory changes, and adjusts the overall project budget as needed
B. Indicates deliverable status, schedule progress, and costs incurred
C. Completes the project upon delivery, performs a service as outlined in the project management plan, and helps generate results
D. Corrects future project performance, helps reduce the negative consequences of project risks, and proves that change requests were implemented

32. The Monitor and Control Project Work process examines processes during which of the following project process groups?

A. Initiating, Planning, Executing, and Closing
B. Initiating, Planning, and Monitoring and controlling
C. Monitoring and Controlling, and Closing
D. Execution, and Monitoring and Controlling

33. You have been assigned to a program in which you'll work with academic researchers. The program itself involves selecting promising research projects, matching available funding to each research proposal, monitoring the progress of each research project, and canceling research projects that cannot meet predefined milestones and benchmarks. During project execution, the earned value management technique will serve as the primary cost control assessment tool to determine whether a project is progressing according to the project management plan.

What must you do as a project manager to facilitate the application of the earned value management technique on various research projects?

A. Compare actual project performance to the project management plan
B. Assess project performance to determine if corrective actions are needed
C. Monitor the implementation of approved changes and manage project risks
D. Establish project baselines, and capture overall progress and variances

34. You have been assigned to a program in which you'll work with academic researchers. The program itself involves selecting promising research projects, matching available funding to each research proposal, monitoring the progress of each research project, and canceling research projects that cannot meet predefined milestones and benchmarks. During project execution, the earned value management technique will serve as the primary cost control assessment tool to determine whether a project is progressing according to the project management plan.

Research Project A reported an earned value of $500 and an actual cost of $505. Research Project B reported an earned value of $455 and an actual cost of $450. Research Project C submitted a cost performance index of 1.08. Research Project D achieved a cost performance index of 0.94. Which research project is the *most* cost efficient?

A. Research Project A
B. Research Project B
C. Research Project C
D. Research Project D

35. You need to determine if corrective actions are required for a project you are working on. The project has an earned value of $747 and an actual cost of $691. Calculate the cost variance.

A. $56
B. −$56
C. 1.08
D. 0.93

36. Which configuration management activity is *not* part of change control tools in the Perform Integrated Change Control process?

A. Configuration identification
B. Architecture configuration and control
C. Configuration status accounting
D. Configuration verification and auditing

37. Documented change requests *must* be either _____, _____, or _____ by the change control board.

A. Accepted, deferred, escalated
B. Reviewed, deferred, postponed
C. Reviewed, accepted, deferred
D. Accepted, deferred, rejected

38. The change control board on Paul's marketing campaign project approved the inclusion of television advertisements in addition to radio, print, and online advertisements. As part of integrated change control, which documents should Paul review to determine the impact of this change and whether updates are required?

A. Project management plan and organizational process assets
B. Organizational process assets and project scope statement
C. Project management plan and project scope statement
D. Administrative closure procedure and contract closure procedure

39. Which of the following is *not* a Perform Integrated Change Control process tool or technique?

A. Earned value analysis
B. Meetings
C. Change control tools
D. Expert judgment

40. If you are working on a multiphase project, when is it appropriate to perform the tasks associated with the Close Project or Phase process?

A. At a specific milestone
B. At the end of each phase
C. At the end of the project
D. At the end of the fiscal year

41. The following project documents can be used as inputs when managing the project knowledge *except* for _____.

A. Lessons learned register
B. Project team assignments
C. Resource breakdown structure
D. Organizational process assets updates

42. Within the Manage Project Knowledge process, sharing tacit knowledge is an example of _____.

A. Interpersonal and team skills
B. Information management
C. Expert judgment
D. Knowledge management

43. Which of the following are inputs to the Close Project or Phase process?

A. Project management plan, accepted deliverables, and organizational process assets
B. Contract (when applicable), enterprise environmental factors, and organizational process assets
C. Project charter, enterprise environmental factors, and organizational process assets
D. Project scope statement, enterprise environmental factors, and organizational process assets

44. Expert judgment is a tool and technique used by which processes?

A. Develop Project Charter, and Direct and Manage Project Work
B. Develop Project Charter, Develop Project Management Plan, Direct and Manage Project Work, Manage Project Knowledge, Monitor and Control Project Work, Perform Integrated Change Control, and Close Project or Phase
C. Direct and Manage Project Work, and Monitor and Control Project Work
D. Perform Integrated Change Control, and Direct and Manage Project Work

45. Project audits, transition criteria, and previous project performance information can be found as part of (the) _____.

A. Project management plan
B. Enterprise environmental factors
C. Organizational process assets
D. Contract documentation

46. Six months after you formally closed an office relocation project, you receive a phone call from a collection agency indicating that your company refuses to pay the invoices of one of the vendors. What would be the *best* course of action for you to take?

A. Revisit the procurement management plan of the project in question
B. Refer the collection agency to the accounts payable department
C. Forward the phone call to your company's legal department
D. Terminate the telephone call because the project is no longer your responsibility

47. You spent one week updating the project files, project closure documents, and historical information. These project documents collectively are part of (the) _____.

A. Configuration management system
B. Organizational process assets
C. Work performance data
D. Enterprise environmental factors

48. Which of the following statements is true about the project's final report?

A. Lessons learned register is finalized to include final information on phase or project closure
B. The project team hands over the responsibilities to the operations team
C. It includes the summary level description of the project or phase
D. Organizational process assets are updated such as lessons learned repository

49. You have been assigned to a project to initiate, plan, and execute a national convention for travel agents. One of the immediate tasks that you need to perform is to create and define the work breakdown structure (WBS). The creation of the WBS is part of which Knowledge Area process?

A. Project Integration Management
B. Project Scope Management
C. Project Schedule Management
D. Project Cost Management

50. How are the Define Scope and Create WBS processes different?

A. The outputs of the Create WBS process serve as inputs to the Collect Requirements process; outputs of the Create WBS process can be used as inputs to Define Scope process.
B. Major project deliverables are subdivided during the Define Scope process; the major project deliverables are then created and defined as part of the Create WBS process.
C. A detailed description of the project is developed during the Define Scope process, and the Create WBS process subdivides major deliverables into smaller components.
D. There are no differences between these two processes—both are parts of Project Scope Management, and they interact with each other to produce the WBS.

51. Which of the following are some of the tools and techniques of the Define Scope process?

A. Product analysis, alternatives analysis, and facilitation
B. Decomposition
C. Interviews, focus groups, questionnaires, and surveys
D. Variance analysis

52. Brainstorming, benchmarking, and focus groups are examples of which Collect Requirements tool and technique?

A. Observation/conversation
B. Facilitation
C. Nominal group technique
D. Data gathering

53. You have been assigned to a project to develop a new bicycle that will use the latest technologies available in the market today. You have started working on the work breakdown structure (WBS) by listing "bicycle" on the first level. Items on the second level include "frameset," "crankset," "wheels," "braking system," and "shifting system." What items would be appropriate at the third level, under "wheels"?

A. Front wheel and rear wheel
B. Concept and design
C. Assembly and testing
D. Specification and testing

54. Expert judgment and _____ are tools and techniques of the Create WBS process.

A. Inspection
B. Decomposition
C. Variance analysis
D. Facilitated workshops

55. The _____ hierarchically depicts the project structure in order to properly relate the work packages to the performing organizational units.

A. Work breakdown structure
B. Organizational breakdown structure
C. Risk breakdown structure
D. Resource breakdown structure

56. Which process requires obtaining formal acceptance of the completed project scope and associated deliverables from the stakeholders?

A. Collect Requirements
B. Define Scope
C. Validate Scope
D. Control Scope

57. As part of the Validate Scope process, the project team must measure, examine, and validate the project deliverables to ensure adherence to the requirements. Which tool or technique would be *most* appropriate in performing these tasks?

A. Product analysis
B. Decomposition
C. Inspection
D. Data analysis

58. Which of the following statements is true about the Control Scope process?

A. The following are examples of inputs to the Control Scope process: project management plan, work performance data, project documentation, and organizational process assets
B. The Control Scope process uses the following tools and techniques: product analysis, alternative identification, expert judgment, and stakeholder analysis
C. The following are examples of outputs from the Control Scope process: project scope management plan, performance reports, and work performance data
D. The Control Scope process produces the following outputs: accepted deliverables, requested changes, and recommended corrective actions

59. Project variance analysis is used to assess the _____.

A. Magnitude of variation
B. Effectiveness of the team
C. Experience of the project manager
D. Conformance to requirements

60. As a result of variance analysis, the scope baseline or other parts of the project management plan may need to be modified. The results of this are called _____.

A. Change requests
B. The change control system
C. The configuration management system
D. A requirements traceability matrix

61. Which Project Scope Management process may introduce updates to work performance information, project documents updates, and project management plan?

A. Collect Requirements
B. Define Scope
C. Validate Scope
D. Control Scope

62. Within the Project Scope Management knowledge area, the scope baseline will be created and may be updated by various processes. From the following list, which processes create and update the scope baseline?

A. Collect Requirements and Define Scope
B. Define Scope and Create WBS
C. Create WBS and Control Scope
D. Validate Scope and Control Scope

63. You are trying to determine how to deliver a marketing campaign project on time. You considered using the precedence diagramming method (PDM) to schedule the project activities in logical order. Which process would normally use the PDM technique?

A. Define Activities
B. Sequence Activities
C. Estimate Activity Resources
D. Develop Schedule

64. In one of your projects, you were assigned to decompose the branches of the WBS down to the work package level. You were able to successfully break down four out of the five branches of the WBS. Unfortunately, the project scope did not provide enough details for you to decompose the fifth branch of the WBS. What should you do next?

A. Ask the sponsor to change the project scope so that you can continue
B. Document the insufficient definition of the WBS branch as a project risk
C. Make reasoned assumptions about the WBS branch so as not to delay the project
D. Use the branch to plan at a higher level of the WBS

65. You are sequencing the activities of an instructor-led course development project. Which of the following statements is true about the tools and techniques used in activity sequencing?

A. The precedence diagramming method (PDM) uses nodes to represent activities, and arrows connect the nodes to show the dependencies
B. Leads and lags allows for delays and acceleration of successor activities, respectively
C. The precedence diagramming method (PDM) is used for dependency determination
D. The two main types of dependency determination are mandatory dependencies (hard logic) and discretionary dependencies (soft logic)

66. The precedence diagramming method (PDM) uses different types of dependencies or precedence relationships. What is the most commonly used type of precedence relationship?

A. Finish-to-start
B. Finish-to-finish
C. Start-to-start
D. Start-to-finish

67. Project managers use various tools and techniques to estimate the required resources (people, equipment, and material) in a project. Which statement is correct about the Estimate Activity Resources process?

A. The Estimate Activity Resources process produces the following outputs: activity list, activity attributes, and resource availability.
B. The Estimate Activity Resources process is performed periodically throughout the project as needed.
C. The Estimate Activity Resources process requires the activity resource requirements and activity attributes as inputs.
D. The Estimate Activity Resources process is closely coordinated with the Develop Schedule process.

68. Calculate the overall project duration for Project X by using the following table.

WBS	Task Name	Duration	WBS Predecessor
1	Project X		
1.1	Start	0 day	
1.2	A	2 days	1.1
1.3	B	3 days	1.1
1.4	C	6 days	1.1
1.5	D	7 days	1.2
1.6	E	8 days	1.5
1.7	F	3 days	1.3
1.8	G	4 days	1.7, 1.4
1.9	H	1 day	1.6, 1.7
1.10	I	2 days	1.8
1.11	J	6 days	1.9, 1.10
1.12	End	0 day	1.11

A. 8 days
B. 12 days
C. 24 days
D. 42 days

69. Using beta distribution, calculate the expected (E) value given the following three point estimates: optimistic (O) = 8, most likely (M) = 14, and pessimistic (P) = 16.

A. 12.67
B. 13.33
C. 14.00
D. 16.00

70. Identify the critical path of Project X based on the following table.

WBS	Task Name	Duration	WBS Predecessor
1	Project X		
1.1	Start	0 day	
1.2	A	2 days	1.1
1.3	B	3 days	1.1
1.4	C	6 days	1.1
1.5	D	7 days	1.2
1.6	E	8 days	1.5
1.7	F	3 days	1.3
1.8	G	4 days	1.7, 1.4
1.9	H	1 day	1.6, 1.7
1.10	I	2 days	1.8
1.11	J	6 days	1.9, 1.10
1.12	End	0 day	1.11

A. A, B, C, and J
B. A, B, C, and I
C. C, D, E, and J
D. A, D, E, H, and J

71. You need to present the monthly status of your construction project to the steering committee. The chair of the committee indicated that she is only interested on the start and finish dates of key project deliverables. What format should you use to present the project's monthly status?

A. Project schedule network diagrams
B. Bar charts
C. Milestone schedule
D. Project schedule

72. Which of the following are outputs of the Develop Schedule process?

A. Schedule data (updates), schedule baseline (updates), and performance measurement baseline (updates)
B. Project schedule, schedule baseline, schedule data, and project documents updates
C. Work performance information, schedule forecasts, and change requests
D. Assumption log (updates), basis of estimates (updates), and project schedule (updates)

73. Which of the following statements is correct about the Control Schedule process?

A. The Control Schedule process enables the project manager to evaluate, influence, and manage changes in the project schedule
B. The Control Schedule process occurs prior to the development of the activity list, activity attributes, and milestone list
C. The Estimate Activity Resources and Develop Schedule processes occur after the Control Schedule process
D. The Control Schedule and Control Cost processes are the most important processes in the Executing Process Group

74. The Control Schedule process is performed as part the _____ process.

A. Executing
B. Monitoring and Controlling
C. Planning
D. Initiating

75. You are working on a network installation project for a major telecommunications company. What do you need in order to determine if updates are required in the project management plan and project documents during the Control Schedule process?

A. Organizational process assets, project scope statement, and activity list
B. Activity attributes, project schedule network diagrams, and activity resource requirements
C. Schedule baseline, scope baseline, work performance data, and organizational process assets
D. Resource calendars, activity duration estimates, and enterprise environmental factors

76. The project sponsor asked you to audit the schedule of a project in a chocolate factory. The project manager provided you with an earned value of $1,234. The number appeared to be correct. The project baseline shows a planned value of $1,540. What should you do next?

A. Do not trust the project manager; calculate the earned value yourself to be sure
B. Calculate the SPI and tell the project manager that no corrective actions are required
C. Present your findings and recommend corrective actions to the project sponsor
D. Confirm the earned value and thank the project manager for doing a great job

77. What should a project manager do if a project has an SPI of 1.29?

A. Confirm that the EV and PV are correct just to be sure
B. Introduce corrective actions to bring the project back on track
C. Ask the project team to crash the overall project schedule
D. Perform resource smoothing to avoid working overtime

78. What is the schedule variance of a project if the earned value is 888 and the planned value 999?

A. -111.00
B. 111.00
C. 0.889
D. 1.125

79. The four Project Cost Management knowledge area processes are _____.

A. Plan Cost Management, Estimate Costs, Determine Budget, and Control Costs
B. Estimate Costs, Determine Budget, Performance Reporting, and Close Project
C. Define Scope, Estimate Costs, Control Costs, and Performance Reporting
D. Plan Cost Management, Plan Procurements, Control Costs, and Administration Procurements

80. The accuracy of estimates will get refined as the project progresses because more detailed information will become available. You were asked to provide cost estimates during the initiation phase of a parasailing expedition project. This is the first time your company has undertaken such a project. At this point in the project, your cost estimates will have a rough order of magnitude (ROM) in what range?

A. -5 to +5%
B. -10 to +10%
C. -25 to +25%
D. -25 to +75%

81. You asked several construction companies to provide estimates for how much it will cost to finish your basement. They asked you for the square footage of the house and whether you want the floor to be finished in carpet, tiles, or hardwood. The construction estimator paused briefly, entered some numbers using a simple calculator, and then gave you a cost estimate. The construction estimator *most likely* used what type of estimating technique?

A. Analogous estimating
B. Bottom-up estimating
C. Parametric estimating
D. Vendor bid analysis

82. Project managers may use analogous or parametric estimating to predict the overall cost of a project. Estimates derived using analogous or parametric models are considered accurate and reliable when _____.

A. The model is prepared by an expert, a certified project management professional collects the parameters, and the calculations allow for subjective measures (for example, aesthetics)
B. The project being estimated is almost exactly the same as previous projects not just in appearance but also in actual fact (for example, a similar four-bedroom house in the same area)
C. The assumptions, constraints, and limitations of the three-point estimates (optimistic, most likely, and pessimistic) have been reviewed, discussed, and finalized by the project team
D. The parameters are quantifiable, the calculations are based on precise historical information, and the model can be used on projects regardless of size (for example, small vs. large project)

83. After performing the Control Costs process, which of the following may be updated?

A. Cost forecasts, project management plan, and project documents
B. Project funding requirements and performance measurement baseline
C. Work performance data and organizational process assets
D. Lessons learned register and work performance data

84. Given EAC = 500 and AC = 450, what is the expected cost to finish all the remaining project work?

A. 1.11
B. 0.90
C. -50
D. 50

85. Which Project Quality Management process uses the cost of quality (COQ) technique?

A. Plan Quality Management
B. Quality Function Deployment
C. Quality Control
D. Quality Audit

86. All of the following are commonly used quality improvement initiatives *except* _____.

A. Total Quality Management
B. Six Sigma
C. Lean Six Sigma
D. PDCA

87. _____ are also called cost of poor quality.

A. Failure costs
B. Internal failures
C. External failures
D. Cost of quality

88. As part of the Plan Quality Management process, which of the following project documents may be updated?

A. Lessons learned register and requirements traceability matrix
B. Requirements traceability matrix and risk management plan
C. Risk management plan and risk register
D. Risk register and scope baseline

89. The quality management plan may include the following components, *except* _____.

A. Quality objectives of the project
B. Quality roles and responsibilities
C. Quality tools
D. Assumption log

90. Data gathering, audits, and quality improvements methods, are used in the _____ process to convert inputs into outputs.

A. Plan Quality Management
B. Manage Quality
C. Control Quality
D. Control Costs

91. As a project manager of a major environmental project, you met with local government agencies to address their concerns about the impact of the project on the migration patterns of birds. After the meeting, three change requests were documented and subsequently approved. After reviewing the change requests in detail, however, your team realized that the three change requests cannot be implemented without an additional environmental study. What should you do next?

A. Include the environmental study in the project scope because it is necessary to complete the documented and approved change requests
B. Check the project's contingency reserve to determine if the cost of the environmental study can be included without additional funding
C. Ask the team to immediately work on the environmental study so as not to delay the implementation of the three change requests
D. Do not proceed or implement the environmental study until it has gone through the Integrated Change Control process

92. As part of your company's ISO-compliant project management processes, a project quality auditor visits all large projects at least once a month. The project auditor visited your project for five consecutive months and found it to be in compliance with the company's project management processes, but the project auditor did not show up last month. What would be an appropriate course of action?

A. Wait until the next month because the audit is not critical to the project and its deliverables
B. Do not address it at this time because the project has been compliant in the past
C. Contact the project quality auditor and ask him/her to perform the monthly project audit as planned
D. Report the project quality auditor to the quality management office

93. A _____ is an assessment performed by an unbiased individual or entity to determine if the project activities conform to organizational and project policies and procedures.

A. Quality audit
B. Configuration management system
C. Change control system
D. Process analysis

94. In the Manage Quality process, project managers execute quality activities to ensure that the project will meet the requirements for which it was undertaken. Such activities could result in continuous process improvement and produce the following outputs:

A. Quality reports, requested changes and an updated scope baseline
B. Quality management plan, quality metrics, and risk management plan
C. Risk management plan, scope baseline, and lessons learned register
D. Requirements traceability matrix, risk register, and stakeholder register

95. The project management team monitors specific project results to ensure compliance with pertinent quality standards. Which of the following statements is correct about the Control Quality process?

A. The Plan Quality Management process is executed throughout the project
B. The Control Quality process identifies standards that are relevant to the project
C. Continuous process improvement is part of the Control Quality process
D. The Control Quality process requires knowledge of sampling and probability

96. Your company established an acceptable budget variance of +/− 5% for every project. On a monthly basis, projects may have a budget variance outside the acceptable range, provided this does not happen more than twice in a row. What quality tool should you use to evaluate your project's cost variances over the past two years?

A. Ishikawa diagram
B. Cause-and-effect diagram
C. Control chart
D. Flowcharting

97. Certain characteristics help identify many tools of quality. Which list accurately enumerates the key components of a control chart?

A. Major defect, and potential causes and effect
B. Upper control limit, x axis, and lower control limit
C. Activities, decision points, and order of processing
D. Graphical representation, number of defects per deliverable, number of times each process is noncompliant

98. Your project team was responsible for automatically installing a popular desktop application on 25,000 computers in six countries in Asia, North America, and Europe. Most of the computers have the same configuration, but there might be slight variations in each country and in each line of business within that country. The lead technical architect suggested that you send a technical support representative to verify the installation of every 100th computer. What type of sampling method was recommended?

A. Quota sampling
B. Simple random sampling
C. Stratified sampling
D. Systematic sampling

99. The Project Resource Management knowledge area deals with organizing the project team and has many processes. Which of the following is not a resource management process?

A. Manage Team
B. Control Resources
C. Estimate Activity Resources
D. Sequence Activities

100. Certain constraints may limit the project manager's ability to select project team members. In a trade/labor union environment, which of the following constraints will directly impact the roles and responsibilities that team members may perform in a project?

A. Organizational structure
B. Collective bargaining agreement
C. Economic conditions
D. Interpersonal relationships

101. The project manager may use the following tools and techniques to acquire the project team:

A. Pre-assignment, negotiation, multicriteria decision analysis, and virtual teams
B. Meetings, training, and co-location
C. Individual and team assessments, virtual teams, and recognition and rewards
D. Influencing, team building, and negotiation

102. You are in the process of forming a project team that includes employees and contractors. A subject matter expert strongly suggested that all of your team members acquire a special technical certification to minimize potential mistakes in the project. What would be the *most* appropriate next step for you to take?

A. Pay for the employees' technical certifications and ask the contractors to pay on their own
B. Require all employees to earn the technical certification, but not necessarily the contractors
C. Ask all employees and contractors to earn the technical certification as soon as possible
D. Prepare a training plan to ensure that all team members have the technical certification

103. A vendor's response to a request for proposal (RFP) identified three key team members by name who will be working on a project. One team member will perform the initial analysis at the corporate headquarters, and two team members will perform the detailed analysis at various field offices across the country. With regard to acquiring the project team members, the three key team members are considered _____.

A. Preassigned
B. Negotiated
C. Acquired
D. Virtual

104. There are several ways of acquiring project team members. From the options, which statement *best* describes negotiation as it relates to acquiring project team members?

A. Ask the vendors to list the subject matter experts who will be working in the project in their responses for the request for proposal (RFP)
B. Request functional managers to provide technical specialists with specific skills to work on the project during project initiation
C. Convince senior managers to hire senior technical consultants and to subcontract parts of the work that are not critical to the schedule
D. Influence the leadership team to allow some of the team members to work remotely to minimize the travel expenses in the project

105. The tool or technique used in acquiring resources by incorporating employees who work from home is called (a) _____.

A. Pre-assignment
B. Negotiation
C. Virtual teams
D. Acquisition

106. Some of your project team members work in their home offices. Because of the urgency of the project, you have teams that work on three different shifts. Your project is essentially operating _____.

A. As a 24x7 operation
B. In a fast-track mode
C. Effectively and efficiently
D. As a virtual team

107. Early in the project, you started to identify the training needs of your project team and you established an efficient communication framework to optimize the efficiency and effectiveness of your project team. By performing these actions, you are performing the _____ process.

A. Resource Planning
B. Acquire Resources
C. Develop Team
D. Manage Team

108. The Develop Team process produces the _____ output.

A. Team performance assessments
B. Physical resources assignments
C. Resource calendars
D. Change requests

109. Developing the project team includes training. The following statements are accurate about training *except* _____.

A. Formal training produces the best results in a project environment
B. Training methods include classroom, mentoring, and coaching
C. Training requirements may be found in the staffing management plan
D. Unplanned training may be scheduled as a result of an observation

110. Which of the following tools or techniques is used in the Develop Team process?

A. Pre-assignment
B. Decision making
C. Training
D. Multicriteria decision analysis

111. During a team meeting, a senior director said, "Great job on the report, John." This type of recognition is considered _____.

A. Formal
B. Informal
C. Tangible
D. Monetary

112. You are in the process of drafting a recognition program for your project team. The project sponsor would like to recognize the success of team performance at the end of the project. Given this, what would be your best response?

A. This is a good approach as the morale will be high at the end of the project
B. A better approach would be to recognize team members throughout the project
C. A better method would be a wait-and-see approach to see if the project is a success
D. Indicate that the project team would prefer a monetary bonus as the recognition method

113. A senior project manager suggested that you incorporate informal assessments to measure the project team's effectiveness. From the following list, which is an example of an informal performance assessment?

A. MBWA
B. ACWP
C. CWBS
D. CPPC

114. In your organization, a team performance assessment serves as a critical input to the annual performance review. As a project manager, you are responsible for conducting the team performance assessment. What can you do to ensure that your project team members will receive a favorable performance assessment?

A. Focus on the positive performance behaviors of all team members
B. Incorporate interim formal reviews throughout the project life cycle
C. Set challenging and aggressive goals for all project team members
D. Coach the team formally and informally whenever opportunities arise

115. In a weak matrix organization, proper management of the dual reporting relationship can determine the success of a project. In such situations, team members are accountable to the _____.

A. Functional manager
B. Project manager
C. Human resource manager
D. Project leader and end users

116. You are working in a strong matrix organization. Who is primarily responsible for managing the dual reporting relationship of project team members?

A. Functional manager
B. Project manager
C. Project sponsor
D. Human resource manager

117. Your project uses the principles of 360-degree feedback. Based on these principles, performance evaluations can come from various sources but *not* from _____.

A. Superiors
B. Peers
C. Subordinates
D. The individual being evaluated

118. A project team member announced her pregnancy during the regular weekly project meeting. She also indicated that she will be taking a maternity leave at the end of the year. The project manager will need to manage the staffing changes using which process?

A. Perform Integrated Change Control
B. Develop Resource Plan
C. Develop Team
D. Manage Team

119. Which of the following are processes in the Project Communications Management knowledge area?

A. Plan Communications Management, Manage Communications, and Monitor Communications
B. Collect Requirements, Plan Communications, Plan Procurements, and Control Procurements
C. Plan Communications Management, Manage Communications, and Manage Stakeholder Engagement
D. Identify Stakeholders, Plan Procurements, Control Procurements, and Control Communications

120. The Plan Communications Management process determines how and when to communicate information to project stakeholders. Which statement below is correct about the Plan Communications Management process?

A. The Plan Communications Management process produces the communications management plan as an output
B. The Plan Communications Management process requires the communications management plan as an input
C. The Plan Communications Management process produces the resource management plan as an output
D. The Plan Communications Management process requires the project schedule as an input

121. A new manager who just joined the project was looking for guidelines on how to distribute the monthly progress reports to the steering committee. Such guidelines can be found in the _____.

A. Project management plan
B. Communications management plan
C. Organizational process assets
D. Performance reports

122. The project manager prepared the weekly progress reports and distributed the same to key project stakeholders. The project manager also responded to an ad hoc request by the finance department to provide an itemized list of capital expenditures. Which process is *best* characterized by these tasks?

A. Control Communications
B. Control Costs
C. Manage Quality
D. Manage Communications

123. You are managing a government project that impacts three other government agencies. Over time, you developed good professional relationships with the other project managers. In fact, you often find yourself discussing project-related information during your lunch breaks. Such discussions are considered _____ communication.

A. Internal, vertical
B. Informal, horizontal
C. External, formal
D. Oral, external

124. The following are examples of electronic tools for project management *except* _____.

A. Web interfaces to project management software
B. Meeting and virtual office support tools
C. Hard-copy document distribution systems
D. Collaborative work management tools

125. The lessons learned register allows current and future projects to avoid repeating the same mistakes. Who is ultimately responsible for conducting lessons learned sessions?

A. Project manager
B. Project sponsor
C. Quality manager
D. Project auditor

126. You are working on a major project to upgrade the facilities of a regional beverage distributor. Within the first three months, you realized that it takes a long time to get approvals on purchase orders if the total amount is more than $10,000. Such knowledge should be _____.

A. Documented in the lessons learned register
B. Noted in the organizational process assets
C. Included in the project records
D. Recorded in the project reports

127. During the execution phase of the project, the project sponsor requested that a monthly progress report be sent to the regulatory compliance department. Which statement *best* describes the proper course of action for the project manager to take?

A. Review the overall project scope to determine if the monthly report is outside the original project scope
B. Investigate the total effort required to produce the report and distribute it if no extra effort is required
C. Modify the communications management plan as needed, using the Perform Integrated Change Control process
D. Ask the project sponsor to fill out a change request form and submit it to the change control board

128. The Manage Communications process collects data and distributes performance information to project stakeholders. Which statement below is correct about the tools and techniques that are used in the Manage Communications process?

A. The Manage Communications process uses communication technology, communication methods, and project reporting
B. The most important tools in the Manage Communications process are time reporting systems and cost reporting systems
C. The tools and techniques of the Manage Communications process include communication methods and information distribution tools
D. The Manage Communications process utilizes communications requirements analysis, communications technology, and communication models

129. Which of the following lists include some of the Manage Communications process inputs?

A. Communications management plan, work performance reports, and organizational process assets
B. Quality control measurements, enterprise environmental factors, and project scope statement
C. Performance measurement baseline, communications management plan, and forecasted completion
D. Approved change requests, organizational process assets, and forecasted completion

130. _____ is an approved plan for the project work against which project execution is compared and against which deviations are measured for management control.

A. Project management plan
B. Work performance data
C. Quality control measurements
D. Performance measurement baseline

131. A document contains a table with the following columns: WBS element, PV, EV, AC, cost variance, schedule variance, CPI, and SPI. The document is *most likely* _____.

A. A performance report
B. A forecast analysis
C. A risk register
D. An issue log

132. As an information technology project manager, you have used monetary values whenever you perform earned value analysis. Your brother is a civil engineer, and he works mostly on roads and highways. On his projects, it is more important to measure performance based on the length of paved roads and highways instead of costs. Will it be appropriate for him to use earned value analysis on his projects?

A. No, because earned value analysis requires monetary values for planned value, earned value, and actual cost for every WBS element
B. Yes, but he will need to convert the length of paved roads and highways into monetary values for every WBS element
C. Yes, the length of paved roads and highways also can be used for the planned budget, earned value, and actual cost
D. No, because earned value analysis is applicable only to information technology projects and not construction projects

133. Project managers need to manage the expectations of stakeholders. Which communication method is the most effective means of resolving issues with stakeholders?

A. Face-to-face meetings
B. Telephone calls
C. Electronic mails
D. Issue tracking logs

134. Which list below contains outputs of the Manage Stakeholder Engagement process?

A. Change requests, forecasts, and communications management plan
B. Stakeholder register, issue log, and project documents updates
C. Project management plan updates, change requests, and project documents updates
D. Performance reports, change requests, and organizational process assets updates

135. Which knowledge area process attempts both to increase the probability and impact of favorable events and to decrease the likelihood and effect of events that can have adverse consequences on the project?

A. Project Quality Management
B. Project Risk Management
C. Project Procurement Management
D. Project Integration Management

136. In the Project Risk Management knowledge area, the initial risk register is produced during the _____ process.

A. Plan Risk Management
B. Identify Risks
C. Perform Qualitative Risk Analysis
D. Perform Quantitative Risk Analysis

137. During which Project Risk Management knowledge area processes can the project documents be updated?

A. Plan Risk Management, Identify Risks, and Perform Qualitative Risk Analysis
B. Identify Risks, Perform Qualitative Risk Analysis, and Plan Risk Management
C. Perform Qualitative Risk Analysis, Plan Risk Response, and Monitor Risks
D. Identify Risks, Plan Risk Responses, and Plan Risk Management

138. Your project used linear values of 0.1, 0.3, 0.5, 0.7, and 0.9 in analyzing the probability and impact of risks. A project risk with a moderate probability of 0.5 and a high impact of 0.7 will have a risk rating of _____.

A. 1.20
B. 0.71
C. 0.20
D. 0.35

139. The Identify Risks process uses several tools and techniques. Which data gathering technique would be most appropriate if you need to work with a multidisciplinary set of experts in addition to the project team to identify the project risks?

A. Checklists
B. Brainstorming
C. Interviewing
D. Root cause analysis

140. Your project used linear values of 0.1, 0.3, 0.5, 0.7, and 0.9 in analyzing the probability and impact of risks. From the following list of descriptions, which will *most likely* be assigned to the values respectively?

A. Moderate, neutral, average, high, and avoid
B. Low, medium, high, average, and very low
C. Very low, low, moderate, high, and very high
D. Very high, high, moderate, low, and very low

141. Using decision tree analysis, you calculated that Project A has an expected monetary value (EMV) of $65,000. In contrast, Project B has an EMV of $75,000. Which project is a better option?

A. Project A, because it has a lower EMV
B. Project B, because it has a higher EMV
C. Neither project, because the difference in EMV is not significant
D. Both, in order to maximize the results

142. Given a false decision node with a cost of $−50M with scenario probabilities of A (55%, $100M) and B (45%, $25M), what is the EMV for this decision node?

A. 0.00
B. 16.25
C. 66.25
D. 75.00

143. Given a false decision node with a cost of $–50M with scenario probabilities of A (55%, $100M) and B (45%, $25M), what are the net path values for A and B, respectively?

A. $27.50M and $–11.25M
B. $50.00M and $–25.00M
C. $55.00M and $11.25M
D. $72.50M and $2.50M

144. Which of the following risk response strategies are appropriate for negative risks or threats?

A. Avoid, transfer, and/or mitigate
B. Exploit, share, and/or enhance
C. Avoid, transfer, and/or recognize
D. Share, enhance, and/or recognize

145. Which risk response strategies are appropriate for positive risks or opportunities?

A. Avoid, transfer, and/or mitigate
B. Exploit, share, and/or enhance
C. Avoid, transfer, and/or recognize
D. Share, enhance, and/or recognize

146. Which risk response strategy can be applied to both negative risks (threats) and positive risks (opportunities)?

A. Mitigate
B. Exploit
C. Share
D. Accept

147. Which of the following statements *best* characterizes residual risks and secondary risks?

A. Secondary risks arise if the risk response generated a residual risk that is much larger than the original risk that was identified in the risk register
B. Secondary risks remain after the implementation of planned responses, whereas residual risks arise as a direct outcome of implementing a risk response
C. Residual risks remain after the implementation of planned responses, whereas secondary risks arise as a direct outcome of implementing a risk response
D. Risk response strategies for negative risks or threats generate residual risks, whereas positive risks or opportunities result in secondary risks

148. In the middle of your project, you noticed that some risks positively and negatively impacted your budget and schedule contingency. What do you need to perform to determine if you have adequate contingency to cover the remaining project risks?

A. Risk reassessment
B. Risk audits
C. Variance and trend analysis
D. Reserve analysis

149. The lists below contain outputs of the Control Risks process *except* for _____.

A. Risk register updates and change requests
B. Project management plan updates and change requests
C. Organizational process assets updates and project management plan updates
D. Risk register updates and make-or-buy decisions

150. The previous project manager left you a spreadsheet that summarized uncertain events with the following columns: probability, impact, priority, and ownership. You are *most likely* looking at what type of document?

A. Risk register
B. Requested changes
C. Recommended corrective actions
D. Recommended preventive actions

151. Which Project Procurement Management knowledge area process produces the procurement documents?

A. Conduct Procurements
B. Plan Procurements
C. Close Procurements
D. Control Procurements

152. Your project issued a purchase order for computer hardware to be delivered at the end of the month. The unit cost is based on the manufacturer's suggested retail price. The purchase order includes an incentive for early delivery. This is an example of a _____ contract.

A. Fixed-price
B. Cost-reimbursable
C. Time and material
D. Cost-plus-incentive-fee

153. Your company hired an offshore company to develop a hardware prototype for a new product line. The project contract states that the seller will be paid based on approved expenses. A fee will be paid depending on the total expenses plus a certain amount based on broad subjective criteria as defined by the buyer. What type of contract did the project use?

A. CPAF
B. CPFF
C. CPIF
D. T&M

154. Your health care project requires a very complex service. Technical capability, management approach, financial capacity, references, and proprietary rights are examples of _____.

A. Procurement documents
B. Source selection criteria
C. Procurement statement of work
D. Procurement document package

155. The Project Procurement Management knowledge area deals with purchasing or acquiring products, services, or results from outside the project team. Which statement is correct about obtaining responses to bids and proposals?

A. The Plan Procurements process produces the procurement management plan
B. The Conduct Procurements process generates the selected sellers and the procurement contract award
C. The Conduct Procurements process uses bidder conferences and proposal evaluation techniques
D. The Control Procurements process uses a contract change control system and claims administration

156. Which statement is correct about the tools and techniques that are used in the Conduct Procurements process?

A. The qualified sellers list contains all sellers that the buyer asked to submit a response to a request for proposal or a request for quotation
B. The Conduct Procurements process uses the following tools and techniques: bidder conferences, proposal evaluation techniques, and procurement negotiations
C. The buyer prepares the procurement document package and formally invites the sellers to prepare a bid for the requested products or services
D. The seller prepares a proposal in response to procurement document package; the proposal constitutes a formal and legally binding offer

157. Bidder conferences normally are held with prospective sellers prior to the preparation of bids and proposals. Other names for bidder conferences include all of the following *except* _____.

A. Contractor conferences
B. Vendor conferences
C. Pre-bid conferences
D. Virtual conferences

158. Which Project Procurement Management knowledge area process uses the following tools and techniques: expert judgement, advertising, and procurement negotiations?

A. Plan Procurements
B. Conduct Procurements
C. Control Procurements
D. Close Procurements

159. Which documents are prepared by the sellers and highlight their ability and willingness to deliver a product, service, or result for the buyer?

A. Agreements
B. Memos of understanding
C. Proposals
D. Letters of intent

160. You are in the process of negotiating with potential suppliers of plastic raw materials for your project. You separated the criteria into technical, economic, experience, and reputation categories. At this stage, what process are you performing?

A. Plan Procurements
B. Conduct Procurements
C. Define Activities
D. Estimate Costs

161. When selecting sellers, the source selection criteria may include all of the following *except* _____.

A. Product and lifecycle cost
B. References from previous customers
C. Credentials of the management team
D. Copies of contracts from other clients

162. Your organization drafted a procurement document package in anticipation of upcoming legislation that will drastically impact how you perform your day-to-day operations. If you distribute the procurement document package to selected sellers, what can you expect in return?

A. Proposals
B. Invoices
C. Quotations
D. Requirements

163. The project sponsor suggested that the selection committee evaluate sellers based solely on quantitative criteria. Which criterion below should be *excluded* in the evaluation process?

A. Assign a numerical weight to each requirement
B. Perform forced ranking of all sellers on each criterion
C. Rate each seller based on the size of previous projects
D. Solicit expert opinions from key industry leaders

164. Several publishers provided different estimates for your project's training manuals. If the range of estimates is too wide, what should you do?

A. Select the seller with the lowest estimate
B. Award the contract to the highest bidder
C. Perform your own independent estimate
D. Pick the seller that you are familiar with

165. Assume that you are the leader of the proposal evaluation team. You asked your team members to come up with ideas on how to evaluate sellers. From the following list, which evaluation technique would be *less preferred* compared to the other source selection criteria?

A. Include both subjective and objective evaluation criteria
B. Rate and score the proposals based on multiple categories
C. Assess the proposal based on the evaluator's narrative summary
D. Assign predefined weightings to business and user requirements

166. A contract obligates the seller to provide the services to the buyer, and it requires the buyer to pay the seller upon receipt of the services. A contract remains valid unless _____.

A. The buyer cannot pay the seller because of unforeseen financial difficulties
B. The contract contains clauses that will violate existing laws and regulations
C. The seller does not have the financial resources to deliver the service
D. One party's legal department cancels the contract with sufficient notice

167. What is the main purpose of the Control Procurements process?

A. To commit the seller to deliver the services as agreed
B. To make sure that the buyer lists the project requirements
C. To get a better price from sellers of the same products
D. To ensure both parties meet their contractual obligations

168. You received a contract from a seller to provide human resources consulting services for your project. There is a clause in the contract that can potentially impact your organization. Your project could be delayed if you ask the legal department to review the contract. What should you do?

A. Proceed with the contract because you have already been authorized to do so in the project charter
B. Ask for a delay in the project schedule so that the legal department can review the contract
C. Cross out the contract clause in question, initial it, and then sign the contract to avoid delays
D. Seek legal advice on what to do with the contract and assess the impact to the schedule

169. Which statement is true about the procurement management plan?

A. The procurement management plan is a subsidiary of the project management plan
B. The procurement management plan is similar to the project management plan
C. The procurement management plan is a subsidiary of the communications management plan
D. The procurement management plan is an output of the Control Procurements process

170. The procurement management plan, as part of the project management plan, is used as an input by the _____.

A. Control Procurements and Close Procurements processes
B. Conduct Procurements and Close Procurements processes
C. Conduct Procurements, and Control Procurements processes
D. Plan Procurements Conduct Procurements, and Close Procurements processes

171. You are working on a small web development project. Who would normally be responsible for paying the seller in accordance with the terms in the contract?

A. The company's accounts payable system
B. The senior leadership team
C. The functional owner of the project
D. The sponsor of the web development project

172. Within the Project Procurement Management knowledge area, procurement documents are an output of the _____ process and an input to the _____ process.

A. Plan Procurement Management; Close Procurements
B. Control Procurements; Close Procurements
C. Plan Procurement Management; Conduct Procurements
D. Conduct Procurements; Control Procurements

173. Trends and emerging practices for Project Procurement Management include the following except _____.

A. Long-term engagements
B. More advanced risk management
C. Advance in tools
D. Changing contracting processes

174. The prototype tests conducted for your project by a seller failed. You have no choice but to terminate the contract early. What should you do next?

A. Mutually terminate the contract early and close the project
B. Consider the seller in default because of the failed prototype tests
C. Pay the seller an early termination fee as stated in the contract
D. Review the contract's terms and conditions for early termination

175. You closed a contract during an early phase of the project, despite some unresolved claims with the seller. You reasoned that the seller will rectify the unresolved claims during the next project phase. If you still cannot agree on how to resolve the issues after the next phase, what should you do?

A. Convince the seller to go to arbitration
B. Threaten the seller with possible legal actions
C. Withhold all payments to the seller immediately
D. Review the contract's terms and conditions

176. Disagreements may arise between the seller and the buyer. If both parties accepted and signed a contract, which outcome is *least* desirable in case of disagreements?

A. Mutually resolve the disagreements
B. Ask the other party to pay a penalty
C. Convince the other party that there position is wrong
D. Take the issue to binding arbitration

177. The Control Procurements process uses several tools and techniques. Which list below contains the correct set of inputs?

A. Expert judgement, data analysis, and inspection
B. Inspection, audits, and change requests
C. Change requests, expert judgement, and claims payments
D. Claims payments, expert judgment and data analysis

178. Which statement is correct about the tools and techniques used in Project Procurement Management?

A. The Plan Procurements process uses standard forms and expert judgment.
B. The Conduct Procurements process uses Expert judgment, data analysis, and bidder conferences
C. The Plan Procurements process uses bidder conferences and records management systems.
D. The Conduct Procurements process uses weighting systems and independent estimates.

179. Procurement audits are structured reviews that recognize good practices and identify questionable items during the preparation and administration of procurement contracts. Which Project Procurement Management process uses procurement audits as a tool or a technique?

A. Plan Procurement Management
B. Conduct Procurements
C. Close Procurements
D. Control Procurements

180. As part of the Plan Procurement process, certain project documents may be updated. Which of the following lists identifies the correct portions of the project documentation that may be updated as part of Plan Procurement outputs?

A. Lessons learned, milestone list, risk register, and stakeholder register
B. Correspondence, payment schedules and requests, and risk register
C. Seller performance evaluation documentation and stakeholder register
D. Payment schedules and requests, lessons learned, and correspondence

181. The Conduct Procurements process was completed for your project. What output should be produced in the next Project Procurement Management process?

A. Closed procurements and organizational process assets updates
B. Procurement documentation and project management plan updates
C. Select sellers and procurement management plan updates
D. Qualified sellers list and procurement document package

182. Which two Project Procurement Management knowledge area processes update the organizational process assets?

A. Plan Procurement Management and Conduct Procurements
B. Conduct Procurements and Begin Procurements
C. Plan Procurement Management and Begin Procurements
D. Control Procurements and Finish Procurements

183. Which Project Stakeholder Management process produces the stakeholder register?

A. Plan Stakeholder Management
B. Control Stakeholder Management
C. Identify Stakeholders
D. Manage Stakeholder Engagement

184. The _____ and _____ are inputs to the Plan Stakeholder Engagement process.

A. Project charter; procurement documents
B. Project management plan; agreements
C. Project management plan; issue log
D. Stakeholder management plan; change log

185. Stakeholder analysis is among the tools & techniques of Identify Stakeholders process. The analysis results in a list of the stakeholders. Stakeholders' overall stake in the project s can include a combination of the following except:

A. Influence
B. Interest
C. Ownership
D. Contribution

186. You are working on a public safety project for a local government. On an extremely rare occasion, one of your project deliverables may violate a privacy law, but you know, in good faith, that it will not necessarily cause any personal harm. What should you do?

A. Monitor the situation since it may only happen on extremely rare occasions
B. There is no need to bring it up because it will not cause any personal harm
C. Disclose only when asked, so as not to delay the project and cause unnecessary panic
D. Inform the project management team about the scenario and address it accordingly

187. You are very excited to work on a large, multi-million-dollar project. Shortly after taking on the role, you realized that you do not have the experience to deliver it successfully. If you remove yourself from the project, it could be the end of your career with the company. You really want this project to be successful, and you are willing to do anything to make it work, but you do not want to look incompetent. What should you do?

A. Schedule special training to get the necessary skills
B. Ask a more senior project manager to mentor you
C. Inform key stakeholders of the gap in your experience
D. Work extra hours to make up for your deficiencies

188. The stakeholder register is an output of the Identify Stakeholders process. The document contains the following information except:

A. Identification information
B. Assessment information
C. Stakeholder influence
D. Stakeholder classification

189. You have always had suspicions about the professional relationship of another project manager with a major supplier. You strongly feel that other project managers share the same suspicions regarding this person. What is the *most appropriate* course of action in this situation?

A. Ask other project managers if they share the same suspicions
B. Report the suspicions to the company's ethics review committee
C. Start gathering facts to substantiate your personal suspicions
D. Stop being envious of the other project manager's relationship

190. During one of your weekly meetings, one of your team members shared a very funny but racial joke. The other person for whom the joke was intended did not mind it, and he started laughing as well. As a project manager, you are expected to _____.

A. Laugh with the team to foster team development
B. Ask for similar jokes to relieve the stress of the project team
C. Tell the team member not to do it again, outside the meeting
D. Remind the team, at the meeting, that such jokes are not tolerated

191. You serve on the board of directors of a professional association's local chapter. The chapter was voting on a motion that could potentially benefit your employer but not you personally. As part of your duty as a professional project management practitioner, you should _____.

A. Support the board's motion and highlight the benefits of hiring your employer
B. Abstain from the discussions to avoid the perception of conflict of interest
C. Point out the deficiencies on all proposals, including your employer's proposal
D. Assess all options and then offer your impartial and expert opinion to the group

192. You realized that you have *not* been fair to one of your project team members. What would be an appropriate course of action?

A. Apologize to the other project team member
B. Remind yourself to be fair next time
C. Do not do anything, as it was a one-time event
D. Take corrective actions as appropriate

193. You were hired to assess a software integration project. Based on your review, it became obvious that the project should be cancelled. If you make such recommendation, however, your contract will be terminated as well. You really need the money, and you cannot afford to lose this contract. You should _____.

A. Tell the truth even if it means losing your contract
B. Make suggestions on how to correct the problems
C. Prolong the contract until you can find another one
D. Ask the project sponsor to redefine the overall scope

194. Professional project managers have aspirational and mandatory standards. From the following list, which one is an aspirational standard of fairness?

A. Proactively disclose any potential conflict of interest
B. Demonstrate transparency when making decisions
C. Not discriminate against others based on race or gender
D. Apply rules of the organization without prejudice

195. From the following list, which action is an example of a mandatory standard of honesty?

A. Make commitments and promises in good faith
B. Make others feel safe to tell the truth
C. Provide accurate information in a timely manner
D. Do not engage in dishonest behaviors

196. A project management contractor did not lie in her presentation but withheld some information to convince the buyer to purchase her services. Such behavior demonstrates failure to meet the _____.

A. Aspirational standard of honesty
B. Mandatory standard of responsibility
C. Mandatory standard of honesty
D. Aspirational standard of fairness

197. Which of the following statements is *not* acceptable with regard to aspirational and mandatory standards of honesty?

A. Provide accurate information in a timely manner
B. Sometimes make implied commitments in good faith
C. Remain truthful in all project communications
D. Avoid dishonest behavior for personal gain

198. A project manager makes it a point to remind his foreign workers that they can be deported if they do not finish their deliverables on time. Can this behavior be considered abusive?

A. No, because it meets the aspirational and mandatory standards of honesty
B. Yes, because it creates an intense feeling of fear on the part of the foreign workers
C. No, because his duty of loyalty requires him to give the timely reminders
D. Yes, because foreign workers place little importance on project deadlines

199. What is the *best* way to resolve issues that may arise when there is a potential clash between duty of loyalty and conflict of interest?

A. Adhere to the duty of loyalty
B. Disclose the conflict entirely
C. Avoid the conflict of interest
D. Do not engage in the discussion

200. A person's responsibility, legal or moral, to promote the best interest of an organization or other person with whom he or she is affiliated is called _____.

A. Duty of loyalty
B. Social obligation
C. Membership affinity
D. Professional responsibility

Bonus Questions

201. A(n) _____ is a collection of projects, programs, subportfolios, and operations.

A. Program management office
B. Program
C. Portfolio
D. Organizational process assets

202. In weak and balanced matrix structures, the project manager's titles are _____ and _____ respectively?

A. Project coordinator, project manager
B. Project leader, project expeditor
C. Project expeditor, project manager
D. Project leader, project manager

203. Which statement is correct with regard to process names and project management process groups?

A. Develop Project Charter is a process within the Planning process group
B. Develop Project Management Plan is a process within the Initiating process group
C. Direct and Manage Project Work is a process within the Monitoring and Controlling process group
D. Develop Project Charter is a process within the Initiating process group

204. Which of the following processes is *not* part of the Planning project management process group?

A. Validate Scope
B. Collect Requirements
C. Define Scope
D. Create WBS

205. Which statement accurately describes interviews and focus groups?

A. Interviews are one-on-one; focus groups are cross-functional
B. Interviews are one-one-one; focus groups are usually facilitated by a moderator
C. Interviews are cross-functional; focus groups are usually facilitated by a moderator
D. Interviews are usually facilitated by a moderator; focus groups are cross-functional

Chapter 4: Answers to Practice Test A

1. **A.** Within the context of a project, the Project Integration Management knowledge area unifies and consolidates the various project management process groups (Initiating, Planning, Executing, Monitoring and Controlling, and Closing) from the beginning until the end of the project.

   The Project Scope Management knowledge area entails identifying all of the work required in order to bring the project to a successful completion. The Project Quality Management knowledge area determines and defines the quality policies, objectives, activities, and responsibilities within the project. The Project Resource Management knowledge area deals with the resourcing, organization, and management of the project team and resources.

   Reference: *PMBOK® Guide*, 6th Ed., page 69

2. **D.** Experienced project managers apply various project management tools and techniques depending on the context of the project. Therefore, it is the project manager's responsibility to seek professional expertise as needed, as well as to adjust the degree of rigor of various processes and procedures depending on the context of the project.

   Reference: *PMBOK® Guide*, 6th Ed., page 72

3. **B.** The project charter serves as the formal authorization for a project or a project phase. The Perform Integrated Change Control process includes reviewing, approving, and managing changes in the project. The project management plan captures the actions required to consolidate and coordinate various subsidiary plans, the project development approach, and baselines. Directing and managing project work occurs after the initiation and planning of the project.

   Reference: *PMBOK® Guide*, 6th Ed., page 70

4. **C.** The development of the project charter occurs during project initiation, whereas the development of the project management plan happens during project planning and the performance of integrated change control takes place during project monitoring and controlling. Managing stakeholder engagement is part of the executing process group within the Project Stakeholder Management knowledge area.

   Reference: *PMBOK® Guide*, 6th Ed., pages 70, 25

5. **D.** The outputs of the Perform Integrated Change Control process include approved change requests, project management plan updates, and project documents updates. The outputs of the Close Project or Phase process include organizational process assets updates.

   Reference: *PMBOK® Guide*, 6th Ed., pages 113, 121

6. A. Expert judgment is used in all of the Project Integration Management knowledge area processes. The project management information system is used in the Direct and Manage Project Work process. Change control tools belong to the Perform Integrated Change Control process. Product analysis is part of the Define Scope process.

Reference: *PMBOK® Guide*, 6th Ed., pages 71, 130

7. C. After the development of the project management plan, the project manager may proceed with the Direct and Manage Project Work process. The Project Integration Management knowledge area processes flow as follows: Develop Project Charter, Develop Project Management Plan, Direct and Manage Project Work, Manage Project Knowledge, Monitor and Control Project Work, Perform Integrated Change Control, and Close Project or Phase.

Reference: *PMBOK® Guide*, 6th Ed., page 70

8. D. Inputs of the Close Project or Phase process consist of the project charter, project management plan, project documents, accepted deliverables, business documents, agreements, procurement documentation, and organizational process assets. The expert judgment technique mentioned in the question is common to all seven processes in the Project Integration Management knowledge area and across the vast majority of *PMBOK® Guide* processes.

Reference: *PMBOK® Guide*, 6th Ed., pages 71, 121

9. A. The project initiator or sponsor will either create the project charter or delegate that duty to the project manager. The sponsor's or initiator's signature on the charter authorizes the project. The project manager may assist in developing the project charter, but the project initiator or sponsor is the one who can authorize it.

Reference: *PMBOK® Guide*, 6th Ed., pages 77, 81

10. B. As a result of internal business needs or external influences, an organization may initiate some sort of business case or benefits management plan prior to the development of the project charter. The project scope statement and the project management plan are developed after the project charter. Likewise, detailed cost estimates and work breakdown structure occur later in the project management processes.

Reference: *PMBOK® Guide*, 6th Ed., pages 77-78

11. A. The project charter normally includes direct and indirect references to the project purpose or justification, measurable project objectives and success criteria, high-level requirements and project description, high-level risks, a summary milestone schedule, preapproved financial resources, key stakeholders, project exit criteria, name of the sponsor and the project manager, and a summary budget. The rest of the options are associated with the development of the project scope statement and not the project charter.

Reference: *PMBOK® Guide*, 6th Ed., page 81

12. D. For an external customer, a project manager will need an agreement (when applicable), typically a contract, in order to prepare the project charter. The project scope statement is an output of Define Scope, which is part of the Planning process group. Work performance reports are used as inputs to the Perform Integrated Change Control process.

Reference: *PMBOK® Guide*, 6th Ed., page 78

13. A. The project business case summarizes the objectives and reasons for project initiation. It helps gauge the project success against the set objectives. The other options are enterprise environmental factors which serve as inputs to every process.

Reference: *PMBOK® Guide*, 6th Ed., pages 30-32, 77

14. B. Enterprise environmental factors internal and external factors. The other options list organizational process assets which include processes, policies, procedures, and organizational knowledge areas.

Reference: *PMBOK® Guide*, 6th Ed., pages 38-41

15. C. Financial control procedures entail time reporting, reviewing expenditures, reviewing disbursements, and assigning accounting codes using standard provisions for contracts. Examples of project closure guidelines include auditing the final project and validating the product. Risk control procedures aim to categorize and assess risks using information about probabilities and impact. Organizational standard processes impact the entire organization through standards, policies, checklists, and so on.

Reference: *PMBOK® Guide*, 6th Ed., pages 40-41

16. D. The two categories of organizational process assets are processes, policies and procedures, and organizational knowledge bases. The other options are examples of organizational processes and procedures.

Reference: *PMBOK® Guide*, 6th Ed., page 39

17. B. An organizational knowledge repositories includes configuration management, financial data, historical information and lessons learned, issue and defect management data, metrics data, project files from previous projects, and more. The other options are incorrect because they include organizational processes and procedures—not organizational corporate knowledge base.

Reference: *PMBOK® Guide*, 6th Ed., page 40

18. A. The business case summarizes the objectives and reasons for project initiation. It helps gauge the project success against the set objectives. A document that formally initiates the project and identifies the project manager describes the project charter. The project scope baseline describes the procurement statement of work, and the project's deliverables and the work required to create those deliverables are included within the project scope statement.

Reference: *PMBOK® Guide*, 6th Ed., pages 30, 77

19. A. The process used to define and document the high-level requirements and risks of the project is the Develop Project Charter process.

Reference: *PMBOK® Guide*, 6th Ed., page 75

20. A. The correct answer is the project charter. Items in the project charter include the project purpose, measurable project objectives, high-level requirements, high-level project description, overall project risk, summary milestone schedule, preapproved financial resources, key stakeholder list, project approval requirements, project exit criteria, assigned project manager, and name and authority of the sponsor.

In contrast, the project management plan deals with the remaining process groups that follow the initiating and planning of the project: executing, monitoring and controlling, and closing. The project scope statement contains, among other things, the detailed product scope description, project deliverables, acceptance criteria and exclusions.

Reference: *PMBOK® Guide*, 6th Ed., page 81

21. A. The project initiator or sponsor may delegate the creation of the project charter to the project manager. However, he or she is the primary source for the information needed in the charter. The project manager may leverage organizational process assets and take enterprise environmental factors into account, but they are not specific to the project.

Reference: *PMBOK® Guide*, 6th Ed., page 77

22. A. The business case, benefits management plan, agreements, enterprise environmental factors, and organizational process assets are inputs to the development of the project charter. The project scope statement, requirements documentation, and approved changed requests are part of scope planning. Project management processes are not an input in the development of the project charter. The project management plan, work performance data, and rejected change request are inputs to the Monitor and Control Project Work process.

Reference: *PMBOK® Guide*, 6th Ed., pages 75

23. C. The project management plan encompasses all of the outputs of the Planning Process Group and includes the description and tailoring of all processes the project will be executing.

Reference: *PMBOK® Guide*, 6th Ed., page 83

24. C. The Direct and Manage Project Work process, as the name implies, deals with the actual execution of the project management plan by the project manager and the project team. They will act to produce the project deliverables, as outlined in the project scope statement. The other processes are incorrect because they are parts of the Monitoring and Controlling Process Group.

Reference: *PMBOK® Guide*, 6th Ed., pages 90-92

25. A. Projects may produce or deliver tangible and intangible deliverables during project execution. From the options provided, public benefit is the only intangible deliverable. Highway lighting, traffic signs, and paved roads are tangible deliverables.

Reference: *PMBOK® Guide*, 6th Ed., pages 4, 7, 33

26. C. Collecting the project data and facilitating the forecasting of cost and schedule are actions that are associated with the Direct and Manage Project Work process, which is part of the Executing Process Group.

Reference: *PMBOK® Guide*, 6th Ed., pages 90-92

27. C. Change requests include corrective actions, preventive actions, defect repairs, and updates, thus making change requests the correct answer. Approved corrective actions are documented, authorized directions that the project manager and the project team must perform in order to bring the project back on the path defined in the project management plan. Preventive actions help reduce the likelihood of risks that can contribute to an unfavorable project outcome. Approved change requests deal with the expansion and contraction of project scope. Approved defect repairs aim to correct product defects that were found during the quality inspection or the audit process.

Reference: *PMBOK® Guide*, 6th Ed., page 96

28. C. Approved change requests deal with the expansion and contraction of project scope, among other approved changes. Approved corrective actions are documented, authorized directions that the project manager and the project team must perform in order to bring the project back on the path defined in the project management plan. Approved preventive actions help reduce the likelihood of risks that can contribute to an unfavorable project outcome. Approved defect repairs aim to correct product defects that were found during the quality inspection or the audit process.

Reference: *PMBOK® Guide*, 6th Ed., page 93

29. D. Expert judgment is one of the tools and techniques in the Direct and Manage Project Work process. Deliverables, work performance data, and issue log along with change requests, project management plan updates, and organizational process updates are outputs of the same process.

Reference: *PMBOK® Guide*, 6th Ed., pages 94-97

30. A. Because the initiating and planning phases already were completed, the project manager is likely to be at the execution phase of the project. One process during project execution is Direct and Management Project Work, which produces the following outputs: deliverables, work performance data, issue log, project management plan updates, project document updates, organizational process assets updates and change requests, which include corrective and preventive actions, and defect repair. The other options are incorrect because they list outputs for the Monitoring and Controlling, and Closing processes of a project.

Reference: *PMBOK® Guide*, 6th Ed., page 90

31. B. As defined in the project management plan, work performance data are the raw observations and measurements identified during execution. It is routinely collected to determine which deliverables have been delivered, to record costs that have been incurred, and to gain an understanding of the extent of the remaining tasks. Changes in the project scope, policies, and other factors are normally documented as change requests. Deliverables are unique products, results, or capabilities that complete the project upon delivery. Implemented change requests prove that change requests were implemented, implemented corrective actions correct future project performance, and implemented preventive actions help reduce the negative consequences of project risks.

Reference: *PMBOK® Guide*, 6th Ed., page 95

32. A. The Monitor and Control Project Work process is performed throughout the project, across the project's initiating, planning, executing, and closing processes.

Reference: *PMBOK® Guide*, 6th Ed., page 105

33. D. Although comparing actual performance to the project management plan, assessing project performance, and monitoring the implementation of approved changes and managing project risks are important components of project monitoring and control, they do not necessarily relate to the question. To facilitate earned value management techniques, the project manager must establish project baselines from which overall progress and variances can be calculated and compared.

Reference: *PMBOK® Guide*, 6th Ed., pages 261-266

34. C. Cost performance index (CPI) = earned value (EV) / actual cost (AC)

Research Project A = $500 / $505 = 0.99
Research Project B = $455 / $450 = 1.01
Research Project C = 1.08
Research Project D = 0.94

A CPI value less than 1.0 indicates a cost overrun—the project is spending more than the planned estimates. In contrast, a CPI value less than 1.0 signifies cost underrun of the estimate. Therefore, Research Project C is the most cost efficient. Essentially, the project receives $1.08 in value of actual completed work for every dollar that it spends.

Reference: *PMBOK® Guide*, 6th Ed., page 263

35. A. Cost variance (CV) = earned value (EV) – actual cost (AC)

CV = $747 – $691 = $56

Reference: *PMBOK® Guide*, 6th Ed., page 262

36. B. Important change control tools are configuration identification, configuration status accounting, and configuration verification and auditing. Architecture configuration and control is vague relative to the other options.

Reference: *PMBOK® Guide*, 6th Ed., page 118

37. D. Documented change requests must be either accepted, deferred, or rejected by the change control board. If change requests are documented, it is implied that they must be reviewed. Deferring a change request is essentially a rejection.

Reference: *PMBOK® Guide*, 6th Ed., page 115

38. C. The project management plan, which contains the project scope statement as part of the scope baseline, need to be updated as a result of an approved change request. Closing the project may require updates to organizational process assets. Note that the administrative closure procedure and contract closure procedure are components of the Close Project process and not the Perform Integrated Change Control process.

Reference: *PMBOK® Guide*, 6th Ed., page 137

39. A. Perform Integrated Change Control process tools and techniques include alternatives analysis, cost-benefit analysis, voting, multi-criteria decision analysis and meetings. Earned value analysis helps assess the overall health of the cost and schedule performance as a part of the Control Costs process—not the Perform Integrated Change Control process.

Reference: *PMBOK® Guide*, 6th Ed., page 113

40. B. The Close Project process must be performed at the end of each phase, especially on a multiphase project, and at the end of the overall project. Such closure includes finalizing a specific portion of the project scope and all of its associated activities. By doing so, Lessons Learned from a phase can then be applied to the succeeding phase. If the Close Project or Phase process is performed only at the end of the project, then the project team will not be able to formally take advantage of Lessons Learned during project execution.

Reference: *PMBOK® Guide*, 6th Ed., page 123

41. D. Project documents that can be used as inputs when managing the project knowledge are lessons learned register, project team assignments, resource breakdown structure, and source selection criteria. Organizational process assets updates is an output, not an input.

Reference: *PMBOK® Guide*, 6th Ed., pages 98, 101

42. D. Sharing tacit knowledge is an example of knowledge management. Expert judgment, knowledge management, information management, and interpersonal and team skills are tools and techniques of the Manage Project Knowledge process.

Reference: *PMBOK® Guide*, 6th Ed., pages 102-104

43. A. Inputs to the Close Project or Phase process include the project charter, project management plan, project documents, accepted deliverables, business documents, agreements, procurement documentation, and organizational process assets.

Reference: *PMBOK® Guide*, 6th Ed., page 121

44. B. Technically, all options are correct because expert judgment is a tool and technique used by all Project Integration Management knowledge area processes. The option that lists all of the processes is considered "more correct" compared to the other options.

Reference: *PMBOK® Guide*, 6th Ed., page 71

45. C. Organizational process assets that can influence the Close Project or Phase process include, but are not limited to, project or phase closure guidelines or requirements (for example, project audits, project evaluations, and transition criteria), along with the historical information and Lessons Learned knowledge base (for example, project records and documents, all project closure information, information regarding previous project selection decisions, previous project performance information, and information from the risk management effort). The other options are incorrect.

Reference: *PMBOK® Guide*, 6th Ed., page 126

46. A. The Control Procurements process captures the actions involved in formally closing all contracts. It is important to briefly revisit the procurement management plan to determine if the collection agency's claims have any merit. Although the project is no longer your responsibility, it would be unprofessional to simply terminate the telephone call without having a plan of action.

Reference: *PMBOK® Guide*, 6th Ed., pages 492-501

47. B. Organizational process assets include project files, project closure documents, and historical information. The project manager updates these documents as part of the Close Project or Phase process. The configuration management system is a collection of formal documented procedures for maintaining the functional and physical characteristics of artifacts associated with a project. Work performance data is the raw data surrounding everything that happened related to the creation of the deliverables. Enterprise environmental factors include internal and external factors that can influence the project.

Reference: *PMBOK® Guide*, 6th Ed., page 501

48. C. The project's final report includes the summary level description of the project or phase. The other options are correct statements but they are incorrect relative to the question.

Reference: *PMBOK® Guide*, 6th Ed., page 127

49. B. The creation of the WBS is part of the Project Scope Management knowledge area process called Create WBS.

Reference: *PMBOK® Guide*, 6th Ed., page 129

50. C. The Project Scope Management knowledge area processes include the following: Plan Scope Management, Collect Requirements, Define Scope, Create WBS, Validate Scope, and Control Scope. A detailed description of the project is created and defined during the Define Scope process, producing the project scope statement, and the Create WBS process subdivides the major project deliverables into smaller components. The other options are incorrect.

Reference: *PMBOK® Guide*, 6th Ed., page 129

51. A. The Define Scope process uses the following tools and techniques:

- Alternative analysis
- Multicriteria decision analysis
- Product analysis

Tools and techniques for the Collect Requirements process include:

- Brainstorming
- Interviews
- Focus groups
- Questionnaires & surveys
- Benchmarking
- Document analysis
- Multicriteria decision analysis
- Affinity diagrams
- Mind mapping
- Nominal group technique
- Context Diagrams

The Create WBS process entails use of decomposition. The Control Scope process uses variance and trend analysis as tools and techniques.

Reference: *PMBOK® Guide*, 6th Ed., page 150

52. D. The Data Gathering tool and technique uses brainstorming, interviews, focus groups, questionnaires and surveys, and benchmarking. Nominal group technique, observation/conversation and facilitation are decision making techniques.

Reference: *PMBOK® Guide*, 6th Ed., pages 142, 144-145

53. A. The WBS is a hierarchical decomposition of the work to be performed on a project. Because the second level of the WBS listed the major parts of a bicycle, it would be reasonable to assume that the succeeding level will further break down each major part into smaller parts (front wheel and rear wheel).

Reference: *PMBOK® Guide*, 6th Ed., page 156

54. B. Expert judgment and decomposition are the only tools and techniques of the Create WBS process. Inspection is for the Validate Scope process and variance analysis is for the Control Scope process. Within the Project Scope Management knowledge area, facilitation (i.e., facilitated workshops) is one of the tools and techniques of the Collect Requirements and Define Scope processes.

Reference: *PMBOK® Guide*, 6th Ed., page 156

55. B. The work breakdown structure (WBS) is a hierarchical decomposition of the work to be performed on a project. In contrast, an organizational breakdown structure (OBS) hierarchically depicts the project organization in order to properly relate the work packages to the performing organizational units. As their names imply, the risk breakdown structure and resource breakdown structure deal with project risks and resources, respectively.

Reference: *PMBOK® Guide*, 6th Ed., page 316

56. C. Formal acceptance of the completed project scope and associated deliverables from the stakeholders occurs during the Validate Scope process. Sequentially, the Collect Requirements process occurs first, followed by the Define Scope process. Outputs of the Define Scope process serve as inputs to the Create WBS process, which is then followed by the Validate Scope process. The Control Scope process is the last process within Project Scope Management.

Reference: *PMBOK® Guide*, 6th Ed., page 163

57. C. Inspection entails measuring, examining, and verifying that the project deliverables adhere to the requirements. Other industries may adopt similar but different techniques such as reviews, walk-throughs, or audits. Product analysis is a tool or technique for the Define Scope process, decomposition for the Create WBS process, and data analysis for the Control Scope Process.

Reference: *PMBOK® Guide*, 6th Ed., pages 130, 166

58. A. The Control Scope process requires the following inputs: project management plan, project documents, work performance data, and organizational process assets. The tools and techniques for this process are data and trend analysis. Through the use of this tool and technique, the Control Scope process produces the following outputs: work performance information, change requests, project management plan updates, and project document updates.

Reference: *PMBOK® Guide*, 6th Ed., page 167

59. A. Variance analysis is used to assess the degree of difference between the baseline and actual performance. Therefore, the remaining options are incorrect.

Reference: *PMBOK® Guide*, 6th Ed., page 170

60. A. An analysis of project's progress against the project scope can result in issuance of change requests to the scope baseline or components of the project management plan. The configuration management system is a collection of formal documented procedures for maintaining the functional and physical characteristics of artifacts associated with a project. The change control system works in conjunction with the configuration management system. The requirements traceability matrix is a table that connects requirements to their origins and traces them throughout the lifetime of the project.

Reference: *PMBOK® Guide*, 6th Ed., page 168

61. D. Outputs of the Control Scope process include updates to the following: work performance information, change requests, project management plan updates, and project document updates.

Reference: *PMBOK® Guide*, 6th Ed., page 130

62. C. As a result of performing the Create WBS processes, the scope baseline will be created. As part of the Control Scope process, the scope baseline may need to be updated (as part of the project management plan updates) if an approved change request will have an impact on the scope. Scope baseline is not an output of Collect Requirements, Define Scope, and Validate Scope processes.

Reference: *PMBOK® Guide*, 6th Ed., pages 130, 171

63. B. The Sequence Activities process uses the PDM. The other options are incorrect.

Reference: *PMBOK® Guide*, 6th Ed., page 187

64. D. Rolling wave planning is a form of progressive elaboration planning where near-term work is planned in more detail and future work is planned at a higher level. As more information becomes known about upcoming events, it can then be decomposed into activities. In contrast, WBS branches with sufficient definition should be decomposed to the work package level.

Reference: *PMBOK® Guide*, 6th Ed., page 185

65. A. The PDM uses nodes (boxes or rectangles) to represent activities; arrows connect the nodes to show the dependencies. Leads and lags allows for acceleration and delays of successor activities, respectively. The four types of dependency determination used to define the sequence of activities include mandatory (hard logic), discretionary (soft logic) and internal and external dependencies.

Reference: *PMBOK® Guide*, 6th Ed., pages 189-192

66. A. Finish-to-start is the most commonly used type of precedence relationship in the PDM. The other options are incorrect.

Reference: *PMBOK® Guide*, 6th Ed., pages 189-190

67. B. The Estimate Activity Resources process is performed periodically throughout the project as needed. Inputs of the Estimate Activity Resources process include: project management plan, project documents, enterprise environmental factors, and organizational process assets. Outputs of the Estimate Activity Resources process include resource requirements, basis of estimates, resource breakdown structure, and project document updates.

Reference: *PMBOK® Guide*, 6th Ed., pages 582-583

68. C. Draw a network diagram based on the table. The critical path includes tasks A, D, E, H, and J. The sum of durations of each of these tasks is 24 days.

Reference: *PMBOK® Guide*, 6th Ed., pages 198-199, 208, 218

69. B. $E = (O + 4M + P) / 6 = (8 + 4*14 + 16) / 6 = 13.33$

Reference: *PMBOK® Guide*, 6th Ed., pages 200-202

70. D. Draw a network diagram based on the table. The critical path includes tasks A, D, E, H and J. The sum of the durations of each task in the critical path is 24 days.

Reference: *PMBOK® Guide*, 6th Ed., pages 198-199

71. C. Graphical representations of the project schedule consist of project schedule network diagrams, bar charts, and milestone schedule. The project schedule is too broad relative to the correct answer. Milestone charts, the correct answer, show the start or completion dates of major deliverables and key external interfaces. Project schedule networks diagram are suited for showing task dependencies, whereas bar charts are ideal for showing the duration of the tasks.

Reference: *PMBOK® Guide*, 6th Ed., pages 218-219

72. B. Outputs of the Develop Schedule process include schedule baseline, project schedule, schedule data, project calendars, change requests, project management plan updates, and project documents updates. The other options are incorrect because the lists contain outputs from the Control Schedule process.

Reference: *PMBOK® Guide*, 6th Ed., pages 205, 222

73. A. The Control Schedule process allows the project manager to assess the current status of the project schedule, influence the factors that create schedule changes, ascertain changes in the project schedule, and manage actual changes. The rest of the statements are incorrect.

Reference: *PMBOK® Guide*, 6th Ed., pages 222-223

74. B. The Control Schedule process is performed as part of the Monitoring and Controlling process group. The other options are incorrect.

Reference: *PMBOK® Guide*, 6th Ed., pages 25, 222

75. C. As part of the Control Schedule process, the following inputs are required: project management plan (schedule management plan, schedule baseline, scope baseline, and performance measurement baseline), project documents (lessons learned register, project calendars, project schedule, resource calendars, and schedule data), work performance data, and organizational process assets.

Reference: *PMBOK® Guide*, 6th Ed., page 222

76. C. Schedule performance index (SPI) = earned value (EV) / planned value (PV) = 0.80

The project is 80% on schedule, meaning 20% behind. Therefore, corrective actions most likely will be required to bring the project back on track. The other options are incorrect.

Reference: *PMBOK® Guide*, 6th Ed., pages 261-267

77. A. An SPI higher than 1.0 indicates that the project is getting more value (earned value) than the budgeted cost for the work scheduled to be completed at that point in time (planned value). If the earned value and planned value are indeed accurate, then there is nothing to worry about in terms of schedule progress.

Reference: *PMBOK® Guide*, 6th Ed., page 263

78. A. Schedule variance (SV) = earned value (EV) − planned value (PV) = 888 − 999 = −111

Reference: *PMBOK® Guide*, 6th Ed., page 262

79. A. The Project Cost Management knowledge area processes are Plan Cost Management, Estimate Costs, Determine Budget, and Control Costs.

Reference: *PMBOK® Guide*, 6th Ed., page 231

80. D. The range of the ROM will be wide during the initiation phase of a project—particularly if there is no historical data from which to base the estimates. Given this, the range of -25 to +75 percent appears to be reasonable.

Reference: *PMBOK® Guide*, 6th Ed., page 241

81. C. Parametric estimating relies on historical data to come up with estimates, plus a specific value of the existing project. Depending on the estimating model, the estimates can be accurate. It is likely that the construction estimator came up with the cost estimate based on square footage and material (for example, carpet, tiles, or hardwood).

Analogous cost estimating derives estimates based on comparable projects. Such a perception of similarity must be based on facts and not just appearance; otherwise, the estimates will not be accurate. Bottom-up estimates are based on estimates of each lower-level activity. The estimates are then rolled up to come up with the estimates. Vendor bid analysis is based on comparing the estimates of multiple vendors.

Reference: *PMBOK® Guide*, 6th Ed., page 244

82. D. The accuracy and reliability of analogous or parametric estimating is dependent on the correctness of the historical information and the scalability of the model (for example, applicability to small, medium, or large projects). It is also imperative that parameters are based on quantifiable factors.

Reference: *PMBOK® Guide*, 6th Ed., page 244

83. A. After performing the Control Costs process, the following outputs may be updated: work performance information, cost forecasts, change requests, project management plan (cost management plan, cost baseline, and performance measurement baseline), and project documents (assumption log, basis of estimates, cost estimates, lessons learned register, and risk register. The remaining options are incorrect because they are inputs, not outputs, of the Control Costs process.

Reference: *PMBOK® Guide*, 6th Ed., page 257

84. D. ETC = EAC − AC = 500 − 450 = 50

Reference: *PMBOK® Guide*, 6th Ed., pages 261-267

85. A. The Plan Quality Management process uses the cost of quality (COQ) technique.

Reference: *PMBOK® Guide*, 6th Ed., page 277

86. D. Total Quality Management, Six Sigma, and Lean Six Sigma are quality improvement initiatives, while PDCA (Plan-Do-Check-Act) cycle is a basis for quality improvement.

Reference: *PMBOK® Guide*, 6th Ed., page 275

87. A. Failure costs are also known as the cost of poor quality. Internal failures and external failures are the two types of failure costs. The cost of quality is a superset of failure costs.

Reference: *PMBOK® Guide*, 6th Ed., pages 274, 282

88. A. The following project documents may be updated during the Plan Quality Management process: lessons learned register, requirements traceability matrix, risk register, and stakeholder register. The other options are incorrect because they include project management plan components such as risk management plan and scope baseline.

Reference: *PMBOK® Guide*, 6th Ed., page 287

89. D. Quality objectives of the project, quality roles and responsibilities, and quality tools are included in the Quality Management Plan as an output to Plan Quality Management process. Assumption log is an input to the Plan Quality Management process.

Reference: *PMBOK® Guide*, 6th Ed., pages 277, 286

90. B. The Project Quality Management knowledge area includes the following processes: Plan Quality Management, Manage Quality, and Control Quality. Data gathering, audits, and quality improvements methods are used in the Manage Quality process to convert inputs into outputs.

Reference: *PMBOK® Guide*, 6th Ed., page 272

91. D. Change requests are outputs of both the Manage Quality and Control Quality processes and, as such, need to follow the Perform Integrated Change Control processes before they can be approved and implemented. Any undocumented changes should not be processed or implemented.

Reference: *PMBOK® Guide*, 6th Ed., page 296

92. C. Project quality audits may be scheduled or random. Given that the project quality audit was scheduled to occur at least once a month, the project manager needs to contact the project quality auditor to conduct the audit as planned.

Reference: *PMBOK® Guide*, 6th Ed., pages 294-295

93. A. A quality audit is an assessment performed by an unbiased individual or entity to determine if project activities conform to organizational and project policies and procedures. A configuration management system is a collection of formal documented procedures for maintaining the functional and physical characteristics of artifacts associated with a project. A change control system works in conjunction with configuration management to define the mechanics of managing changes on the project. Process analysis processes work to analyze and identify opportunities for improvement.

Reference: *PMBOK® Guide*, 6th Ed., pages 294-295

94. A. The quality activities stated in the question characterize the Manage Quality process. Managing quality in a project produces the following outputs: quality reports, test and evaluation documents, change requests (recommended corrective actions and/or preventive actions), project management plan updates, and project documents updates. The other options are outputs of the Plan Quality Management process, not the Manage Quality process; hence, they are incorrect answers.

Reference: *PMBOK® Guide*, 6th Ed., pages 288, 277

95. D. Project quality control requires knowledge of statistical quality control to determine the causes of unsatisfactory results. The other options are incorrect.

Reference: *PMBOK® Guide*, 6th Ed., pages 298-300

96. C. An Ishikawa diagram is another name for a cause-and-effect diagram, so both choices can be eliminated as correct answers. Flowcharting helps to analyze how problems occur. Given this, control chart is the correct answer because it can be used to determine if a process is stable—in this particular case, the monthly project budget.

Reference: *PMBOK® Guide*, 6th Ed., pages 293-294, 304

97. B. Control Charts leverage an upper control limit, x axis, and lower control limit. The following characteristics are associated with the tools noted:

- Cause and effect diagram—major defect, potential causes and effect
- Control chart—upper control limit, x axis, and lower control limit
- Flowcharting—activities, decision points, and order of processing
- Histograms—graphical representation, number of defects per deliverable, number of times each process is noncompliant

Reference: *PMBOK® Guide*, 6th Ed., pages 293-294, 304

98. D. Systematic sampling selects every n^{th} element within the sampling frame. In this particular example, the technical support representative will check every 100th computer within the sampling frame of 25,000 computers.

Reference: *PMBOK® Guide*, 6th Ed., page 303

99. D. The Project Resource Management processes include Plan Resource Management, Estimate Activity Resources, Acquire Resources, Develop Team, Manage Team, and Control Resources. The Sequence Activities process is part of the Project Schedule Management knowledge area.

Reference: *PMBOK® Guide*, 6th Ed., pages 307, 174

100. B. In a unionized organization, the collective bargaining agreement will directly impact the roles and responsibilities that team members may perform in a project. The collective bargaining agreement is basically a labor contract between an employer and one or more unions that defines the parties' relationships in a workplace environment.

Reference: *PMBOK® Guide*, 6th Ed., page 329

101. A. The Acquire Resources process uses the following tools and techniques: decision making (multicriteria decision analysis), interpersonal and team skills (negotiation), pre-assignment and virtual teams. The other options are incorrect because they are tools and techniques used in the Develop Team process.

Reference: *PMBOK® Guide*, 6th Ed., pages 328, 336

102. D. Although the other options may be acceptable but the most correct answer—partly because of its generalized nature—is to prepare a training plan to make sure that all team members have the technical certification. The plan can also include ways to help team members obtain certifications that would benefit the project. The other options potentially can be included as part of the training plan.

Reference: *PMBOK® Guide*, 6th Ed., page 336, 342

103. A. The three key team members are considered preassigned because their assignments to the project are known in advance. Staff negotiation entails getting the project team members from various functional or departmental areas. Acquired staff means hiring consultants or subcontracting the work. Although two of the team members will be working as a virtual team, but the fact that they were known in advance makes preassigned a better answer than virtual.

Reference: *PMBOK® Guide*, 6th Ed., page 333

104. B. Pre-assignment involves knowing the project team members prior to the start of the project. Hiring consultants or subcontracting the work is considered an acquisition. Virtual teams work remotely. Although all of these may require some form of negotiation, the correct answer is requesting the functional managers (or similar roles) to provide the staff with the proper skills to work in a particular time frame.

Reference: *PMBOK® Guide*, 6th Ed., page 333

105. C. Virtual teams, although working on the same project, perform the work in different locations.

Reference: *PMBOK® Guide*, 6th Ed., page 333

106. D. The project team is basically working around the clock and in a fast-track mode. We know that they are working 24 hours per day (8 hours × 3 shifts = 24 hours). However, it is not known if they work on weekends as well. Thus, 24x7 is incorrect. We also do not know if the project is running effectively and efficiently. Given this, virtual team is the best answer because home offices and shift work are characteristics of a virtual team.

Reference: *PMBOK® Guide*, 6th Ed., page 333

107. C. Enhancing the competencies of team members and facilitating the interactions among them, especially when performed early in the project, enhance the overall project team performance. Such actions are part of the Develop Team process.

Reference: *PMBOK® Guide*, 6th Ed., page 336

108. A. Outputs of the Develop Team process include team performance assessments, change requests, project management plan updates, project documents updates, enterprise environmental factors updates, and organizational process assets updates. The other options are incorrect because they are outputs of the Acquire Resources process.

Reference: *PMBOK® Guide*, 6th Ed., pages 336, 328

109. A. Although training can be formal or informal, it is inaccurate to claim that formal training produces the best results in a project environment. In some cases, informal training may be comparable to or even better than formal training.

Reference: *PMBOK® Guide*, 6th Ed., page 342

110. C. Training is one of the tools and techniques for the Develop Team process. Pre-assignment, negotiation, and virtual teams are tools and techniques of the Acquire Resources process.

Reference: *PMBOK® Guide*, 6th Ed., pages 336, 328

111. B. An unplanned recognition of a staff during a team meeting is considered informal, as opposed to a formal, planned, and management-decided award. It is also not monetary, which is also be viewed as a tangible reward.

Reference: *PMBOK® Guide*, 6th Ed., pages 341-342

112. B. A good strategy for project managers is to give team recognition throughout the life cycle of the project rather than waiting until the project is complete. The other options reflect various methods at the end of the project.

Reference: *PMBOK® Guide*, 6th Ed., pages 341-342

113. A. Actual cost of work performed (ACWP), contract work breakdown structure (CWBS), and cost-plus-percentage of cost (CPPC) are not informal performance assessments. Only management by walking around (MBWA) is an example of an informal assessment.

Reference: *PMBOK® Guide*, 6th Ed., page 343

114. D. All of the options are essentially correct, but coaching the team formally and informally throughout the project will help keep team members focused on achieving individual and collective project goals. Good work can be recognized and rewarded, and poor work can be adjusted as needed.

It is good to focus on positive performance, but negative performance should not be hidden or ignored. Formal reviews throughout the project are needed and should be complemented with informal reviews. In addition to being challenging and aggressive, goals must be achievable and realistic.

Reference: *PMBOK® Guide*, 6th Ed., page 343

115. A. In a weak matrix organization, team members are accountable to a functional manager because the project manager has a low authority in this particular organizational structure. The other options are incorrect.

Reference: *PMBOK® Guide*, 6th Ed., page 47

116. B. In a strong matrix organization, the project manager is primarily responsible for managing the dual reporting relationship of project team members. The other options are incorrect.

Reference: *PMBOK® Guide*, 6th Ed., page 47

117. D. Based on the 360-degree feedback principles, performance evaluations can be received from all sources that interact with the person being evaluated, such as superiors, peers, and subordinates, but not from the individuals being evaluated. However, there are cases where the individual being evaluated can be asked to perform a self-assessment so that it can be compared to the assessments provided by others. She then work her manager to try to narrow the gap between the self-assessment and the assessments of others.

Reference: *PMBOK® Guide*, 6th Ed., page 347

118. A. Change requests such as staffing changes are handled through the Perform Integrated Change Control process. The other options are incorrect.

Reference: *PMBOK® Guide*, 6th Ed., page 350

119. A. Project Communications Management knowledge area processes include Plan Communications Management, Manage Communications, and Monitor Communications.

Reference: *PMBOK® Guide*, 6th Ed., page 359

120. A. The Plan Communications Management process produces the communications management plan as an output.

Reference: *PMBOK® Guide*, 6th Ed., pages 366

121. B. The communications management plan, a subsidiary of the overall project management plan, contains the guidelines on how to distribute information within the project. Organizational process assets are too broad and performance reports are too narrow (too specific) to be correct answers.

Reference: *PMBOK® Guide*, 6th Ed., page 377

122. D. The Manage Communications process entails gathering and disseminating relevant project information as outlined in the communications management plan. The Manage Communications process also includes ad hoc or unplanned requests for information.

Reference: *PMBOK® Guide*, 6th Ed., pages 379-380

123. B. Communication can be verbal, informal (ad hoc conversation), and horizontal (with peers). Although the other project managers work for other government agencies, it is not clear if the professional relationships can be considered internal or external. We know that the communication is not vertical and not formal. Therefore, the correct answer is informal, horizontal.

Reference: *PMBOK® Guide*, 6th Ed., pages 360-361

124. C. Hard copy is not an electronic tool.

Reference: *PMBOK® Guide*, 6th Ed., pages 366-367

125. A. Project managers have a professional obligation to conduct Lessons Learned sessions for all projects with key internal and external stakeholders, particularly if the project yielded less than desirable results.

Reference: *PMBOK® Guide*, 6th Ed., pages 382, 387

126. A. The purchase order approval process obviously merits a review. Although improvement of the process may be outside the project scope, such knowledge should be documented in the lessons learned register. The other choices are incorrect because organizational process assets include the lessons learned register, project records, project reports, and other documentation. Lessons learned are considered parts of project records. Project reports may include lessons learned. Lessons learned is a better answer because it is closest to the question at hand. The other options, although can be argued as correct, are supersets of the lessons learned register.

Reference: *PMBOK® Guide*, 6th Ed., pages 382, 387

127. C. The best answer is to modify the communications plan as needed, as defined in the Perform Integrated Change Control process. The Perform Integrated Change Control process defines how to handle change requests, including changes that may impact the project scope and effort. Depending on the magnitude of the changes, a change request may not be needed if it falls with the guidelines stipulated in the change management plan.

Reference: *PMBOK® Guide*, 6th Ed., page 393

128. A. The Manage Communications process uses the following tools and techniques: communication technology, communication methods, communication skills, project management information system, project reporting, interpersonal and team skills, and meetings.

Reference: *PMBOK® Guide*, 6th Ed., page 379

129. A. Inputs of the Manage Communications process include project management plan (communications management plan and stakeholder engagement plan), project documents (change log, issue log, lessons learned register, quality report, risk report, and stakeholder register), work performance reports, enterprise environmental factors, and organizational process assets.

Reference: *PMBOK® Guide*, 6th Ed., page 379

130. D. Performance measurement baseline is an approved plan for the project work against which the project execution is compared, and deviations are measured for management control. The project management plan includes performance measurement baseline information. The other options are incorrect.

Reference: *PMBOK® Guide*, 6th Ed., pages 88, 169, 171, 224, 229

131. A. Based on the columns, it appears that the project is using earned value management to determine the performance of the project. The document could very well be a forecast, but the lack of estimate at completion and estimate to complete make performance report a better answer. The columns indicate that the document is not a risk register or an issue log.

Reference: *PMBOK® Guide*, 6th Ed., pages 26, 382

132. C. Monetary value (dollar amount) is the most common unit of measure in earned value analysis. It is also possible, however, to use other units of measure such as labor hours, square footage, and cubic meters of concrete for calculation purposes.

Reference: *PMBOK® Guide*, 6th Ed., page 267

133. A. If distance is not an issue and availability is not an issue, face-to-face meetings are ideal for resolving issues with stakeholders.

Reference: *PMBOK® Guide*, 6th Ed., pages 535

134. C. Outputs of the Manage Stakeholder Engagement process includes change requests, project management plan updates, and project documents updates.

Reference: *PMBOK® Guide*, 6th Ed., page 504

135. B. The Project Risk Management knowledge area process deals with increasing the probability and impact of favorable project events as well as decreasing the probability and impact of adverse project events.

Reference: *PMBOK® Guide*, 6th Ed., page 396

136. B. The Identify Risk process produces the risk register as an output.

Reference: *PMBOK® Guide*, 6th Ed., page 396

137. C. Project documents get updated in all Project Risk Management knowledge area processes except for the Plan Risk Management process.

Reference: *PMBOK® Guide*, 6th Ed., page 396

138. D. Risk rating = probability × impact = 0.5 × 0.7 = 0.35

Reference: *PMBOK® Guide*, 6th Ed., pages 407-408

139. B. The project team normally performs brainstorming, often with a multidisciplinary set of external experts outside of the team to generate ideas on potential project risks. Interviewing and root cause analysis can augment the list of project risks that were identified as part of the brainstorming process. Checklists are used as a reminder of the items, actions or points to be considered.

Reference: *PMBOK® Guide*, 6th Ed., pages 414-415

140. C. In ascending order, 0.1 usually represents very low probability/impact compared to 0.9, which normally equates to very high probability/impact. Therefore, the correct descriptive labels for the values are very low, low, moderate, high, and very high, respectively. The other options are incorrect because the descriptions are not in the correct ascending order.

Reference: *PMBOK® Guide*, 6th Ed., pages 407-408

141. B. With all other things being equal, a project with a higher EMV is more favorable than a project with a lower EMV. EMV, a statistical concept used in quantitative analysis, is used to analyze potential outcomes based on uncertain conditions.

Reference: *PMBOK® Guide*, 6th Ed., page 435

142. B. Calculate the net path value for A and B.

A = −50 + 100 = $50M
B = −50 + 25 = $−25M

Multiply the net path value by the probability of each scenario.

A = 50 × 55% = $27.5M
B = −25 × 45% = $−11.25M

The EMV for the false decision node is 27.5 + −11.25 = $16.25M.

Reference: *PMBOK® Guide*, 6th Ed., page 435

143. B. Calculate the net path value for A and B.

A = −50 + 100 = $50M
B = −50 + 25 = $−25M

The probabilities of 55 percent and 45 percent, respectively, are not relevant in this question.

Reference: *PMBOK® Guide*, 6th Ed., page 435

144. A. Risk response strategies for negative risks or threats include escalate, avoid, transfer, mitigate, and/or accept. Risk response strategies for positive risks or opportunities include escalate, exploit, share, enhance, and/or accept. Recognize is not a risk response strategy.

Reference: *PMBOK® Guide*, 6th Ed., page 442-443

145. B. Risk response strategies for negative risks or threats include escalate, avoid, transfer, mitigate, and/or accept. Risk response strategies for positive risks or opportunities include escalate, exploit, share, enhance, and/or accept. Recognize is not a risk response strategy.

Reference: *PMBOK® Guide*, 6th Ed., pages 443-444

146. D. Risk response strategies for negative risks or threats include escalate, avoid, transfer, mitigate and/or accept. Risk response strategies for positive risks or opportunities comprise escalate, exploit, share, enhance and/or accept. If a risk cannot be reduced or eliminated, acceptance can be adopted as a risk response strategy. Acceptance can be applied to both threats and opportunities.

Reference: *PMBOK® Guide*, 6th Ed., pages 442-444

147. C. Residual risks remain after the implementation of planned responses, whereas secondary risks arise as a direct outcome of implementing a risk response.

Reference: *PMBOK® Guide*, 6th Ed., page 448

148. D. Reserve analysis compares the remaining contingency reserve in the budget and/or schedule to determine if the remaining amount can adequately cover the remaining risks in the project.

Reference: *PMBOK® Guide*, 6th Ed., page 456

149. D. Make-or-buy decisions are outputs of the Plan Procurement Management process.

Reference: *PMBOK® Guide*, 6th Ed., pages 453, 460

150. A. A risk register normally contains descriptions of project risks along with probability, impact, priority, and ownership. Status (open, closed, and so forth), dates (open date, trigger date, etc.), and notes may also be included in the risk register. Probability, impact, priority, and ownership are not likely to be part of the other options.

Reference: *PMBOK® Guide*, 6th Ed., page 417

151. B. The Plan Procurement Management process produces the procurement documents along with procurement management plan, procurement statement of work, source selection criteria, make-or-buy decisions, changes requests, and procurement documents updates.

Reference: *PMBOK® Guide*, 6th Ed., page 460

152. A. The situation above is not a time and material contract. Cost-reimbursable is a superset of cost-plus-incentive-fee, so it can be eliminated as a choice. The situation as described can very well be a fixed-price (lump-sum) or a cost-plus-incentive-fee contract. However, the latter is typically associated with purchases when actual work needs to be performed (for example, paving a road, computer programming, and so forth) instead of simply shipping a regular product. Therefore, fixed-price is considered correct.

Reference: *PMBOK® Guide*, 6th Ed., pages 471-472

153. A. The situation above is not a time and material (T&M) contract. The project used a cost-plus-award-fee (CPAF) because the seller will be reimbursed for its expenses and will be paid a fee based on broad subjective criteria as defined by the buyer. Cost-plus-fixed-fee (CPFF) means that the seller will be reimbursed for its expenses (costs) plus a fixed fee regardless of costs. In contrast, cost-plus-incentive-fee (CPIF) pays the seller a predetermined incentive based on the achievement of certain milestones.

Reference: *PMBOK® Guide*, 6th Ed., page 472

154. B. Within the context of the Plan Procurement Management process, source selection criteria incorporate several factors, including the seller's technical capability, management approach, financial capacity, and references. Other source selection criteria may also consider the ownership of intellectual property rights and proprietary rights.

Reference: *PMBOK® Guide*, 6th Ed., pages 478-479

155. C. All of the choices are true statements. However, the question asks about obtaining responses to bids and proposals. Bidder conferences and proposal evaluation techniques describe actions that relate to requesting seller responses.

Reference: *PMBOK® Guide*, 6th Ed., page 487

156. B. All of the statements are true statements. However, only one option lists some of the tools and techniques that are used in the Conduct Procurements process—bidder conferences, proposal evaluation techniques, expert judgment, advertising, analytical techniques, and procurement negotiations.

Reference: *PMBOK® Guide*, 6th Ed., page 482

157. D. Other names for bidder conferences include contractor conferences, vendor conferences, and pre-bid conferences.

Reference: *PMBOK® Guide*, 6th Ed., page 487

158. B. The Conduct Procurements process uses the following tools and techniques: bidder conferences, proposal evaluation techniques, expert judgment, advertising, analytical techniques, and procurement negotiations.

Reference: *PMBOK® Guide*, 6th Ed., page 482

159. C. Prepared by the sellers, proposals highlight their ability and willingness to supply a product, service, or result to the buyer. The proposal constitutes a contract if accepted by the buyer.

Reference: *PMBOK® Guide*, 6th Ed., page 486

160. B. The Conduct Procurements process includes deciding which vendor or supplier the project will use. The process considers several factors including price, technical approach, and management style in the negotiation process. The Plan Procurements process is incorrect because it deals with what to purchase, when and how—not the negotiation process itself. The Define Activities and Estimate Costs processes are incorrect.

Reference: *PMBOK® Guide*, 6th Ed., page 482

161. D. When selecting sellers, the buyer may consider several factors to properly evaluate the sellers' ability to supply the products, services, or results that the project needs. Copies of contracts from other clients are generally not available privacy laws and confidentiality agreements.

Reference: *PMBOK® Guide*, 6th Ed., page 478-479

162. A. Sellers prepare proposals in response to a procurement document package. The proposal will then be used to evaluate and select one or more bidders (sellers).

Reference: *PMBOK® Guide*, 6th Ed., page 486

163. D. All of the options can be quantified (numerical weight, forced ranking, and seller ratings) except for soliciting opinions from key industry leaders.

Reference: *PMBOK® Guide*, 6th Ed., page 489

164. C. In the case of widely varying estimates from multiple suppliers, you should perform your own independent estimate. An independent estimate (should-cost estimate) enables the buyer to assess the validity of the seller's estimate. Low price may mean that the seller did not understand the requirements. In contrast, high price may indicate that the seller is proposing a higher-quality product or service.

Reference: *PMBOK® Guide*, 6th Ed., pages 475, 479, 485, 708

165. C. It is acceptable to include both subjective and objective evaluation criteria when selecting sellers. Objective criteria such as ratings, scores, and weights generally are preferred to subjective criteria. Given this, the evaluator's narrative summary is less preferred relative to the other options.

Reference: *PMBOK® Guide*, 6th Ed., page 478

166. B. A signed contract is mutually binding, and any modifications must be accepted by both parties. A contract or portions of it may become invalid if it contains clauses or provisions that will violate existing laws and regulations.

Reference: *PMBOK® Guide*, 6th Ed., page 489

167. D. The Control Procurements process ensures that both parties, the buyer and the seller, meet their contractual obligations. It is imperative that the buyer stipulates the project requirements in the contract and that the seller delivers the services as agreed upon. Negotiating price is a component of selecting the sellers and the Control Procurements process.

Reference: *PMBOK® Guide*, 6th Ed., pages 492-494

168. D. Although contractual terms are met within a project, contracts that can have organizational impacts should be reviewed by legal professionals. The project charter authorizes the project manager to expend resources to deliver the project. The project manager, however, may not be in a position to enter into a binding contract with other parties. It is also premature to ask for delays in the project schedule without first getting input from legal professionals. Crossing out a contract clause can also be problematic without proper legal advice.

Reference: *PMBOK® Guide*, 6th Ed., pages 492-494

169. A. The procurement management plan is a subsidiary of the project management plan. It is produced as an output of the Plan Procurement Management process. The other options are incorrect.

Reference: *PMBOK® Guide*, 6th Ed., pages 87, 475

170. C. The Conduct Procurements and Control Procurements processes all use the procurement management plan, part of the project management plan, as an input. There is no Close Procurements process.

Reference: *PMBOK® Guide*, 6th Ed., page 460

171. A. On smaller projects, the company's accounts payable system would normally pay the seller. The project management team reviews and approves the payment to ensure adherence to the terms of the contract.

Reference: *PMBOK® Guide*, 6th Ed., pages 497, 501

172. D. Within the Project Procurement Management knowledge area, procurement documents are an output of the Plan Procurement Management process and an input to the Conduct Procurements and Control Procurements processes. There is no Close Procurements process.

Reference: *PMBOK® Guide*, 6th Ed., pages 477-479

173. A. Trends and emerging practices for Project Procurement Management include advance in tools, more advanced risk management, changing contracting processes, logistic and supply chain management, technology and stakeholder relations, trial engagements.

Reference: *PMBOK® Guide*, 6th Ed., pages 463-464

174. D. The failure of the prototype test may not be the fault of the seller. At this point, it is important to review the contract's terms and conditions for early termination to determine the appropriate course of action.

Reference: *PMBOK® Guide*, 6th Ed., page 499

175. D. A well-written contract normally will stipulate the terms and conditions on how to deal with unresolved claims or issues. It is important, therefore, to review the contract prior to proceeding with any further actions.

Reference: *PMBOK® Guide*, 6th Ed., pages 494, 499

176. D. If at all possible, it is usually more cost effective for both parties to avoid legal actions in case of contract disagreements. Taking the issue to binding arbitration, therefore, is the least desirable outcome because it is a legal action.

Reference: *PMBOK® Guide*, 6th Ed., pages 494, 496, 498

177. A. Control Procurements process uses tools and techniques including expert judgement, claims administration, data analysis, inspection, and audits.

Reference: *PMBOK® Guide*, 6th Ed., page 460

178. B. The Conduct Procurements process uses Expert judgment, advertising, bidder conferences, data analysis, and interpersonal and team skills.

Reference: *PMBOK® Guide*, 6th Ed., pages 460

179. D. Tools and techniques of the Control Procurements process include audits, inspection, data analysis, claims administration, and expert judgement.

Reference: *PMBOK® Guide*, 6th Ed., page 460

180. A. The correct portions of the project documentation that may be updated as part of Plan Procurement outputs include Lessons learned, milestone list, requirements documentation, requirements traceability matrix, risk register, and stakeholder register.

Reference: *PMBOK® Guide*, 6th Ed., page 480

181. A. The next process after Conduct Procurements is Control Procurements. The Control Procurements process produces closed procurements and organizational process assets updates as outputs.

Reference: *PMBOK® Guide*, 6th Ed., page 460

182. A. Within the Project Procurement Management knowledge area, the Conduct Procurements and Control Procurements processes update the organizational process assets. The other options are incorrect.

Reference: *PMBOK® Guide*, 6th Ed., page 460

183. C. The stakeholder register is an output of the Identify Stakeholders process.

Reference: *PMBOK® Guide*, 6th Ed., page 504

184. B. Project charter, project management plan, project documents, agreements, enterprise environmental factors, and organizational process assets are inputs to the Plan Stakeholder Engagement process.

Project charter and procurement documents are inputs to the Identify Stakeholders process. Project management plan and issue log are inputs to the Control Stakeholder Engagement process. Lastly, stakeholder management plan and change log are input to the Management Stakeholder Engagement process.

Reference: *PMBOK® Guide*, 6th Ed., page 504

185. A. Stakeholders' stakes can include a combination of interest, rights, ownership, knowledge, and contribution.

Reference: *PMBOK® Guide*, 6th Ed., page 512

186. D. As a project management practitioner, one of your mandatory responsibilities is to make decisions and take actions that will uphold applicable laws and regulations.

Reference: *Code of Ethics and Professional Conduct*, page 3

187. C. Key stakeholders should be informed in a timely manner and provided accurate information in instances where there is an experience gap or the objective has been stretched.

Reference: *Code of Ethics and Professional Conduct*, page 5

188. C. The stakeholder register is an output of Identify Stakeholders process and contains information that includes identification information, assessment information, and stakeholder classification.

Reference: *PMBOK® Guide*, 6th Ed., page 514

189. C. The *Code of Ethics and Professional Conduct* states to report only ethical complaints that can be substantiated by facts.

Reference: *Code of Ethics and Professional Conduct*, page 2

190. D. The *Code of Ethics and Professional Conduct* specifically states that "We inform ourselves about the norms and customs of others and avoid engaging in behaviors they might consider disrespectful." Even though the person to whom the joke was directed was not personally offended, others might find it offensive.

Reference: *Code of Ethics and Professional Conduct*, page 3

191. B. The *Code of Ethics and Professional Conduct* specifically states that "Fairness is our duty to make decisions and act impartially and objectively." Given that your employer may benefit from the outcomes of the motion, it is best to abstain from the discussions altogether to avoid the perception of conflict of interest.

"When we realize that we have a real or potential conflict of interest, we refrain from engaging in the decision-making process or otherwise attempting to influence outcomes, unless or until: we have made full disclosure to the affected stakeholders; we have an approved mitigation plan; and we have obtained the consent of the stakeholders to proceed."

Reference: *Code of Ethics and Professional Conduct*, page 5

192. D. Project management practitioners are expected to take corrective actions as appropriate if they feel that they have not been fair in their actions. Apologizing to the other party might be a correct course of action, but taking corrective actions includes that option, as well as other potential options, so it is the better answer.

Reference: *Code of Ethics and Professional Conduct*, page 5

193. A. As project managers, we are expected to be truthful in our communications and in our conduct.

Reference: *Code of Ethics and Professional Conduct*, page 5

194. B. One example of an aspirational standard of fairness is to demonstrate transparency when making decisions. The other options are mandatory standards of fairness.

Reference: *Code of Ethics and Professional Conduct*, page 4

195. D. It is a mandatory standard of honesty to not engage in dishonest behaviors. The other options are aspirational standards of honesty.

Reference: *Code of Ethics and Professional Conduct*, page 6

196. C. Telling half-truths or withholding some information to influence the outcome of a discussion is a violation of the mandatory standard of honesty.

Reference: *Code of Ethics and Professional Conduct*, page 6

197. B. All options are essentially correct except for B. Commitments must be made, implicitly and explicitly, in good faith all the time—not some of the time.

Reference: *Code of Ethics and Professional Conduct*, page 6

198. B. Conduct that results in physical harm or creates an intense feeling of fear or humiliation is considered abusive behavior.

Reference: *Code of Ethics and Professional Conduct*, page 8

199. B. The best way to resolve conflicting duties of loyalty is to fully disclose the conflict. Fully disclosing the conflict can help one adhere to the duty of loyalty, thus avoiding any potential or actual conflict of interest. Avoiding the discussion altogether violates the duty of honesty.

Reference: *Code of Ethics and Professional Conduct*, pages 5, 8

200. A. A person's responsibility, legal or moral, to promote the best interest of an organization or other person with whom he or she is affiliated is called duty of loyalty. The other options are incorrect.

Reference: *Code of Ethics and Professional Conduct*, pages 5, 8

Bonus Questions

201. C. A portfolio is a collection of projects, programs, subportfolios, and operations.

Reference: *PMBOK® Guide*, 6th Ed., page 714

202. A. Individuals coordinating a project in a weak matrix organization may be referred to as a project coordinator or project expeditor. We first see the title of project manager appear in a balanced matrix organization.

Reference: *PMBOK® Guide*, 6th Ed., page 47

203. D. Develop Project Charter is a process within the Initiating process group. Develop Project Management Plan process is part of the Planning process group while the Direct and Manage Project Work is part of the Executing process group.

Reference: *PMBOK® Guide*, 6th Ed., page 25

204. A. The Validate Scope process is part of the Monitoring and Controlling process group.

Reference: *PMBOK® Guide*, 6th Ed., page 25

205. B. Interviews are usually conducted one-on-one while focus groups require a trained moderator.

Reference: *PMBOK® Guide*, 6th Ed., page 142

Chapter 5: Practice Test B

1. You have been asked to initiate a business-critical project for your organization. Historically the organization has survived by creating ad hoc processes and documents, with mixed results. You want to use best practices wherever possible on this project to maximize the chances of success. Which of the following would you do first?

    A. Calculate the project timeline and initial budget
    B. Recruit the key project skills as early as possible
    C. Develop the project charter and high-level requirements
    D. Establish a comprehensive change control process

2. A project manager, new to an organization, is employed on a project to refurbish an office block. What is one of the first things that the project manager should do?

    A. Develop a project work breakdown structure
    B. Write and get approval of a project charter
    C. Estimate the initial budget for the project work
    D. Produce a project schedule for the work required

3. A project manager is developing a project charter for a project. The project is to be paid for by an external customer of the organization she works for. Which of the following items should be in place to complete the project charter?

    A. The detailed features list to be delivered
    B. The final price quoted for the project
    C. The agreed-upon contract for the project
    D. The estimated labor costs of the project

4. As a project manager, you have been given an approved business case for a project you are assigned to manage. Who will have provided you with this approved business case?

    A. The end-user group
    B. Your functional manager
    C. The project director
    D. The project sponsor

5. You have been given a short time to write a project charter. The project is new to your organization and will develop an IT system to help the sales department close leads. Which of the following would be *least* likely to help you clarify the influences on the project when writing the project charter?

A. Escalating costs of acquiring new customers
B. Regulatory standards that are about to be approved
C. The infrastructure in place to support an IT solution
D. Introduction of a new internal training offering

6. You must present your project budget to the project sponsor for approval. You are anticipating some of the questions that she may ask about the project benefits to the organization. The following data shows expected cash flow for the next five years. What is the payback period for this project?

End of Year	Cash In	Cash Out
1	-	450,000
2	250,000	200,000
3	450,000	50,000
4	350,000	50,000
5	300,000	50,000

A. Two years
B. Three years
C. Four years
D. Five years

7. The project charter you have developed has not yet been approved by the project sponsor. Your direct line manager insists that you start work on the project immediately because he thinks time is tight. What is the best course of action for you?

A. Review and adapt the organization's change control process
B. Immediately begin to work on time-critical work packages
C. State the likely impact of proceeding without approval
D. Continue to work only on approved project work packages

8. As part of developing a project charter, you have leveraged the company's project management methodology to help you. Which of the following categories does the project management methodology fall under?

A. Internal quality standards
B. Documentation management system
C. Integrated change control process
D. Organizational process assets

9. The project you have been asked to develop a charter for a complex project that has many inputs that are beyond your direct knowledge. Which of the following tools and techniques would you use to help you proceed with the project chartering process?

A. Matrix management structure
B. Available project templates
C. Previous project schedules
D. Expert judgment of others

10. When planning and implementing a project, you must consider a number of influences. Which of the following activities would help you understand the project environment?

A. Schedule and resources
B. Cultural and social issues
C. Project budget approval process
D. Detailed requirements analysis

11. You have been asked to analyze a project charter that has been developed by another part of your business. Which of the following would you consider essential for the project charter to be approved?

A. Detailed work and schedule estimates
B. A list of all the resources required
C. The business need for the project
D. A list of all the risks in the project

12. One planning process that the project manager should complete is to develop the work breakdown structure (WBS) for the project. This WBS will be used to do which of the following?

A. Show the constraints on the resources in the organization
B. Define and organize the total scope of the project
C. Indicate the logical dependencies between project tasks
D. Describe the scope of the new project to the customer

13. On your project, configuration verification and configuration audits have been scheduled. A team member asks you what this process entails. Your response should indicate that the configuration verification and configuration audits accomplish which of the following?

A. Involve reviewing deliverables with the customer or sponsor to ensure they are completed satisfactorily and obtaining formal acceptance by the customer or sponsor
B. Ensure that the composition of a project's configuration item is correct and that corresponding changes are registered, assessed, approved, tracked, and correctly implemented
C. Monitor and record the results of executing quality activities to assess performance and recommend necessary changes, and the configuration validation and configuration audit are done throughout the project
D. Include the process of tracking, reviewing, and regulating the progress to meet the performance objectives defined in the project management plan, and the configuration validation and configuration audit are done throughout the project

14. You have to develop a scope statement for a cross-department project. Many people will be involved in this project. Who would approve the project scope statement that you have developed?

A. The project team members
B. The project sponsor
C. The project manger
D. The financial manager

15. You have been provided with a document that contains the market demand and cost-benefit analysis that justifies the go-ahead of the project. What is this document called?

A. A contract
B. A project business benefit plan
C. A business case
D. An organizational asset

16. As a result of comparing planned results to actual results, change requests may be issued that expand, adjust, or reduce project or product scope. All of the following are changes that are included as change requests *except* _____.

A. Corrective action
B. Situational action
C. Defect repairs
D. Preventive action

17. A project manager has been given a completed project scope statement that she has not seen before. She has been asked to manage this project from now on. What is the first action she should take at this point?

A. Create a complete network diagram for the tasks and milestones in the project
B. Confirm that the project management team developed this statement
C. Develop a detailed project plan based on the new work breakdown structure
D. Call a meeting of the project management team to agree on a procurement plan

18. The project you are managing has a WBS. A new team member asks you the purpose of the WBS. You explain its primary purpose is:

A. To clarify the responsibility for project tasks
B. To communicate 100 percent of the project scope
C. To define the business need for the project
D. To detail the dates for the work packages

19. You are the project manager for a small project team. In one of the regular status meetings, a team member proposes an additional feature to the system you are developing. As a project manager, you remind the team to formally document the proposed additional feature. Which process is this an example of?

A. Control Quality
B. Monitor and Control Project Work
C. Control Scope
D. Control Configuration

20. The organization you work for is very traditional, and projects must be managed within a functional organizational structure. Your functional manager assigned you to a project that is in trouble. What is your likely level of authority over the management of this project?

A. High
B. Moderate
C. Limited
D. Little or none

21. The project has produced a requirements traceability matrix that links requirements to their origin and tracks them throughout the project life cycle. Which statement describes the purpose of this document?

A. It describes, in detail, the project's deliverables and the work required to create those deliverables and includes product and project scope description
B. It ensures that requirements approved in the requirements documentation are delivered at the end of the project and helps manage change to product scope
C. It is a narrative description of products or services to be delivered by the project and is received from the customer for external projects
D. It provides the necessary information from a business standpoint to determine whether or not the project is worth the required investment

22. You have been developing a project scope statement for a project you have been given authority to manage. During this process, you came across areas of technical detail that you were not familiar with. Which of the following you would use to help clarify the related issues and their impact on the project scope?

A. Experienced managers
B. Special interest groups
C. Expert judgment
D. Similar project plans

23. You have been given a document for a project to review. The document contains details of how the project will be executed, monitored, controlled, and closed. What is this document called?

A. Project charter document
B. Project management plan
C. Project benefits management plan
D. Scope management plan

24. You have been assigned to develop a new configuration management system that will address both configuration control and change control. Which of the following identifies the functions of change control?

A. Identifying, proving, approving, tracking, and validating changes
B. Submitting, approving, tracking, measuring, and validating changes
C. Identifying, requesting, assessing, validating, and communicating changes
D. Reviewing, approving, tracking, validating, and proving changes

25. You are managing the execution of a project in your organization. You work with many people and groups regularly during this stage of a project. Whom do you work most closely with to direct, manage, and execute the project?

A. The project initiator or sponsor
B. The business unit as the customer
C. No one; as project manager, you assume full responsibility
D. The project team

26. You have been given the responsibility for a project that you have not been involved with to date. The project is at the beginning of the execution stage. What is the main document to which you would refer to guide you on what you should be doing on this project?

A. Project management plan
B. Procurement management plan
C. Communications management plan
D. Project scope management plan

27. You are asked by your functional manager to describe your current activities as a project manager. You replied that you are currently collecting requirements, estimating costs, and planning risk responses. What project stage would you likely be in?

A. Starting the project
B. Organizing and planning
C. Carrying out the work
D. Ending the project

28. During the process of executing a project, a number of influences drive a project manager's activities. Which of the following is an input to this process?

A. Outstanding defects and faults
B. Administrative procedure edits
C. Approved change requests
D. Postponed change requests

29. You are managing a project that is time critical and essential for the survival of the business. You have a number of changes on this project. Which of the following do you spend your time scheduling into the work for the project team?

A. Likely changes to the schedule
B. Change requests to the scope
C. Requested changes to budget
D. Approved change requests

30. You are involved in a project and regularly receive regular work packages to complete from the project manager. The project manager describes some of the results of your work as project deliverables. The processes that describe project deliverables from your work are defined in which of the following?

A. The completed task contract form
B. The initial work breakdown structure
C. The project management plan
D. The initial project scope document

31. You are leading a team on a project that is directing and managing the project work. A new team member has joined the team and asks you what the project deliverables are. Which of the following is the *best* answer to this question?

A. All items consumed in the project during the execution
B. The goods that are delivered to the shipping dock and are signed for
C. A product purchased according to the procurement plan
D. Something that is produced to complete the project

32. You are managing a project that is in progress. Many tasks have been completed, some are in progress, and others are yet to start. You are reviewing your workload by monitoring the activities in the project. When is the best time to collect this information?

A. At the start of the activity
B. Routinely and regularly
C. At the end of the task only
D. Monthly, for progress reports

33. When running a project, the project manager must manage the project work. Which of the following statements is part of effectively monitoring and controlling the project progress?

A. Email the team the schedule according to the plan
B. Record the actual progress on tasks on a daily basis
C. Compare actual activity performance against plan
D. Report only completed activity, schedule, and costs

34. One of the tools you use managing your project is earned value analysis. Your functional manager asks you to justify the time you spend on reporting progress. Which of the following statements *best* explains why you are using the earned value analysis technique?

A. Future performance can be made to correspond to the plan
B. Past performance can be measured to an accuracy of less than 5 percent
C. Future performance can be predicted to within 10 percent of the budget
D. Future performance can be forecasted based on past performance

35. Which statement below *best* describes the purpose of using preventive actions in a project?

A. They reduce the probability of negative consequences related to risks
B. They reduce the impact of negative consequences related to risks
C. They increase the project budget to allow for some overrun on costs
D. They increase the reporting frequency on activities that are critical

36. You are planning a project and wish to introduce the concept of integrated change control to your team. The team is used to a casual management style, and you anticipate some questions. What is the best way to describe the use of integrated change control to the team?

A. Integrated change control applies to the early stages of the project to help define the scope.
B. Integrated change control applies from the beginning of the project to the end, and formally addressed through this process once the baselines are established
C. Integrated change control is used only when there are large changes to budget, scope, or schedule
D. Change control is used during the execution of the project to control schedule creep

37. You are managing a section of a large project and have adopted an integrated change control system to address the flow of changes from the project team. Which of the following describes how you would act on changes?

A. Approve changes that cost less than 10 percent of budget
B. Automatically approve all changes to the schedule
C. Review, then approve, or reject, project changes
D. Reject all changes to the budget, scope, or deliverables

38. You are asked to describe why you are using the Perform Integrated Change Control process in your projects. You refer to the systems and processes that are in place in your workplace. Which of the following *best* describes your reasons for using change control?

A. There is a form that is always used on every project
B. Change control is always used to limit budget overspend
C. It is required on the entire project because of legislation
D. It is part of the project management methodology

39. A project that is using the Perform Integrated Change Control process will have a number of outputs. A member of your team suggests that the project management plan is an output of this process. What should your answer be?

A. Disagree because updates to the project management plan are outputs
B. Disagree because the project management plan is not an output
C. Agree that the project management plan is an output
D. Disagree because project management plan is not used in this process

40. Your organization has implemented best practices in project management processes. One function that has been set up is the Project Management Office (PMO). What is the function of the PMO?

A. To provide hot desk facilities for all project managers
B. To coordinate the management of projects
C. To close project accounts at the end of the projects
D. To provide standard stationery for project paperwork

41. You are at the end of a project that has been successfully delivered. One of the processes that you have to manage is the Close Project or Phase process. You are not certain what this entails. Where would you get guidance on the process to help you close the project?

A. The procurement management plan
B. The project scope management plan
C. The project management plan
D. The quality management plan

42. You are managing the Close Project or Phase process for a project that you have delivered and are gathering information to allow you to complete this process. Which of the following is an input to this process?

A. Final product/service
B. Project management plan updates
C. Change request status updates
D. Accepted deliverables

43. The project management team is performing the Collect Requirements process. As part of the process, ideas and thoughts brought up in the brainstorming session are written onto a single map to reflect common understanding, as well as generate new ideas. What is this technique called?

A. Observation technique
B. Facilitated workshops
C. Mind mapping
D. Monte Carlo technique

44. The project management team has produced a requirements management plan. What is the purpose of this document?

A. To link requirements to their origin and trace them throughout the project
B. To document how requirements will be analyzed, documented, verified, and managed throughout the project
C. To describe how individual requirements meet the business need for the project
D. To provide guidance on how project scope will be defined, documented, verified, managed and controlled

45. You are responsible for the Close Project or Phase process on a large project. You are asked to report the activities you are performing. These activities include defining how the project will transfer the services produced to the operational division of the organization. What term describes these activities?

A. Contract closure
B. The project management plan
C. Administrative closure
D. Deliverable acceptance

46. You have been managing a project for some time and have been asked to identify the current stage of the project. You have a document that formally indicates that the sponsor has officially accepted the project deliverables. Which of the documents below is this considered a part of?

A. Administrative closure documents
B. Contract closure documents
C. Project closure documents
D. Organizational process assets

47. What is the collection of documents that includes the project management plan, cost baseline, project calendar, and risk register?

A. The project files
B. Historical information
C. Acceptance documents
D. Closure documentation

48. You have been given the responsibility of documenting why a project was terminated. Which of the following documents would you use to record this information?

A. Project contract document
B. Project closure document
C. Contract closure procedure
D. Administrative closure procedure

49. You are discussing your role as a project manager with your peers. In the conversation, another team member describes the process of defining and controlling what is, and what is not, included in the project. What is this process called?

A. Project documentation management
B. Project change control
C. Project scope management
D. Formal acceptance documents

50. You have been involved in a workshop at which the project management team created an initial work breakdown structure (WBS). Which of the following statements *best* describes the process in which you were involved?

A. Calculating the total duration of the project
B. Determining the total number of work packages in the project
C. Allocating responsibilities for the project work to individuals on the team
D. Subdividing the project work into smaller, more manageable components

51. The scope management plan is produced by the project management team as part of the Plan Scope Management process. Which of the following statements *best* describes the scope management plan?

A. The scope management plan provides guidance on how project scope will be defined, developed, monitored, controlled, and validated.
B. The scope management plan documents how requirements will be analyzed, documented, and managed throughout the project
C. The scope management plan describes the project's deliverables and the work required to create those deliverables
D. The scope management plan is a deliverable-oriented hierarchical decomposition of the work to be executed by the project team

52. A team member who has just joined your team asks what is involved in this project. You refer her to the project scope statement, which contains all of the following *except* _____.

A. Approved change requests
B. Project scope description
C. Project deliverables
D. Acceptance criteria

53. Which of the following descriptions about requirements documentation is *false*?

A. Must be measurable, testable, and traceable
B. Serves as working model of the project's product
C. Can start at a high level and then be refined later
D. Includes the list of prioritized requirements

54. You are assigned to manage a new project. Your line manager suggests that you should use a tool to help you plan the new project. She suggests that you use a work breakdown structure (WBS) template. Which of the following is the *best* description of this tool?

A. A document that lists WBS elements
B. An all-purpose WBS from the Internet
C. A WBS from a previous project
D. A definition of WBS colors and shapes

55. The project meeting you are attending is becoming somewhat heated, and there are disagreements about the work completed and the work to be done. The project manager stops the discussion and refers to a document that is used as a reference. What is this document called?

A. Approved changes
B. The issue log
C. The WBS template
D. The scope baseline

56. The project team you are working with is doing the work of obtaining formal stakeholders' acceptance of the completed deliverables. Each deliverable is reviewed against the requirements to check that it has been completed satisfactorily. What is this process called?

A. Validate Scope
B. Define Scope
C. Control Scope
D. Plan Scope Management

57. You are discussing your project roles with a colleague. She states that she is working on developing a process that ensures all scope changes go through integrated change control. What project process is she performing?

A. Perform Integrated Change Control
B. Control Scope
C. Identify Risks
D. Monitor and Control Project Work

58. The project team is involved in measuring, examining, and verifying that the work and deliverables meet the product and acceptance criteria. Which of the following is the process that the team is executing?

A. Define Scope
B. Perform Integrated Change Control
C. Validate Scope
D. Plan Scope Management

59. The Control Scope process is part of the _____ knowledge area under the _____ process group.

A. Project Integration Management; Monitoring and Controlling
B. Project Quality Management; Planning
C. Project Risk Management; Executing
D. Project Scope Management; Monitoring and Controlling

60. Integrated change control includes two main components: _____, which deals with both deliverables and processes, and _____, which ensures proper administration of the changes in the project and product baselines.

A. Configuration control; change control
B. Change requests; change control
C. Configuration control; change requests
D. Change control; configuration control

61. A number of changes to the project schedule and requirements have been suggested by the project team and the customer. These are urgent, and all impact the resources you are using. What is the recommended next step to take?

A. Have the changes go through the Perform Integrated Change Control process for review
B. Notify the project sponsor and recommend that the work starts immediately
C. Disregard the changes and adhere to the approved scope and schedule baselines
D. Reschedule resources to begin the changes immediately

62. After some approved changes to your project scope, you have revised the schedule, costs, and work package assignments. What action do you now complete?

A. Reassign resources as needed
B. Update the project management plan
C. Review potential additional changes to submit
D. Continue the project as planned

63. As you plan a project assigned to your team, you identify the activities, dependencies, and resources needed to produce the project deliverables. What is this process you are doing called?

A. Project Schedule Control
B. Project Risk Management
C. Project Schedule Management
D. Project Cost Planning

64. You have asked a team member to participate in performing a number of actions described within the project management plan. These actions involve decomposing the work packages into smaller components of work called activities. What process is this team member responsible for?

A. Schedule Work
B. Estimate Tasks
C. Schedule Activities
D. Define Activities

65. You note that your weekly time sheet report shows that you have identified activities, defined the work needed on each, and provided sufficient detail to allow a team member to understand what is required to complete that work. What is a description of the work you have accomplished this week?

A. Producing an activity list
B. Defining the project scope
C. Developing the project schedule
D. Identifying the WBS elements

66. You are analyzing a project schedule on which activities are represented on a diagram as boxes and the dependencies between activities are shown as arrows. What is this representation is known as?

A. Activity on arrow
B. Activity-on-node
C. Schedule analysis
D. Critical path method

67. The precedence diagramming method can be used to show the dependencies between activities. One type of dependency used is to ensure that the successor activity does not start until the completion of the predecessor activity. What is the name given to this type of dependency?

A. Start-to-start
B. Finish-to-finish
C. Finish-to-start
D. Start-to-finish

68. Which of the following is a project management deliverable that identifies and describes the types and quantities of each resource required to complete all project work packages?

A. Resource calendar updates
B. Activity attributes updates
C. Resource breakdown structure
D. Resource requirements

69. You are completing the planning for a project schedule. Because you do not have much information about one particular activity, you decide to estimate its duration by referring to the actual duration of a similar activity on another project. What is this technique called?

A. Analogous estimating
B. Expert judgment
C. Parametric estimating
D. Reserve analysis

70. Your project manager asks you to calculate the early start and finish dates, along with late start and finish dates, for all the project activities. He suggests you use a forward and backward pass analysis. What is this technique is known as?

A. Critical chain method
B. Critical path method
C. Schedule compression
D. What-if scenario analysis

71. You are asked to review a project that another department has planned for your organization. Your functional manager asks you to show her a project overview that shows only the start and end dates of major deliverables, along with key external dependencies. This graphic is known as a _____.

A. Network diagram
B. Summary bar chart
C. Milestone chart
D. Schedule baseline

72. You are reviewing the project schedule with your team. One version of the schedules lists the activity identifier, activity description, and calendar units. The start and end date of each activity is depicted by a horizontal bar, which clearly shows the activity duration relative to the project schedule time frame. There is also a vertical line marked "Data Date." What is this graphical representation of schedule called?

A. Milestone schedule
B. Network diagram
C. Detailed schedule with logical relationships
D. Summary schedule or bar chart

73. Which of the following statements is correct about a schedule baseline?

A. The schedule baseline is used as a basis for comparison.
B. The schedule baseline is the basis from which the project management team calculates the project completion date based on optimistic, most likely, and pessimistic estimates.
C. Reviewed and approved by the project sponsor, the schedule baseline includes the corporate calendar, project calendar, resource calendar, and a list of statutory holidays.
D. The project calendar is exactly the same as a regular calendar except that Saturdays are always used in the preparation of the overall project schedule.

74. The project team used schedule network analysis, the critical path method, the schedule compression, and other tools to produce the project schedule and schedule baseline. These tools and techniques, and the resulting outputs, compose the _____ process.

A. Define Activities
B. Develop Schedule
C. Control Schedule
D. Estimate Activity Durations

75. As a project manager, your responsibilities include gathering data on actual start and finish dates of activities, along with remaining durations for work in progress. The work you are doing is involved with _____.

A. Cost variance analysis
B. Performance measurement
C. Performance reviews
D. Critical path analysis

76. What does the term *variance analysis* mean for a project manager, in reference to the schedule?

A. Recording the actual start date of critical activities in the project
B. Analyzing the calendar contract start date and finish date
C. Calculating the difference between total slack and free slack
D. Comparing activity target start date with actual start date

77. You are managing a project that is running late. You have proposed corrective actions that will affect the schedule baseline. What are these actions called?

A. Change requests
B. Action change control
C. Schedule baseline updates
D. Project scope updates

78. The project archive you are reviewing shows that the project has had a number of changes to the start and finish dates of the schedule baseline. What are these changes are known as?

A. Schedule variance analysis
B. Schedule baseline updates
C. Approved change requests
D. Performance reviews

79. Which knowledge area includes processes that ensure the completion of the project within the approved budget?

A. Project Risk Management
B. Project Schedule Management
C. Project Cost Management
D. Project Resource Management

80. You have been working on a project in the planning stage, developing the cost estimates. The project sponsor expects a more definitive estimate of the costs because more information is now known. Which of the following is considered a suitable range for this request?

A. −25 percent to +75 percent
B. −5 percent to +10 percent
C. −25 percent to +25 percent
D. −50 percent to +50 percent

81. A project team member is building the costs for a current project, based only on costs from a previous similar project that has been completed in your organization. What is this process known as?

A. Analogous estimating
B. Bottom-up estimating
C. Parametric estimating
D. Three-point estimating

82. Building cost estimates for a current project using metrics from the current project, along with historical information from past similar projects, is known as _____.

A. Analogous estimating
B. Bottom-up estimating
C. Parametric estimating
D. Three-point estimating

83. What factors are needed to calculate the estimate to complete (ETC) for a project?

A. EAC and PV
B. BAC, AC, and PV
C. BAC, EV, and AC
D. EAC and AC

84. You have been asked to report to the project sponsor on the schedule performance of a project. Which of the following would help you provide this information?

A. Cost performance index (CPI)
B. Schedule performance index (SPI)
C. Estimate to complete (ETC)
D. Estimate at completion (EAC)

85. Which value is used as part of the CV, SV, CPI, and SPI calculations?

A. Planned value
B. Actual cost
C. Earned value
D. Schedule variance

86. A new team member is monitoring and recording results of executing quality activities to assess performance and recommend necessary changes. He asks for clarification on what his activities are related to. Which of the following is the *best* answer to his question?

A. Control Quality
B. Manage Quality
C. Plan Quality Management
D. Improve Quality

87. A team member has been given the task of identifying which quality standards are relevant to this project and determining how to satisfy these standards. In which of the following activities is she engaged?

A. Control Quality
B. Manage Quality
C. Plan Quality Management
D. Develop Quality

88. As a project manager you must audit the quality requirements and the results from quality control measurements to ensure that appropriate quality standards and operational definitions are used. This is part of which of the following processes?

A. Control Quality
B. Manage Quality
C. Plan Quality Management
D. Improve Quality

89. Which of the following is *not* an output of the Plan Quality Management process?

A. Quality management plan
B. Project documents updates
C. Quality metrics
D. Change requests

90. You have been asked to perform quality planning for a project. One of your first actions will be to clarify some of the project or product attribute measurements on the project are and how the Control Quality process will measure these attributes. The output of the Plan Quality Management process as described here is known as _____.

A. Quality metrics
B. Quality checklists
C. Quality management plan
D. Process improvement plan

91. Which of the following is an input to Manage Quality process?

A. Project documents
B. Project requirements
C. Change requests
D. Verified deliverables

92. An external team is assessing whether your project activities comply with organizational and project quality polices, processes and procedures. They are working to determine best practices being implemented and any nonconformities or gaps. This tool or technique is called _____.

A. Quality metrics
B. Quality audit
C. Quality control measurements
D. Quality checklists

93. A team member is following the steps outlined in the process improvement plan. This is needed to improve organizational and project performance. What technique will the team member use to help with this activity?

A. Quality metrics
B. Quality audits
C. Process analysis
D. Quality reports

94. In the Control Quality process, when is time normally allocated to do this work?

A. At every project milestone
B. At termination of the project
C. At the end of each phase of the project
D. Throughout the project

95. You are coaching a new team member in your project. One of her functions is to recommend corrective actions to increase the effectiveness and efficiency of the organization. This falls under the Manage Quality process. This list of actions that results from carrying out this process is documented as _____.

A. Change requests
B. Organizational process assets updates
C. Project management plan updates
D. Recommended preventive actions

96. The project you are managing has a serious problem that will compromise the delivery of a key component. Your team is trying to find the reasons for the failure of the system, using a tool consisting of a diagram that shows how various factors might be linked to the problem or the effects. What is this diagram is called?

A. Scatter diagram
B. Cause and effect diagram
C. Control chart
D. Statistical sampling

97. Your mentor suggests that you use a diagram that can organize potential causes of defects into groups showing areas of similarity or commonality. What is the name for this diagram?

A. Scatter diagram
B. Flowchart
C. Affinity diagram
D. Control chart

98. A common tool used in analyzing problems on a project is a diagram that shows the relationship between two variables. What is this diagram called?

A. Control chart
B. Pareto chart
C. Run chart
D. Scatter diagram

99. You are identifying and documenting project roles, responsibilities, and reporting relationships for a project. Which process is responsible for these activities?

A. Plan Resource Management
B. Acquire Team
C. Manage Team
D. Develop Team

100. As part of the Resource Management Plan, you find a chart that illustrates the link between work packages and project team members. What is this chart called?

A. Hierarchy-type chart
B. Assignment matrix
C. Organizational chart
D. Network diagram

101. You are planning the staff for a project. One of the diagrams you produce illustrates the number of hours that each person will be needed each week over the course of the project schedule. What is this chart is commonly known as?

A. Work breakdown structure
B. The project schedule network diagram
C. Resource histogram
D. Detailed Gantt chart

102. Your team has proposed that a resource leveling technique should be adopted for the project schedule from this point on. Which of the following statements best describes what they are suggesting?

A. No change to the resources and reducing the project schedule
B. Adding resources and reducing the project schedule
C. Reducing resources but not changing the project schedule
D. Balancing out the peaks and valleys of resource usage

103. You meet with the project sponsor, and the conversation covers the following topics: availability, competencies, prior experience, and resource costs of the potential project team members. The items referenced are part of which of the following?

A. Enterprise environmental factors
B. Project resource histogram
C. Responsibility assignment matrix
D. Organizational breakdown structure

104. Some of the project staff assignments are defined within the project charter. What is this assignment of tasks is known as?

A. Resource management
B. Pre-assignment
C. Resource leveling
D. Responsibility assignment matrix (RAM)

105. You are managing a team whose members all have a shared goal, and they all perform their roles, spending little or no time meeting face to face. What is this type of team environment called?

A. Composite organization
B. Matrix organization
C. Virtual team
D. Remote team

106. You are working on your resource management plan. Which of the following establishes clear expectations regarding acceptable behavior by project team members?

A. Recognition plan
B. Assignment matrix
C. Resource control
D. Team charter

107. You have been asked to give details of how you propose to develop the project team. Which of the following descriptions best describes what you should be doing?

A. Improve the competencies of team members
B. Document the resource calendars of team members
C. Assign the appropriate people to activities on the project
D. Finalize roles and responsibilities in the project plan

108. Which process uses the following tools and techniques: interpersonal and team skills, team-building activities, and co-location?

A. Identify Stakeholders
B. Develop Team
C. Plan Human Resource Management
D. Manage Stakeholder Engagement

109. At your personal performance review, your functional manager suggests a number of areas in which you can improve. These include better understanding the feelings of the project team members and acknowledging their concerns. These skills are most related to _____.

A. Team building
B. Ground rules
C. Interpersonal and team skills
D. Co-location

110. Which of the following tools and techniques is not part of developing a project team?

A. Interpersonal and team skills
B. Training
C. Team-building activities
D. Project management information system

111. You are preparing a budget item for your project to support a facilitated offsite meeting designed to improve interpersonal relationships within the project team. The title for this budget line item should be _____.

A. Team building
B. Soft skills training
C. Effective team working
D. Improving team competencies

112. You are required to develop a recognition and reward system for your project office. Which of the following is an appropriate basis for this system?

A. Reward only desirable behavior
B. Establish and reward a "team member of the month"
C. Reward all team members who work overtime
D. Reward individualism, regardless of culture

113. Which of the following organizational structures creates a more complicated environment for managing the project team?

A. Functional organization
B. Matrix organization
C. Projectized organization
D. Hierarchical organization

114. Tracking team performance, providing feedback, resolving issues, and coordinating changes to enhance project performance are all part of which process?

A. Develop Team
B. Acquire Resources
C. Manage Team
D. Plan Resource Management

115. Measuring the effectiveness of the project team, recording current competencies, and monitoring reduction in team turnover rates are related to _____.

A. Project staff assignments
B. Project team-building activities
C. Recognition and reward systems
D. Team performance assessments

116. Results from schedule control, cost control, quality control, and scope validation are all examples of inputs that can be included in _____ to help manage the project team.

A. Work performance reports
B. Team performance assessment
C. Resource management plan
D. Organizational process assets

117. Certificates of appreciation, corporate apparel, and other organizational perquisites are examples of _____ that can influence the management of the project team.

A. Staff roles and responsibilities
B. Organizational process assets
C. Staffing management plan
D. Team performance assessments

118. To help you manage the project team, you are documenting who is responsible for resolving a specific problem by a target date. The project team will most likely refer to the resulting document as a _____.

A. Project risk register
B. Change request
C. Project issue log
D. Performance report

119. A project manager must develop an approach for addressing stakeholder's information needs and requirements; creating, collecting, distributing, storing, and retrieving project information; and monitoring and controlling communications. These activities are considered part of which of the following knowledge areas?

A. Project Scope Management
B. Project Resource Management
C. Project Stakeholder Management
D. Project Communications Management

120. Which of the following are inputs and outputs of the Plan Communications Management process?

A. Project charter, project management plan, communications management plan, and project document updates
B. Stakeholder register, communication models, enterprise environmental factors, and organizational process assets
C. Communications requirements analysis, communication technology, communication models, and communication methods
D. Communication models, communication methods, communications management plan, and project document updates

121. A section of your project management plan lists methods and technologies to be used to convey information such as memos, email, and press releases, and how frequently these should be used. What is the document that defines these called?

A. Communications management plan
B. Organizational process assets
C. Communications technology
D. Stakeholder management plan

122. During the planning stage of a project you assign a member of your project team to be responsible for the distribution of information about the project. This responsibility is defined in a document called (a) _____.

A. Resource management plan
B. Communications management plan
C. Project roles and responsibilities document
D. Staffing management plan

123. When sending information to project stakeholders, the project manager is responsible for making the information clear and complete so that the recipient can understand it correctly. What attribute of a project manager does this statement describe?

A. Influence skills
B. Negotiating skills
C. Communications skills
D. Delegation skills

124. When managing project stakeholders, you may use a number of different techniques to convey information, including written and verbal, formal and informal, official and unofficial, internal and external to the organization. These are all examples of _____.

A. Influence skills
B. Communication methods
C. Delegation skills
D. Communications dimensions

125. The document that covers the topics of identifying project successes and failures, and making recommendations on how to improve future performance on other projects, is referred to as the _____.

A. Lessons Learned register
B. Stakeholder management plan
C. Communications management plan
D. Change log

126. You have completed an end-of-phase review meeting. Several actions and suggestions have been given to you as the project manager. You must document these so that they are considered for use on future projects. These actions and suggestions are called (the) _____.

A. Project issues list
B. Lessons learned
C. Risk register items
D. Project documentation

127. Which of the following is the recommended way of reporting on project progress to stakeholders?

A. Regularly, at preset times
B. Comprehensively, at the end of the project
C. Regularly and on an exception (ad hoc) basis
D. On exception (ad hoc) and at the end of project

128. You have been asked to collect and provide performance information to the project stakeholders. The process responsible for compiling reports is called _____.

A. Baselining the schedule
B. Stakeholder management
C. Team performance assessments
D. Project reporting

129. Which of the following are inputs to the Manage Communications process?

A. Project reporting
B. Work performance reports
C. Change requests
D. Lessons learned register

130. Work performance reports that indicate the status of deliverables and what has been accomplished to date in the project is part of which process group?

A. Initiating
B. Executing
C. Closing
D. Planning

131. You have a number of documents and data, including status reports, memos, justifications, bar charts, S-curves, histograms, and tables for the data analyzed against the performance measurement baseline. The collective name for this information is _____.

A. Performance measurements
B. Forecast completion
C. Work performance reports
D. Deliverable Status

132. As part of your role as project manager, you must frequently update and reissue work performance information that has been analyzed and integrated in the Monitor and Control Project work process as the project proceeds. This information concerns how the project's past performance could impact the project in the future. This information is documented as _____.

A. Work performance reports
B. Corrective actions
C. Change requests
D. Variance analysis

133. To ensure comprehensive identification and listing of stakeholders, judgment and expertise should be sought from individuals or groups except from _____.

A. The competitors
B. The project manager
C. Subject matter experts (SMEs)
D. Senior management

134. Which of the following is a tool that a project manager uses to help document and monitor the resolution of issues in the project?

A. Risk register
B. Issues log
C. Change requests
D. Corrective actions

135. The set of project management activities including identification, analysis, planning responses, and monitoring and controlling of risks in the project is part of carrying out _____.

A. Risk identification
B. Project risk analysis
C. Project risk management
D. Project risk mitigation

136. In order to be successful, how often should an organization address risk management?

A. At every management meeting
B. Only in the planning phase of the project
C. On high-risk projects only
D. Consistently throughout the project

137. The project director advises you that your project should be working to maximize opportunities and minimize threats. . This policy is implemented in a project using which of the following?

A. Risk responses
B. Risk analysis
C. Risk identification
D. Risk classification

138. One of the tools used to assess risks in a project is a table showing the various levels of likelihood and consequences for risks identified in the project. What is this table called?

A. Risk register
B. Risk probability and impact matrix
C. Issues log
D. Impact scales

139. Who is responsible for identifying risks in a new project?

A. Project manager
B. Project sponsor
C. Any project personnel
D. The main stakeholders

140. What is the document that contains a list of identified risks, potential risk owners, list of potential responses to the risks, and additional information about the identified risks called?

A. Risk management plan
B. Project issues log
C. Risk-related procurement decisions
D. Risk register

141. As part of your responsibility for managing risks in your project, you rate risks as low, medium, or high. What tool would you typically use to define these ratings?

A. Risk probability and impact matrix
B. Project documents updates
C. Assumption analysis
D. Checklist analysis

142. A new member of your project team suggests that you should use a specific technique for quantitative risk analysis. She says that you should calculate information on the lowest, highest, and most likely costs, duration, or resource requirements and be represented as a probability distribution. This technique is an example of _____.

A. Representations of uncertainty
B. Probability and impact assessment
C. Probability distributions
D. Sensitivity analysis

143. What is the process of project planning that involves developing options, determining actions to enhance opportunities, and reducing threats to project objectives called?

A. Perform qualitative risk analysis
B. Plan risk responses
C. Perform quantitative risk analysis
D. Probability impact matrix

144. You have been given responsibility for developing a risk register for your project. Through which process is this document started?

A. Plan Risk Responses
B. Perform Quantitative Risk Analysis
C. Identify Risks
D. Perform Qualitative Risk Analysis

145. A common risk management strategy is to shift the negative impact of a threat, and ownership of the response, to a third party. What is this technique is called?

A. Exploit
B. Avoid
C. Mitigate
D. Transfer

146. Your team is developing a part of the risk management plan. For some of the risks, the team decides that a response plan will be executed only when certain predefined conditions exist. What is the term given to this type of risk strategy?

A. Contingent
B. Share
C. Exploit
D. Enhance

147. You are managing risk on a project using the risk management plan. How often should you monitor the project work for new and changing risks?

A. At the beginning of project planning
B. Continuously throughout the project lifecycle
C. At the beginning of each project phase
D. At the end of each project phase

148. Information such as outcomes of risk reassessments, risk audits, and periodic risk reviews are examples from which of the following?

A. Risk management plan
B. Approved change requests
C. Project documents updates
D. Work performance information

149. Identifying and documenting the effectiveness of risk responses in dealing with identified risks and the root causes, and of the effectiveness of the risk management process, is called (a) _____.

A. Risk mitigation
B. Risk identification
C. Risk analysis
D. Risk audit

150. A consultant has been reviewing outputs that resulted from carrying out the Monitor Risks process. She lists a number of actions that are required to bring the project into compliance with the project management plan. What are these actions called?

A. Recommended project plan updates
B. Project documents updates
C. Recommended corrective actions
D. Project management plan updates

151. You are part of a team running a complex project spanning a number of years and involving a number of subcontractors. The contracts signed for this project might or will end _____.

A. During any phase of the project
B. During the completion phase
C. During the execution phase
D. During the acceptance phase

152. During the Plan Procurement Management process for a project, you make a decision based on whether a particular product or service can be produced by the project team or instead should be purchased. This decision-making process is called _____.

A. Procurement management
B. Expert judgment
C. Risk management
D. Make-or-buy analysis

153. The contract you are negotiating with a subcontractor involves a set price for a well-defined requirement. There are also incentives for meeting selected objectives. This type of agreement is a _____.

A. Time and material contract
B. Cost-reimbursable contract
C. Fixed-price contract
D. Cost plus incentive fee contract

154. This procurement-related process involves asking such questions as how well the seller can meet the requirements in the procurement statement of work, whether the seller has the capacity to meet future requirements, and whether the seller can provide references from previous customers. What is the name given to this list and/or its use?

A. Contract management
B. Source selection criteria
C. Make-or-buy decisions
D. Contract negotiation

155. What is the procurement process that involves obtaining seller responses, selecting a seller, and awarding a contract called?

A. Qualified sellers list
B. Bidder conference
C. Conduct procurements
D. Selected sellers

156. A list of prospective and previously qualified sellers and information on relevant past experience with sellers, both good and bad, is known as _____.

A. Procurement management plan
B. Procurement documentation
C. Organizational process assets
D. Preferred sellers list

157. The project sponsor asks you that all prospective sellers have a clear and common understanding of the procurement you require. He suggests you have a structured meeting to do this. What is this meeting called?

A. Change control meeting
B. One-on-one meeting
C. Project status meeting
D. Bidder conference

158. The document containing information on specific prescreened sellers who are previous qualified or approved is known as:

A. A prequalified sellers list
B. A procurement document
C. An organizational process assets
D. A procurement statement of work

159. The sellers in a project have prepared documents that describe their ability and willingness to provide the requested products, services, or results described in the procurement documents. What is the generic name for the documents that the sellers provided?

A. Requirements
B. Responses
C. Requests
D. Proposals

160. Your contract and procurement consultant recommends that you establish source selection criteria for each of your sellers' proposals. What part of procurement management is this a part of?

A. Bidder conference
B. Plan Procurement Management
C. Conduct Procurements
D. Control Procurements

161. Within the Conduct Procurements process, the procurement management plan, seller proposals, and source selection criteria are examples of _____.

A. Contract types
B. Conduct Procurements tools
C. Conduct Procurements inputs
D. Conduct Procurements outputs

162. In a project where there are a number of sellers, the responses to a bid document are called _____.

A. Proposals
B. Presentations
C. Requests
D. Bidding

163. You have commissioned a consulting organization to check on the proposed pricing for a new contract. You request that their report highlight differences between the pricing suggested by the consultants and the proposed pricing from the seller. This technique makes use of _____.

A. Independent estimates
B. Bidder conference
C. Screening system
D. Expert judgment

164. Project management processes are organized into multiple groups. Which of the following statements is incorrect?

A. The process groups are independent of a knowledge area
B. Individual process in the groups are often iterated
C. Processes fall into multiple knowledge area
D. All process groups could not be represented within a phase

165. A mutually binding legal agreement that obligates the seller to provide the specified services and also obligates the buyer to pay the seller is called _____.

A. Request
B. Tender
C. Contract
D. Proposal

166. The specific technique for evaluating sellers' proposals that involves evaluation of the proposals by a multidiscipline team including members with specialized knowledge in each of the areas covered by the proposed contract is called (a) _____.

A. Seller rating system
B. Expert judgment
C. Screening system
D. Bidder conference

167. The procurement management plan for a project is a subset of (the) _____.

A. Procurement documentation
B. Project management plan
C. Claims administration
D. Request for proposal

168. You have been asked by the project sponsor to ensure that the seller's performance meets the contractual requirements and that your organization performs according to the contract. The process responsible for these activities is called _____.

A. Control Procurements
B. Plan Procurement Management
C. Conduct Procurements
D. Close Procurements

169. The procurement management plan for a project describes how the procurement processes will be managed _____.

A. At the seller selection stage
B. Throughout the project lifecycle
C. Throughout the lifetime of the contract
D. During contract documentation

170. The project you are managing has a problem that requires the contract with a seller to be modified. The alteration to the contract is in accordance with the change control terms of the contract and project. The recommended time to make this change to the contract is _____.

A. Never; the contract cannot be modified at any time
B. At any time regardless of the response from the seller
C. At any time prior to the contract being awarded to the seller
D. At any time prior to contract closure by mutual consent

171. Control procurements uses a set of tools and techniques which include the following except:

A. Audits
B. Inspection
C. Claims transfer
D. Expert judgment

172. As part of the Control Procurements process, contested changes may arise where the buyer and seller cannot reach an agreement on compensation for the change, or cannot agree that a change has occurred. These are called claims, disputes, or appeals. If the parties cannot resolve a claim by themselves, it may need to be resolved using what method?

A. Alternative dispute resolution
B. Compromising technique
C. Integrated change control
D. Economic price adjustment

173. A document produced by the buyer that rates how well each seller is performing the project work is called (a) _____.

A. Source selection criteria
B. Seller performance evaluation
C. Procurement management plan
D. Work performance information

174. The project you have been working on is near completion. One activity that you must manage involves finalizing open claims by sellers. This activity is part of a process called _____.

A. Close Project or Phase
B. Control Procurements
C. Lessons Learned
D. Validate Scope

175. There are many inputs to the Conduct Procurements process, such as the project management plan, lessons learned register and requirements documentation. Which of the following is not an input to the Conduct Procurements process?

A. Cost baseline
B. Seller proposals
C. Bidder conferences
D. Procurement documentation

176. When managing a contract in a project, the process that involves archiving the seller performance for future use is called _____.

A. Close Project or Phase
B. Validate Scope
C. Lessons Learned
D. Close Procurements

177. The project office wants to do a structured review on your project of the procurement-related activities, from the Plan Procurement Management, Conduct Procurements, and Control Procurements processes. This review is called (a) _____.

A. Performance reporting
B. Contract management
C. Procurement audit
D. Claims administration

178. You are about to perform the Control Procurements process on a project. Which of the following is a key input to that process?

A. Procurement documentation
B. Closed procurements
C. Work performance information
D. Lessons learned register

179. Which of the following tools and techniques is *not* part of the Control Procurements process?

A. Audits
B. Claims administration
C. Inspection
D. Risk register

180. Your project is near completion. You have been authorized to provide the vendor for one of the project deliverables with formal notice that the contract has been completed. What process is this?

A. Lessons Learned
B. Close Project or Phase
C. Control Procurements
D. Deliverable acceptance

181. Your project is near completion. You have been authorized to provide the seller of one of the project deliverables with formal notice that the deliverables have been accepted. The action that you took is called _____.

A. Lessons Learned
B. Procurement management
C. Deliverable acceptance
D. Contract management

182. As part of the Control Procurements process, you have provided a list of recommendations for process improvements for future contracts and purchases. What is this called?

A. Contract documentation
B. Procurement audit
C. Lessons learned register
D. Claims administration

183. The expected monetary value (EMV) of what your organization will earn if it builds a new manufacturing plant is $63M and to upgrade it is $64M. What is the EMV of the decision to build or upgrade?

A. $63M
B. $64M
C. $63.5M
D. $127M

184. Your company needs to make a decision whether to spend $120K to build a new mobile app or to enhance an existing one for $50K. With the new mobile app, there is a 60 percent chance to generate revenue of $200K if the app store reviews are positive. Your company expects revenue of $90K if the reviews are not so positive. If the company enhances the existing mobile app, the expected revenue is $120K and $60K respectively with the same probabilities as the building of a new mobile app. What is the net path value for enhancing the existing mobile app with app store reviews that are not so positive?

A. $80K
B. $-30K
C. $70K
D. $10K

185. Your company needs to make a decision whether to spend $120K to build a new mobile app or to enhance an existing one for $50K. With the new mobile app, there is a 60 percent chance to generate revenue of $200K if the app store reviews are positive. Your company expects revenue of $90K if the reviews are not so positive. If the company enhances the existing mobile app, the expected revenue is $120K and $60K respectively with the same probabilities as the building of a new mobile app. What is the scenario probability for enhancing the existing mobile app with app store reviews that are not so positive?

A. 16 percent
B. 24 percent
C. 36 percent
D. 40 percent

186. Your company needs to make a decision whether to spend $120K to build a new mobile app or to enhance an existing one for $50K. With the new mobile app, there is a 60 percent chance to generate revenue of $200K if the app store reviews are positive. Your company expects revenue of $90K if the reviews are not so positive. If the company enhances the existing mobile app, the expected revenue is $120K and $60K respectively with the same probabilities as the building of a new mobile app. What is the expected monetary value (EMV) for building a new mobile app?

A. $36K
B. $46K
C. $80K
D. -$30K

187. As a project manager, you are expected to take ownership for the decisions you make or fail to make, the actions you take or fail to take, and the resulting consequences. What best fits this description of the conduct of a project manager?

A. Responsibility
B. Respectability
C. Confidentiality
D. Consistency

188. Your company needs to make a decision whether to spend $120K to build a new mobile app or to enhance an existing one for $50K. With the new mobile app, there is a 60 percent chance to generate revenue of $200K if the app store reviews are positive. Your company expects revenue of $90K if the reviews are not so positive. If the company enhances the existing mobile app, the expected revenue is $120K and $60K respectively with the same probabilities as the building of a new mobile app. What is the decision expected monetary value (EMV)?

A. $46K
B. $50K
C. $120K
D. $170K

189. It is the duty of project managers to show high regard for themselves, for others, and for the resources entrusted to them. This behavior can be referred to as _____.

A. Honesty
B. Responsibility
C. Respect
D. Fairness

190. In project meetings, you often take time to listen to others' points of view, seeking to understand them. How would you classify this behavior?

A. Aspirational responsibility
B. Mandatory responsibility
C. Mandatory respect
D. Aspirational respect

191. You are in a project meeting, and another project manager acts in a way that is abusive to another member of the team. You decide to remind the team member, outside the meeting, that this is a breach of which professional standard?

A. Mandatory responsibility
B. Mandatory respect
C. Mandatory fairness
D. Mandatory honesty

192. It is the duty of a project manager to act impartially and objectively when making decisions and otherwise behaving. This value can be classified as _____.

A. Fairness
B. Honesty
C. Respect
D. Responsibility

193. You advise your team to behave in a manner that provides equal access to information to those who are authorized to have the information. This behavior can be considered as following the value of _____.

A. Aspirational respect
B. Aspirational fairness
C. Aspirational honesty
D. Aspirational responsibility

194. While negotiating a contract with a supplier, you realize that you already know one of the other parties in a professional capacity. You decide you must disclose this as a potential conflict of interest. What professional standard are you applying in this situation?

A. Mandatory honesty
B. Mandatory respect
C. Mandatory fairness
D. Mandatory responsibility

195. It is the duty of a project manager to try to understand the truth and act in a truthful manner in both communications and conduct. Such behavior can be considered as following the value of _____.

A. Fairness
B. Responsibility
C. Respect
D. Honesty

196. When describing the culture that you try to encourage in the project team, you identify trying to create an environment in which others feel safe to tell the truth as an example of appropriate behavior. This behavior can be referred as following the value of _____.

A. Aspirational honesty
B. Aspirational respect
C. Mandatory honesty
D. Mandatory respect

197. While managing the contracts for a project, you become aware that a team member is engaging in dishonest behavior for personal gain. You decide that you must disclose this behavior. What professional standard are you applying in this situation?

A. Aspirational fairness
B. Mandatory honesty
C. Mandatory respect
D. Aspirational responsibility

198. Conduct by team members that result in others feeling humiliated is an example of
_____.

A. Abusive manner
B. Allowable behavior
C. Aspirational standards
D. Mandatory standards

199. In a RACI (responsible, accountable, consult, and inform) chart, which role should be assigned only once to a deliverable or activity?

A. Accountable
B. Consult
C. Responsible
D. Inform

200. As you introduce a new team member to the organization, you describe one of the requirements of the role of project manager as responsibility, both legally and morally, to promote the best interests of the organization. What does this type of behavior describe?

A. Aspirational respect
B. Duty of loyalty
C. Aspirational standard
D. Good practice

Bonus Questions

201. What is the most common logical relationship in a precedence diagramming method (PDM)?

A. Finish-to-start (FS)
B. Start-to-finish (SF)
C. Finish-to-finish (FF)
D. Start-to-start (SS)

202. Which of the following Precedence Diagramming Method (PDM) relationship type is rarely used?

A. SS
B. SF
C. FF
D. FS

203. A project activity cannot start until after the resolution of a pending lawsuit. The dependency of the project activity to the lawsuit resolution is an example of a _____ dependency.

A. Discretionary internal
B. Mandatory external
C. Discretionary external
D. Mandatory internal

204. Which of the following is not an input to the Plan Communications Management process?

A. Stakeholder register
B. Enterprise environmental factors
C. Organization process assets
D. Communication technology

205. Which risk response strategy can be used for both negative and positive risks?

A. Avoid
B. Transfer
C. Mitigate
D. Accept

Chapter 6: Answers to Practice Test B

1. C. The development of the project charter is part of project initiation process and is carried out through the Develop Project Charter process. The high-level requirements are a component of the project charter. The other tasks are performed outside the initiating process group after the development of the project charter.

Reference: *PMBOK® Guide* 6th Ed., page 75

2. B. The project charter is the document that formally authorizes a project. The project charter provides the project manager with the authority to apply organizational resources to project activities. A project manager is identified and assigned as early in the project as is feasible. The project manager should always be assigned prior to the start of planning, and preferably while the project charter is being developed. Without approval of the charter, the project manager has no authority to assign resources to the project.

Reference: *PMBOK® Guide* 6th Ed., page 75

3. C. The project charter inputs may include an agreement or contract if the project is being done for an external customer. The other options are all subsets of an agreed-upon contract or calculations that lead to an agreed-upon contract.

Reference: *PMBOK® Guide* 6th Ed., page 78

4. D. The approved business case is provided by the project initiator or sponsor.

Reference: *PMBOK® Guide* 6th Ed., page 77-78

5. D. As a project manager, you must consider many factors such as the standards that are relevant to the project, the current and planned infrastructure of the organization, and prevailing market conditions when developing a project charter. The other options are examples of these factors except for the introduction of a new internal training offering

Reference: *PMBOK® Guide* 6th Ed., page 78

6. B. When developing a project budget, a project manager may need to use a number of tools and techniques of economic analysis on the project benefits. One method is to examine the payback period. To calculate the payback period, identify the point when the project schedule income exceeds the outgoing cash plus the initial investment. For this project, it will take three years for the Cash In (0 + 250,000 + 450,000) to equal the Cash Out (450,000 + 200,000 + 50,000).

Reference: *PMBOK® Guide* 6th Ed., pages 34, 233, 473

7. C. As a project manager you should not start a project without an approved charter. If the project starts without approval, organizational resources may be misdirected or wasted, and rework may be created. Your authority to proceed should be given by the ultimate authority, the project sponsor.

Reference: *PMBOK® Guide* 6th Ed., pages 75-77

8. D. As a project manager, you must adapt the project management methods that exist to help you develop the project charter. Organizational process assets include any or all process-related assets and can include formal and informal plans, policies, procedures, and guidelines. A company's project management methodology falls into this category.

Reference: *PMBOK® Guide* 6th Ed., page 79

9. D. When developing a project charter, the tool or technique of expert judgment is often used to help identify the inputs that must be considered in carrying out the Develop Project Charter process.

Reference: *PMBOK® Guide* 6th Ed., page 79

10. B. When you are planning and implementing a project, one of the considerations is the project environment, including the cultural and social issues that may impact the success of the project. All of the other choices are general organizational or detail items used or evaluated later in the planning processes.

Reference: *PMBOK® Guide* 6th Ed., page 38

11. C. The business need for the project is an essential input to the project charter, which is often stated through a business case. The detailed estimates and lists of risks are produced as part of project planning, which comes after the project chartering process. Human resources are not included – just financial

Reference: *PMBOK® Guide* 6th Ed., page 77

12. B. The WBS is a deliverable-oriented hierarchical decomposition of the project work. It is created through the Create WBS process and defines the total scope of the project.

Reference: *PMBOK® Guide* 6th Ed., page 157

13. B. Configuration verification and configuration audits ensure that the composition of a project's configuration items is correct. This activity also confirms that corresponding changes are registered, approved, tracked, and correctly implemented, to ensure that the functional requirements defined in the Configuration Management Plan have been met. Option A refers to scope validation, option C is the definition of quality control, and option D describes monitoring and controlling project work.

Reference: *PMBOK® Guide* 6th Ed., page 118

14. B. The project sponsors or initiators have the business need for the project. They approve the project scope statement for the project through the approval of a scope baseline. The scope baseline contains the project scope statement, WBS, and WBS dictionary. The roles in the other answers have input to creating the scope statement but do not approve it.

Reference: *PMBOK® Guide* 6th Ed., page 54

15. C. The business case contains the business need and cost-benefit analysis that justifies the go-ahead of the project, and it is created as a result of market demand, organizational need, customer request, technological advance, or legal requirement. All other options refer other inputs used within the Develop Project Charter process.

Reference: *PMBOK® Guide* 6th Ed., pages 77-78

16. B. Change requests can include corrective actions, preventive actions, and defect repairs. Situational action is a made-up term.

Reference: *PMBOK® Guide* 6th Ed., page 96

17. B. The project management team is responsible for taking the project charter and creating a scope statement. They are considered key stakeholders. It is important that all stakeholders provide input to the project scope statement.

Reference: *PMBOK® Guide* 6th Ed., page 151

18. B. The WBS does not show responsibilities for tasks; the business need is defined in the project charter and dates are decided based on more detailed schedule planning. The WBS serves as a communication tool by defining 100 percent of the project scope.

Reference: *PMBOK® Guide* 6th Ed., pages 156-157

19. C. The scope baseline defines the approved work that the project delivers. The Control Scope process is responsible for ensuring that only the approved work is completed—no more, no less. Any changes made through the Control Scope process are processed through Perform Integrated Change Control.

Reference: *PMBOK® Guide* 6th Ed., page 167

20. D. In a functional organization, the person organizing the project has little or no influence on project outcomes. The functional manager controls the budget and coordination of the project is done at the functional manager level.

Reference: *PMBOK® Guide* 6th Ed., page 47

21. B. The requirements traceability matrix ensures that requirements approved in the requirements documentation are delivered at the end of the project. The requirements traceability matrix also ensures that requirements add value by linking them to the business needs they are addressing.

Reference: *PMBOK® Guide* 6th Ed., pages 148-149

22. C. The use of expert judgment is recommended when creating a project scope statement. Experienced managers is not a clear answer. Special interest groups may be a possibility, as is similar project plans, but expert judgment is the best answer because of the technical detail that can be provided by a subject matter expert.

Reference: *PMBOK® Guide* 6th Ed., pages 79, 153

23. B. The project charter does not give the details of how the project will be executed, monitored, controlled, and closed. The Project benefits management plan is an input to the develop project charter and the scope management plans is a component of the project management plan.

Reference: *PMBOK® Guide* 6th Ed., page 83

24. C. Change control is the process of identifying, requesting, assessing, validating, and communicating changes to the project management plan. It does not include measuring and does not include proving.

Reference: *PMBOK® Guide* 6th Ed., pages 118-119

25. D. The project manager, in conjunction with the project management team, directs, manages, and executes the project. The project sponsor or initiator does not manage the day-to-day activities of the project. The business unit/customer receives the deliverables from the project. The project manager cannot do it all. He or she needs to work with the project team to execute the range of project activities to be performed.

Reference: *PMBOK® Guide* 6th Ed., page 92

26. A. The project management plan is the main reference for the project manager during the execution stage of a project. The procurement management plan, communication management plan, and project scope management plan are all subsets of the project management plan.

Reference: *PMBOK® Guide* 6th Ed., pages 82-83

27. B. A generic project life cycle includes starting the project, organizing and planning, carrying out the work, and ending the project. The key deliverable of the organizing and planning the project is the project management plan which requires collecting requirements, estimating costs, planning risk responses, and other planning process group processes.

Reference: *PMBOK® Guide* 6th Ed., page 18

28. C. The Direct and Manage Project Work process has a number of inputs defined. All of these are approved documents or actions. The correct option is approved change requests. The other options are not inputs to the Direct and Manage Project Work process.

Reference: *PMBOK® Guide* 6th Ed., page 93

29. D. Only approved changes should be scheduled into the project activities. Likely changes that have not been approved should not be scheduled into the project workload. Requests for changes are approved only through the formal change control process.

Reference: *PMBOK® Guide* 6th Ed., page 93

30. C. Deliverables are produced as outputs from the processes described in the project management plan. Not all tasks produce project deliverables.

Reference: *PMBOK® Guide* 6th Ed., page 95

31. D. Project deliverables are outputs from the Direct and Manage Project Work process and are defined as a verifiable product, service or result. Options B and C are items obtained to complete the project. All items consumed in the project during the execution are consumables of the project.

Reference: *PMBOK® Guide* 6th Ed., page 95

32. B. Option A does not give progress information. Option C does not give start or variance information. Option D does not allow for progress information on shorter duration activities (less than one month in duration). Reviewing work performance should be done routinely and regularly as part of the execution of the project management plan.

Reference: *PMBOK® Guide* 6th Ed., pages 90-92

33. C. Comparing actual activity performance against the project management plan identifies deviations and problems early. Communicating the plan does not measure progress. Recording progress or completed activities does not provide meaningful information on how the project is performing versus the plan.

Reference: *PMBOK® Guide* 6th Ed., page 107

34. D. Earned value analysis is used to predict future performance based on past performance. Future performance can only be controlled through corrective action and past performance can be measured only as closely as actual data allows.

Reference: *PMBOK® Guide* 6th Ed., pages 261-268

35. A. Preventive actions are a type of change request that are documented actions that aim to reduce the probability of negative consequences associated with project risks.

Reference: *PMBOK® Guide* 6th Ed., page 112

36. B. Although the Perform Integrated Change Control process is conducted from project start through completion, before baselines are established, changes are not required to be formally controlled by this process.

Reference: *PMBOK® Guide* 6th Ed., page 115

37. C. An integrated change control system must have a review step that results in either approval or rejection of changes to the project. The review step is applied not only to budget or to schedule change requests, but also to other change requests that can affect the project.

Reference: *PMBOK® Guide* 6th Ed., page 115

38. D. The Perform Integrated Change Control process is part of the project management methodology. It aids the project team in managing changes to the project.

Reference: *PMBOK® Guide* 6th Ed., page 117

39. A. The Perform Integrated Change Control process has a number of outputs. Among them are project management plan updates. The project management plan is an input to this process, and is used by the change control board in making decisions to accept or reject changes.

Reference: *PMBOK® Guide* 6th Ed., page 120

40. B. The PMO is a central function for the coordination of the management of projects in an organization. The other options are not correct, and the project manager is responsible for closing out his own respective projects.

Reference: *PMBOK® Guide* 6th Ed., page 48

41. C. The Close Project or Phase process is defined within the project management plan. The procurement, scope, and quality management plans are specific plans for each of these areas and do not specify how the project or phase should be closed.

Reference: *PMBOK® Guide* 6th Ed., page 121

42. D. The Close Project or Phase process has accepted deliverables as an input. The final product/service, project management plan updates, and change request status updates are outputs of other processes.

Reference: *PMBOK® Guide* 6th Ed., pages 125, 166

43. C. Mind mapping is a technique wherein ideas created through individual sessions are consolidated into a single map to reflect commonality and differences in understanding, as well as generate new ideas. Observation is the process of directly viewing individuals and how they perform tasks. Facilitated workshops are sessions that bring key cross-functional stakeholders together. Monte Carlo is a computer simulation for what-if scenario analyses.

Reference: *PMBOK® Guide* 6th Ed., page 144

44. B. The requirements management plan documents how requirements will be analyzed, documented, and managed throughout the project. Option A is a definition of the requirements traceability matrix, option C describes the requirements documentation, and option D describes the scope management plan.

Reference: *PMBOK® Guide* 6th Ed., page 137

45. C. The Close Project or Phase process involves administrative closure. This includes methodologies for how the project will transfer the services produced to the operational division of the organization. Contract closure is not concerned with transfer to operations. The project management plan is the superset of these procedures. Deliverable acceptance is not part of the Close Project or Phase process.

Reference: *PMBOK® Guide* 6th Ed., page 123

46. C. The project closure documents include sponsor/customer acceptance documentation from scope validation. Administrative closure, contract closure, and organizational process assets do not require direct involvement of the sponsor.

Reference: *PMBOK® Guide* 6th Ed., page 128

47. A. As part of the Close Project or Phase process, the project manager is responsible for collecting all the documentation resulting from the project activities. These include the project management plan, which itself contains the project's baselines, project calendar, and risk register, among others, which are known collectively as project files. The other options refer to items that are part of the organizational process assets, which project files will later become part of.

Reference: *PMBOK® Guide* 6th Ed., page 128

48. B. Project closure documents are formal documents that indicate the completion or termination of a project. Contract closure and administrative closure are separate activities.

Reference: *PMBOK® Guide* 6th Ed., page 128

49. C. The Project Scope Management knowledge area defines and controls what is and what is not included in the project. Project documentation management and project change control are procedures that allow the control of changes to the project.

Reference: *PMBOK® Guide* 6th Ed., page 129

50. D. The Create WBS process subdivides the major project deliverables into smaller, more manageable components. The WBS does not concern project duration. Determining the total work package count is not a function of the Create WBS process. The allocation of responsibilities is not a function of the WBS, although it may be included as part of the WBS dictionary.

Reference: *PMBOK® Guide* 6th Ed., page 156

51. A. The scope management plan provides guidance on how project scope will be defined, developed, monitored, controlled, and validated. The scope management plan may be formal or informal, highly detailed, or broadly framed, based on the project needs. Option B describes the Collect Requirements process, option C describes the project scope statement, and option D describes the WBS.

Reference: *PMBOK® Guide* 6th Ed., page 134

52. A. The detailed project scope statement includes project scope description, acceptance criteria, project deliverables, and project exclusions. Approved change requests to the scope become part of the scope baseline, a component of the project management plan.

Reference: *PMBOK® Guide* 6th Ed., pages 154-155

53. B. Prototypes, not requirements documentation, serve as a working model of the expected product that the project will deliver prior to the actual build. Prototypes are a tool of the Collect Requirements process. The rest of the options are valid requirements documentation descriptions.

Reference: *PMBOK® Guide* 6th Ed., page 147

54. C. A work breakdown structure template is often a WBS from a previous similar project within your organization because projects within an organization often share many common elements and processes. Generic or general-purpose lists of elements or structures are not always necessarily the best fit for your organization.

Reference: *PMBOK® Guide* 6th Ed., page 156

55. D. The work to be done in a project is defined in the WBS and the approved project scope statement. These two documents, plus the WBS dictionary, make up what is known as the scope baseline. Approved changes are only one part of the scope. Issues do not necessarily impact the immediate work or scope. The WBS template is a generic starting point for defining the scope or final WBS.

Reference: *PMBOK® Guide* 6th Ed., pages 161-162

56. A. Validate Scope is the process of obtaining stakeholders' formal acceptance of the project and associated deliverables. This process is performed at the end of the phase, or before project closure, to determine if the project has delivered the defined scope. Define Scope is the process of determining what the project will deliver. Control Scope is the process of monitoring the status of the project and product scope and managing changes to the scope baseline. Plan Scope Management refers to the overall scope-related efforts, defined in the project management plan, of how the team will define and manage scope.

Reference: *PMBOK® Guide* 6th Ed., page 163

57. B. The act of monitoring and controlling the product and project scope, as well as ensuring that all scope changes go through integrated change control, is part of the Control Scope process.

Reference: *PMBOK® Guide* 6th Ed., page 167

58. C. The Validate Scope process focused on customer acceptance of the project deliverables and uses a number of techniques, including inspection. Inspection is a process of measuring, examining, and verifying that the work and deliverables meet the product and acceptance criteria.

Reference: *PMBOK® Guide* 6th Ed., page 167

59. D. Along with the Validate Scope process, the Control Scope process is part of the Project Scope Management knowledge area. Specifically, these processes occur as part of the Monitoring and Controlling process group.

Reference: *PMBOK® Guide* 6th Ed., pages 167-169

60. A. Option A, configuration control and change control, respectively, is correct. Change requests include corrective actions, preventative actions and defect repairs.

Reference: *PMBOK® Guide* 6th Ed., page 118

61. A. Changes to project scope or requirements must be reviewed by the change control board (or whomever designated in the documented Change Management Plan) through the Perform Integrated Change Control process. They will review and then approve or reject the changes according to the documented guidelines. No work should start until it is approved through the Integrated Change Control process.

Reference: *PMBOK® Guide* 6th Ed., pages 167-169

62. B. Updating the project management plan is an output of the Control Scope process once the changes have been approved. The project management plan includes the Performance Measurement Baseline (of which the Scope Baseline is a component) and approved changes are incorporated into an updated Performance Measurement Baseline within the project management plan.

Reference: *PMBOK® Guide* 6th Ed., page 171

63. C. Identifying the activities, dependencies, and resources needed to produce the project deliverables are some of the actions carried out in the Project Schedule Management knowledge area. Project Risk Management deals with risks and not with identifying and sequencing activities. Project Schedule Control and Project Cost Planning are not knowledge areas.

Reference: *PMBOK® Guide* 6th Ed., page 173

64. D. As part of Project Schedule Management knowledge area, the project team must define activities, which decomposes the work packages from the WBS into smaller components of work. These activities are the basis for estimating, scheduling, and performing work of the project. Scheduling the work/activities and estimating durations are part of subsequent processes.

Reference: *PMBOK® Guide* 6th Ed., page 183

65. A. The activity list is a comprehensive list of all scheduled activities, including the activities' scope and unique identifier that is in sufficient detail for a team member to complete the work. Defining the project scope is accomplished through the approved scope statement, WBS, and WBS dictionary. It does not yet reflect the dependencies identified within the project schedule.

Reference: *PMBOK® Guide* 6th Ed., page 185

66. B. A diagram on which activities are represented as boxes and the dependencies between activities are shown as arrows is known as activity-on-nod and/or a project schedule network diagram.

Reference: *PMBOK® Guide* 6th Ed., page 190

67. C. The type of dependency in which the successor activity does not start until the completion of the predecessor activity is known as finish-to-start.

Reference: *PMBOK® Guide* 6th Ed., page 190

68. D. A list that identifies and describes the types and quantities of each resource required to complete activities is known as the resource requirements. Project document updates, and resource breakdown structure are other outputs of the Estimate Activity Resources process.

Reference: *PMBOK® Guide* 6th Ed., page 316

69. A. Estimating the duration of a project activity by referring to the actual duration of a similar activity on another project is known as analogous estimating. Expert judgment relies on specialists in a specific domain to perform a specialized task. Parametric estimating uses a metric from the current project in combination with historical information. Reserve analysis refers to determining the need for contingency reserve.

Reference: *PMBOK® Guide* 6th Ed., page 200

70. B. Calculating the early start and finish dates and the late start and finish dates for all project activities using a forward and backward pass analysis is known as the critical path method. Schedule compression is about reducing project duration. With the context of project schedule, what-if scenario analysis attempts to answer the question: "If Scenario X occurs, what will be the impact to the project?"

Reference: *PMBOK® Guide* 6th Ed., pages 210

71. C. A project overview that shows only the start and end of major deliverables, along with key external dependencies, is known as a milestone chart. Network diagrams and summary bar charts are used for more detailed presentation, and they also show dependencies and durations of tasks. The schedule baseline refers to the approved and signed-off version of the schedule.

Reference: *PMBOK® Guide* 6th Ed., page 218

72. D. A summary schedule lists the activity identifier, activity description, and calendar units with the length of the duration displayed proportionally as a horizontal bar relative to the project schedule time frame's start and end dates. The network diagram shows dependencies between activities. The detailed schedule with logical relationships shows more details that the summary schedule by displaying milestones and dependencies. The milestone schedule shows the calendar units as zero and only displays the milestones as a point in time.

Reference: *PMBOK® Guide* 6th Ed., page 219

73. A. The schedule baseline is the approved version of the schedule that can only be changed through formal change control and is used as a basis for comparison to actual results.

Reference: *PMBOK® Guide* 6th Ed., page 217

74. B. The Develop Schedule process uses the following tools and techniques: schedule network analysis, critical path method, resource optimization, data analysis, leads and lags, schedule compression, project management information system, agile release planning. The outputs include schedule baseline, project schedule, schedule data, project calendars, change requests, project management plan updates, and project documents updates.

Reference: *PMBOK® Guide* 6th Ed., page 205

75. C. Gathering actual start and finish dates of activities, along with remaining durations for work in progress, is known as a performance review. Cost variance analysis compares baseline to actual data. Performance measurement is a specific earned value technique. Critical path analysis is a planning tool.

Reference: *PMBOK® Guide* 6th Ed., page 227

76. D. Variance analysis is used as part of the Control Schedule process to assess the magnitude of variation from the project schedule and schedule baseline in order to evaluate progress. Recording dates does not compare the plan to actual results. Calendar contract dates do not give variance information and the difference between total and free slack is not the variance that is analyzed in variance analysis.

Reference: *PMBOK® Guide* 6th Ed., page 227

77. A. Schedule variance analysis, along with performance reviews, can result in change requests to the schedule baseline. *Action change control* is a made-up term and does not of itself constitute corrective actions. Updates to the schedule baseline will only occur if the change request is approved. Updates to the project scope are not necessarily implied.

Reference: *PMBOK® Guide* 6th Ed., page 229

78. B. Approved changes to the start and finish dates of the schedule baseline for the project are referred to as schedule baseline updates. Variance analysis is a technique that compares planned to actual dates, and a performance review involves reviewing, measuring, and analyzing schedule performance. The description is not of a list of approved change requests.

Reference: *PMBOK® Guide* 6th Ed., page 229

79. C. Estimating, budgeting, and cost control processes make up the Project Cost Management knowledge area. Project Risk Management is focused on risks, not solely on costs. Project Schedule Management deals with the duration and dependencies of tasks. Project Resource Management involves identifying necessary resources to complete the project.

Reference: *PMBOK® Guide* 6th Ed., page 231

80. B. As more information becomes known later in the project, estimates could narrow to a range of −5 percent to +10 percent, which is referred to as a definitive or control estimate. Earlier in a project, for example in the initiation stage, estimates could use a rough order of magnitude (ROM) range between -25 percent and +75 percent.

Reference: *PMBOK® Guide* 6th Ed., page 241

81. A. Using costs from a previous similar project that has been completed in your organization is known as analogous estimating. Bottom-up estimating aggregates the individual detailed estimates to arrive at the total estimate, whereas parametric estimating relies on statistical relationships to arrive at an estimate based on historical information and other parameters (for example, length, width, square footage, and so forth). Three-point estimating uses three estimates to calculate the expected duration—most likely, optimistic, and pessimistic.

Reference: *PMBOK® Guide* 6th Ed., page 244

82. C. Parametric estimating relies on statistical relationships to arrive at an estimate based on historical information and other parameters (for example, length, width, square footage, and so forth) whereas bottom-up estimating aggregates the individual detailed estimates to arrive at the total estimate. Using only costs from a previous similar project that has been completed in your organization is known as analogous estimating. Three-point estimating uses three estimates to calculate the expected duration—most likely, optimistic, and pessimistic.

Reference: *PMBOK® Guide* 6th Ed., page 244

83. D. The ETC requires the estimate at completion (EAC), and actual costs (AC) to date. The formula is ETC = EAC − AC.

Reference: *PMBOK® Guide* 6th Ed., page 267

84. B. The SPI is the only indicator that would help to measure schedule progress. The others are related only to costs.

Reference: *PMBOK® Guide* 6th Ed., page 263

85. C. Earned value is used as a part of the calculations for CV (EV - AC), SV (EV - PV), CPI (EV / AC), and SPI (EV / PV).

Reference: *PMBOK® Guide* 6th Ed., page 267

86. A. Monitoring and recording results of executing quality activities to assess performance and recommend necessary changes occurs as part of the Control Quality process. Manage Quality is responsible for ensuring that appropriate quality standards are used and for carrying out process improvement. Plan Quality Management involves establishing the quality requirements and/or standards for the project and project product. Quality improvement is an organizational development process, not a project management process.

Reference: *PMBOK® Guide* 6th Ed., page 272

87. C. Plan Quality Management is related to establishing the quality requirements and/or standards for the project. Monitoring and recording results of executing quality activities to assess performance and recommend necessary changes is carried out through the Control Quality process. Manage Quality is responsible for ensuring that appropriate quality standards are used, for carrying out process improvement. Develop quality is not a project management process.

Reference: *PMBOK® Guide* 6th Ed., page 272

88. B. Manage Quality involves ensuring that appropriate quality standards are used and carrying out process improvement. Plan Quality Management is related to establishing the quality requirements and/or standards for the project. Monitoring and recording results of executing quality activities to assess performance and recommend necessary changes is part of the Control Quality process. Quality improvement deals with increasing the effectiveness and efficiencies of organizational policies, processes, and procedures.

Reference: *PMBOK® Guide* 6th Ed., pages 289-290

89. D. Outputs of the Plan Quality Management process include quality management plan, quality metrics, project management plan updates, and project document updates.

Reference: *PMBOK® Guide* 6th Ed., page 277

90. A. Quality metrics clarify what some of the measurements on the project are and how the Control Quality process will measure those metrics. Quality checklists are structured tools used to ensure that a predefined set of steps have been followed to ensure consistent delivery of a particular component. The quality management plan describes how the project will adhere to the organization's quality policy. Process improvement is done as a part of the Manage Quality process.

Reference: *PMBOK® Guide* 6th Ed., page 272

91. A. Project documents are an input to the Manage Quality process. Project requirements are not quality inputs. Change requests are an output of the Manage Quality process. Verified deliverables are an output of the Control Quality process.

Reference: *PMBOK® Guide* 6th Ed., pages 288-289

92. B. An audit is a structured, independent process used to determine if project activities comply with organizational and project policies, processes, and procedures. A quality audit is usually conducted by a team external to the project, such as the organization's internal audit department, PMO, or by an auditor external to the organization.

Reference: *PMBOK® Guide* 6th Ed., page 294

93. C. The technique used to carry out the steps outlined in the process improvement plan to improve processes and project performance is known as process analysis. Quality metrics are an output to Plan Quality Management Performing a quality audit involves identifying inefficient and ineffective policies, processes, and procedures, and auditing the results of the Control Quality process. Quality reports are an output of Manage Quality.

Reference: *PMBOK® Guide* 6th Ed., pages 272, 292

94. D. Quality control should be performed throughout the project to formally demonstrate, with reliable data, that the customer's expectations will be met.

Reference: *PMBOK® Guide* 6th Ed., page 299

95. A. Actions that have been recommended to increase the effectiveness and efficiency of the organization are documented as change requests. Change requests can be used to take corrective or preventative action or to perform defect repair.

Reference: *PMBOK® Guide* 6th Ed., pages 272, 292

96. B. A diagram that shows how various factors might be linked to the problem or the effects is known as a cause and effect diagram. A scatter diagram shows the relationship between two variables only. A control chart is used to determine the stability of a system. Statistical sampling is related to population sampling of components.

Reference: *PMBOK® Guide* 6th Ed., pages 293, 294

97. C. A diagram that can organize potential causes of defects into groups showing areas of similarity is an Affinity Diagram. A scatter diagram shows the relationship between two variables and a flowchart is a graphical representation of a process. A control chart relates to the stability of processes or deliverables.

Reference: *PMBOK® Guide* 6th Ed., page 293

98. D. A scatter diagram shows the relationship or potential correlation between two variables

Reference: *PMBOK® Guide* 6th Ed., page 293

99. A. The Plan Resource Management process defines how the project will estimate, acquire, manage, and use team and physical resources. The process defines roles and responsibilities for the project using hierarchical charts, a Responsibility Assignment Matrix (RAM) or text-oriented format.

Reference: *PMBOK® Guide* 6th Ed., pages 316-137

100. B. A matrix that illustrates the link between work packages and project team members is called an assignment matrix (RAM). A hierarchy-type chart resembles a traditional organizational chart by showing positions and relationships in a top-down format. Organizational charts can take many forms, such as hierarchical, matrix, or text-oriented. Network diagrams show the logical workflow of activities in a project.

Reference: *PMBOK® Guide* 6th Ed., page 317

101. C. A chart that illustrates the number of hours that each person will be needed each week over the course of the project schedule is known as a resource histogram. A WBS does not show resource allocation. A project schedule network diagram is used to show the relationship and interdependencies between tasks. A Gantt or bar chart shows task schedule information.

Reference: *PMBOK® Guide* 6th Ed., page 719

102. D. Balancing out the peaks and valleys of resource usage is a commonly used resource leveling strategy. None of the other strategies listed is a resource-leveling strategy.

Reference: *PMBOK® Guide* 6th Ed., page 211

103. A. Enterprise environmental factors are an input to the Acquire Project Team process. As part of this input, the following is considered: availability, competencies, prior experience, and resource costs of the potential project team. The project resource histogram shows the need for resources over a period of time. The responsibility assignment matrix (RAM) shows which project team member should be working on a particular work package or activity. The organizational breakdown structure does not any information related to availability, experience, or cost.

Reference: *PMBOK® Guide* 6th Ed., page 331

104. B. Pre-assignment is when team members are defined in advance of the project, either based on expertise or having been identified within the Develop Project Charter process. Resource management and resource leveling are activities not included in the project charter. The responsibility assignment matrix (RAM) shows which project team member should be working on a particular work package or activity.

Reference: *PMBOK® Guide* 6th Ed., page 333

105. C. A team whose members all have a shared goal and all perform their roles, spending little or no time meeting face to face, is known as a virtual team. Composite (a blend of functional and projectized) and matrix organizations are types of organizational structures. Remote teams do not necessarily have a shared goal.

Reference: *PMBOK® Guide* 6th Ed., page 333

106. D. The team charter is a document that establishes the team values, agreements, behavioral expectations and operating guidelines. It can additionally include communication guidelines, decision making process, conflict resolution process, meeting guidelines and team agreements.

Reference: *PMBOK® Guide* 6th Ed., pages 319, 320

107. A. The Develop Team process includes activities such as improving the competencies of team members, improving team interaction, and improving the project environment. Creating the resource calendars and assigning team members to the project are outputs of the Acquire Project Team process.

Reference: *PMBOK® Guide* 6h Ed., page 336

108. B. The Develop Team process uses these tools and techniques and works to create an environment that facilitates teamwork and continually motivates the team by providing opportunities, challenges, timely feedback, and support.

Reference: *PMBOK® Guide* 6th Ed., page 336

109. C. Better understanding the feelings of the project team members and acknowledging their concerns are examples of interpersonal and team skills. Team building helps project team members to work more effectively. Ground rules encompass setting clear expectations within the project team. Co-location is placing project team members in one physical location to enhance their interaction and ability to perform as a team.

Reference: *PMBOK® Guide* 6th Ed., page 341

110. D. Interpersonal and team skills, training, and team-building activities are tools and techniques of the Develop Team process. Project management information system is one of the tools and techniques of the Manage Team process.

Reference: *PMBOK® Guide* 6th Ed., pages 336, 345

111. A. An offsite meeting designed to improve interpersonal relationships within the project team is an example of a team building activity. Soft skills training is a specific type of training related to interpersonal skills. Effective team working and improving team competencies are related to developing the project team.

Reference: *PMBOK® Guide* 6th Ed., page 341

112. A. Only desirable behavior should be rewarded in a recognition and reward system. Rewarding a team member of the month and rewarding all team members who work overtime have a narrow focus compared to focusing on desirable behavior. Rewarding individualism, regardless of culture may not always be appropriate.

Reference: *PMBOK® Guide* 6th Ed., pages 341-342

113. B. Managing the project team becomes more complicated when team members are accountable to both a functional and a project manager, as in the case within a matrix organization. Functional, hierarchical, and projectized organizations have clear accountability.

Reference: *PMBOK® Guide* 6th Ed., page 47

114. C. Tracking team performance, providing feedback, resolving issues, and coordinating changes to enhance project performance are all part of the Manage Team process. The Develop Team process focuses on optimizing performance. The Acquire Resources is the process of obtaining team members facilities, equipment, materials, supplies, and other resources necessary to complete project work. Plan Resource Management process addresses how the project will estimate, acquire, develop and manage the physical and human resources needed to execute the project.

Reference: *PMBOK® Guide* 6th Ed., pages 328, 345

115. D. Checking skills improvements, recording current competencies, and monitoring reduction in team turnover rates are part of team performance assessments. Project staff assignments are an input to developing the project team. Recognition and reward systems, as well as team-building activities, are tools and techniques of the Develop Project Team process.

Reference: *PMBOK® Guide* 6th Ed., page 343

116. A. Results from schedule control, cost control, quality control, and scope validation are all examples of inputs that are integrated within the work performance reports that are used to help manage the project team. Team performance assessments are an evaluation of the team's overall performance. The resource management plan provides guidance on how resources will be estimated, allocated, managed and ultimately, released. Organizational process assets are policies, procedures, and systems for reward.

Reference: *PMBOK® Guide* 6th Ed., page 112

117. B. The organizational process assets that can influence the Manage Team process include certificates of appreciation, corporate apparel, and other organizational perquisites (perks). Team performance assessments are appraisals of how the team is performing as a whole. The resource management plan documents how resources will be estimated, acquired, managed and released. Team roles and responsibilities are also documented in the resource management plan.

Reference: *PMBOK® Guide* 6th Ed., page 348

118. C. An issue log is a document where information about issues is recorded and monitored. A project risk register is a used for identifying, tracking, and documenting project risks. A change request is used to document any potential deviation from the approved project management plan. Performance reports or assessments are used to evaluate team performance.

Reference: *PMBOK® Guide* 6th Ed., page 96

119. D. Developing an approach for stakeholder's information needs and requirements; creating, collecting, distributing, storing, and retrieving project information; and monitoring and controlling communications are examples of activities in the Project Communications Management knowledge area.

Reference: *PMBOK® Guide* 6th Ed., page 359

120. A. Inputs to the Plan Communications Management process include the project charter, project management plan, project documents, enterprise environment factors, and organizational process assets. Communications management plan, project management plan updates and project document updates are outputs of the Plan Communications Management process.

Reference: *PMBOK® Guide* 6th Ed., page 360

121. A. Methods and technologies to be used to convey memoranda, email, and press releases, and how frequently these should be used, are examples of the contents of a communications management plan.

Reference: *PMBOK® Guide* 6th Ed., page 377

122. B. The staff member responsible for the distribution of information about the project is defined in the communications management plan. The resource management plan addresses how project resources are going to be acquired, developed and managed. Project roles and responsibilities are related to task responsibilities. A staffing management plan no longer exists in the PMBOK.

Reference: *PMBOK® Guide* 6th Ed., page 377

123. C. Making information clear and complete so that the recipient can understand it correctly is an example of communications skills. Influence skills, negotiating skills, and delegation skills are different attributes of the soft skills set that a project manager should have.

Reference: *PMBOK® Guide* 6th Ed., page 363

124. D. Written and verbal communication, formal and informal, official and unofficial, internal and external to the organization are all examples of communication dimensions. Communication methods include push, pull and interactive. Influence skills and delegation skills are different attributes of the soft skills set that a project manager should have.

Reference: *PMBOK® Guide* 6th Ed., page 361

125. A. Identifying project successes and failures, and making recommendations on how to improve future performance on other projects, is part of the Lessons Learned register. The other choices are all inputs to the Manage Stakeholder Engagement process.

Reference: *PMBOK® Guide* 6th Ed., page 92

126. B. Actions and suggestions that are documented and considered for use on future projects are called Lessons Learned.

Reference: *PMBOK® Guide* 6th Ed., page 92

127. C. Generally, regular reports are required by stakeholders, and exception reports should be issued as appropriate.

Reference: *PMBOK® Guide* 6th Ed., page 385

128. D. Project reporting is the process of collecting and distributing performance information, including status reports, progress measurements, and forecasts. Baselining the project is a specific action to record the signed-off and approved versions of the schedule, budget, and scope. Stakeholder management refers to analyzing and communicating with the stakeholders. Team performance assessments are the output of the Develop Project Team process.

Reference: *PMBOK® Guide* 6th Ed., page 385

129. B. Work performance reports are inputs to the Manage Communications process.

Reference: *PMBOK® Guide* 6th Ed., page 379

130. B. Work performance reports, inputs to the Manage Communications process, indicate the status of deliverables and what has been accomplished to date in the project. The Manage Communications process is part of the Executing process group.

Reference: *PMBOK® Guide* 6th Ed., pages 25, 112, 382

131. C. Documents and data that include status reports, memos, justifications, bar charts, S-curves, histograms, and tables for the data analyzed against the project baseline is known as work performance reports.

Reference: *PMBOK® Guide* 6th Ed., pages 112, 382

132. A. Work performance reports are issued periodically and are the basis for simple status reports to more elaborate reports. More elaborate reports may contain analysis of past performance, forecasted project completion, current status of risks and issues, and results of variance analysis, among other information. Variance analysis, corrective actions, and change requests are not related to forecasting.

Reference: *PMBOK® Guide* 6th Ed., pages 112, 382

133. A. As part of stakeholder analysis, groups or individuals such as senior management, subject matter experts, project team, industry groups, and even technical or professional associations can contribute to the process. Competitors are not part of this process.

Reference: *PMBOK® Guide* 6th Ed., pages 85, 94, 404

134. B. One of the tools used to help document and monitor the resolution of issues in a project is known as the issues log. The risk register captures the outcomes of the risk management processes. Change requests are actions required as a result of issues or risks identified. Corrective actions refer to changes made when executing the project.

Reference: *PMBOK® Guide* 6th Ed., page 96

135. C. Identification, analysis, planning responses, and monitoring and controlling of risks in the project are part of the Project Risk Management knowledge area. Risk identification, analysis, and mitigation refer to various risk-related activities.

Reference: *PMBOK® Guide* 6th Ed., page 395

136. D. An organization should be committed to address risk management proactively and consistently throughout the project.

Reference: *PMBOK® Guide* 6th Ed., pages 397-398

137. A. The objective of the Plan Risk Responses process is to take actions that will potentially maximize opportunities and minimize threats. Risk analysis, risk identification, and risk classification are other risk-related efforts that take place prior to determining the appropriate responses to identified risks.

Reference: *PMBOK® Guide* 6th Ed., pages 397-398

138. B. The risk probability and impact matrix is one of the tools used to assess the probability and impact of both threats and opportunities. A risk register records all identified risks and information about them. An issues log records all issues. The impact scales are used to define the impact of risks relative to major project objectives (for example, cost, time, scope, and so forth).

Reference: *PMBOK® Guide* 6th Ed., pages 423

139. C. Any project personnel can identify risks in a project. The project manager or risk manager manages the risk management process, with input from the sponsor and other stakeholders.

Reference: *PMBOK® Guide* 6th Ed., page 411

140. D. Identified risks, potential risk owners and responses are the basic fields in a risk register. The risk management plan is the overall management document and processes definitions for managing risk in the project. The issues log contains the list of all issues. When a decision is made to transfer risk, risk-related procurements will include agreements to purchase insurance, bonds, and so forth in order to properly mitigate or transfer part of all of the risks.

Reference: *PMBOK® Guide* 6th Ed., page 417

141. A. Rating risks into a low, medium, or high is done using a risk probability and impact matrix. Project documents updates are an output in six of the seven risk management process. Assumption analysis and checklist analysis are tools and techniques used for risk identification.

Reference: *PMBOK® Guide* 6th Ed., pages 408, 423

142. A. A technique that is often used for quantitative risk analysis that calculates or obtains information on the lowest, highest, and most likely impact of a risk event is referred to as a representation of uncertainty. These estimates can then be used for triangular, beta, or other distributions when performing risk simulations. Probability and impact assessment is a ranking of risks. Probability distributions, within the context of project risk management, are used to model and simulate uncertainties in the project, such as duration and cost estimates. Sensitivity analysis is used to test the impact of risk on individual project variables. .

Reference: *PMBOK® Guide* 6th Ed., page 432

143. B. Developing options, determining actions to enhance opportunities, and reducing threats to project objectives is completed as part of the Plan Risk Responses process. Performing qualitative risk analysis and perform quantitative risk analysis are prior steps in the risk management knowledge area. The probability impact matrix is one of the tools used to assess the probability and impact of potential threats and opportunities.

Reference: *PMBOK® Guide* 6th Ed., page 437

144. C. The risk register is first created in the Identify Risks process. Qualitative risk analysis follows this process and provides updates to the risk responses. Plan Risk Responses follows the execution of both the Perform Qualitative and Perform Quantitative Risk Analysis processes.

Reference: *PMBOK® Guide* 6th Ed., page 437

145. D. A common risk management strategy used to shift the negative impact of a threat, and ownership of the response, to a third party is called transfer. Exploit is a risk response used for risk opportunities. Avoid and mitigate are alternative techniques for addressing potential threats.

Reference: *PMBOK® Guide* 6th Ed., page 443

146. A. For some of the threats and opportunities in a project, a response plan that will be executed only when certain predefined conditions exist is called a contingent response strategy. Share, exploit, and enhance are responses to opportunities, also known as positive risks.

Reference: *PMBOK® Guide* 6th Ed., page 445

147. B. The project team should monitor the project work for new and changing risks continuously throughout the project lifecycle. The efforts carried out as part of the Monitor Risk process should be defined in the risk management plan, and it should specify continuous monitoring for new and changing risks.

Reference: *PMBOK® Guide* 6th Ed., page 453

148. C. Information such as outcomes of risk reassessments, risk audits, and periodic risk reviews are examples of project documents updates from the Monitor Risks process. The risk management plan defines the process and resources involved in managing the risks. Approved change requests and work performance information do not match the question items.

Reference: *PMBOK® Guide* 6th Ed., pages 457-458

149. D. The action of identifying and documenting the effectiveness of risk responses in dealing with identified risks and the root causes, and of the effectiveness of the risk management process, is known as a risk audit. Risk mitigation is a type of risk response. Risk analysis can be qualitative (prioritization based on probability and impact) or quantitative (numerically analyzing the effect of a risk relative to project objectives). Risk audits examine and document the effectiveness of the risk management processes.

Reference: *PMBOK® Guide* 6th Ed., pages 294, 293, 456

150. C. Actions that are required to bring the project into compliance with the project management plan are known as recommended corrective actions. Project documents updates and project management plan updates are also outputs of the Control Risk process, but they do not fit the question posed.

Reference: *PMBOK® Guide* 6th Ed., page 703

151. A. In a complex project involving many contracts and subcontractors, each contract lifecycle can end during any phase of the project, or when the deliverables are accepted.

Reference: *PMBOK® Guide* 6th Ed., page 461

152. D. The process of deciding whether a particular product or service can be produced by the project team or instead should be purchased is known as make-or-buy analysis. Procurement management refers to procurement-related activities and effort carried throughout the project lifecycle. Expert judgment is a technique used in many decision-making processes. Risk management refers to all risk-related efforts carried out throughout the project's life cycle in order to identify and manage risks.

Reference: *PMBOK® Guide* 6th Ed., pages 473, 479

153. C. A contract that involves a fixed price for a well-defined requirement, possibly with incentives for meeting selected objectives, is a fixed-price contract. A time and material contract is cross between cost-reimbursable and a fixed-price contract. A cost-reimbursable contract includes payments for costs incurred to complete the work plus a fee to the seller. A cost plus incentive fee contract includes a predetermined incentive based on performance.

Reference: *PMBOK® Guide* 6th Ed., pages 471-472, 476

154. B. How well the seller can meet the requirements defined in the procurement SOW, whether the seller has the capacity to meet future requirements, and whether the seller can provide references from previous customers are examples of contract source selection criteria. Contract management is the overall effort of managing contracts. Make-or-buy decisions capture the conclusion of an evaluation whether a particular component should be built by the project team or acquired externally. Contract negotiation occurs after source selection criteria have been decided and analyzed.

Reference: *PMBOK® Guide* 6th Ed., pages 478-479

155. C. The procurement process involving obtaining seller responses, selecting a seller, and awarding a contract is Conduct Procurements. Qualified sellers list is an input to this process, bidder conferences is a tool or technique used within this process, and selected sellers are an output of the process.

Reference: *PMBOK® Guide* 6th Ed., page 482

156. C. A list of prospective and previously qualified sellers and information on relevant past experience with sellers, both good and bad, is considered to be as an organizational process asset. The qualified sellers list is one part of these assets. The procurement management plan and procurement documents are other inputs to the Conduct Procurements process.

Reference: *PMBOK® Guide* 6th Ed., page 486

157. D. A structured meeting to ensure that all prospective sellers have a clear and common understanding of the procurement requirements is called a bidder conference. Change control meetings are conducted to review whether to approve, defer, or reject proposed changes to the project. One-one-meetings involve a conversation between two individuals. Project status meetings review the status of the project, including progress, issues, risks, costs, etc.

Reference: *PMBOK® Guide* 6th Ed., page 487

158. A. A list of sellers who have been prescreened for their qualifications and past experience, is called a prequalified seller list. Procurement documents and organizational process assets are inputs to the Conduct Procurements process. The procurement statement of work is an output from the Plan Procurement Management process.

Reference: *PMBOK® Guide* 6th Ed., page 501

159. D. Seller proposals are prepared in response to a procurement bid documents, and they include the information that will be evaluated to select the successful bidder(s). Requirements are a list of the needs of the contract or project. Responses are the reply to request for tender. Requests are the initial requests from the customer.

Reference: *PMBOK® Guide* 6th Ed., page 486

160. B. Establishing source selection criteria for each of your sellers' proposals helps to rate or score seller proposals. These source selection criteria are an output of the Plan Procurement Management process and are used as an input to the Conduct Procurements process. The bidder conference is an open meeting prior to the proposals being delivered, where the buyer answers questions from the potential sellers. The Control Procurements process includes managing procurement-related contracts, relationships, and changes.

Reference: *PMBOK® Guide* 6th Ed., pages 478-479

161. C. The procurement management plan, seller proposals, and source selection criteria are examples of the inputs to the Conduct Procurements process.

Reference: *PMBOK® Guide* 6th Ed., page 486

162. A. A response to a bid document, such as a request for proposal (RFP), is called a proposal. While a presentation may be given by potential sellers as part of the proposal, it is not considered a formal response. Requests in this instance refer to the buyer's bid document. Bidding describes the response by potential sellers to a request by a buyer.

Reference: *PMBOK® Guide* 6th Ed., pages 485-486

163. A. Independent estimates are used to highlight differences between the pricing proposed by a seller and either its own internal estimate, or an estimate prepared by an outside provider to serve as a benchmark. Bidder conferences are used to ensure that all prospective sellers have a clear and common understanding of the goods and service being procured. Screening systems are used to establish minimum levels of compliance to requirements. Expert judgment is used to assist in the evaluation of sellers' proposals.

Reference: *PMBOK® Guide* 6th Ed., pages 479, 485

164. D. It is possible that all process groups could be represented within a phase. All processes can be performed one time, multiple times or not at all during any phase or project.

Reference: *PMBOK® Guide* 6th Ed., page 554-555

165. C. A contract is a mutually binding legal agreement that obligates the seller to provide the specified services to the buyer and also obligates the buyer to pay the seller. A request is from the buyer, asking for proposals from sellers. The tender, a formal offer to produce or deliver a service, contains the documents provided by the seller. The proposal is the offering from the seller.

Reference: *PMBOK® Guide* 6th Ed., page 494

166. B. Having proposals evaluated by a multidiscipline team including members with specialized knowledge in each of the areas covered by the proposed contract is known as using expert judgment. Seller rating systems are sometimes based on past performance. Screening systems are based on predefined minimum levels of compliance to requirements. Bidder conferences are used to ensure that all prospective sellers have a clear and common understanding of the procurement.

Reference: *PMBOK® Guide* 6th Ed., page 497

167. B. The procurement management plan is a subset of the project management plan. Procurement documents are part of the project documents. Claims administration deals with the handling of claims, disputes, or appeals. The request for proposal (RFP) is used to solicit proposals from vendors.

Reference: *PMBOK® Guide* 6th Ed., page 89

168. A. The process of ensuring that the seller's performance meets the contractual requirements and that the buying organization performs according to the contract is called Control Procurements. Plan Procurements and Conduct Procurements are processes that precede the Control Procurements process. Close procurements is completed as a part of the Close Project or Phase process.

Reference: *PMBOK® Guide* 6th Ed., page 492

169. C. The procurement activities described within the procurement management plan are managed throughout the duration of the procurement. The project lifecycle may be longer or shorter than the procurement. Seller selection and developing contract documentation are activities that follow the creation of the procurement management plan.

Reference: *PMBOK® Guide* 6th Ed., page 475

170. D. The contract with a seller can be modified at any time, in accordance with the change control terms of the contract and project. Contracts usually are varied or modified during a project, for practical reasons. The contract is not in place until it has been awarded.

Reference: *PMBOK® Guide* 6th Ed., page 496

171. C. Claims administration, not claims transfer, is a tool and technique of Control Procurements.

Reference: *PMBOK® Guide* 6th Ed., page 492

172. A. If the parties cannot resolve a claim by themselves, it may need to be handled in accordance with alternative dispute resolution (ADR), usually following procedures established in the contract. Compromising is a technique for conflict resolution within project teams; integrated change control is the process for handling changes, not claims; and economic price adjustment is a form of a fixed price contract.

Reference: *PMBOK® Guide* 6th Ed., page 498

173. B. A document that rates how well each seller is performing the project work is known as a seller performance evaluation. Source selection criteria are an input to the Conduct Procurements process. The procurement management plan refers to how the procurement processes will be managed. Work performance information contains meaningful and analyzed information from controlling processes.

Reference: *PMBOK® Guide* 6th Ed., pages 501

174. B. Verification that all the work and deliverables supplied by the seller were acceptable is carried out through the Control Procurements process. The Close Project or Phase process deals with information related to administration, communication, and records. Lessons Learned are collected throughout the project. The Validate Scope process formalizes the acceptance of completed deliverables.

Reference: *PMBOK® Guide* 6th Ed., page 649

175. C. Bidder conferences is a tool and technique of, not an input to, the Conduct Procurements process.

Reference: *PMBOK® Guide* 6th Ed., page 482

176. A. Close Project or Phase refers to formalizing the completion of a project or phase, including the formal closure of any associated procurements. Lessons Learned are collected throughout the project and archived as part of performing project closure. The Validate Scope process formalizes the acceptance of completed deliverables. There is not a dedicated Close Procurements process.

Reference: *PMBOK® Guide* 6th Ed., page 634

177. C. A structured review of the procurement processes from the Plan Procurement Management process through the Control Procurements process is called a procurement audit. Contract management is a generic term for the overall procurement management processes. Performance reporting and claims administration are other tools and techniques of procurement management.

Reference: *PMBOK® Guide* 6th Ed., page 498

178. A. Procurement documentation is a key input to the Control Procurements process. Closed procurements, work performance information, and lessons learned register are all outputs of the Control Procurements process.

Reference: *PMBOK® Guide* 6th Ed., page 492

179. D. The Control Procurements process uses the following tools and techniques: expert judgment, claims administration, data analysis (performance reviews, earned value analysis, and trend analysis), inspection and audits.

Reference: *PMBOK® Guide* 6th Ed., page 492

180. B. Providing the seller of one of the project deliverables with formal notice that the contract has been completed is one of the activities of the Close Project or Phase process. The Control Procurements process evaluates completed deliverables against the contracts. In contrast, the close Project or Phase process deals with administration, communication, and records.

Reference: *PMBOK® Guide* 6th Ed., page 649

181. C. Providing the seller of one of the project deliverables with formal notice that the deliverable is acceptable is called deliverable acceptance. Procurement management and contract management are procurement-related efforts.

Reference: *PMBOK® Guide* 6th Ed., pages 41, 562

182. C. The lessons learned register captures recommended process improvements for future contracts and purchases. Contract documentation is the generic term for all documents related to the contracts. Procurement audit and claims administration are parts of running a contract.

Reference: *PMBOK® Guide* 6th Ed., page 500

183. B. The larger EMV, $64M, will drive the decision to upgrade the manufacturing plant.

Reference: *PMBOK® Guide* 6th Ed., page 435

184. D. The decision to be made is to build a new mobile app (invest $120K) or to enhance an existing one (invest $50K). These two options are the decision nodes. These two decision nodes have two chance nodes each. The first chance node of the first decision node has a 60 percent scenario probability of getting positive app store reviews with potential revenue of $200K, and the second chance node has 40 percent (100 percent - 60 percent = 40 percent) scenario probability of getting not so positive app store reviews with an expected revenue of $90K. For the second decision node, with the same scenario probabilities (60 percent and 40 percent split), the expected revenues are $120K (positive reviews) and $60K (not so positive reviews) respectively. The net path value for enhancing the existing mobile app with not so positive reviews equals $60K (expected revenue from not so positive reviews) less $50K (investment for this decision node). Thus, the net path value for this decision node is $10K.

Reference: *PMBOK® Guide* 6th Ed., page 435

185. D. If the scenario probability for enhancing the existing mobile app with positive app reviews is 60 percent, then the not so positive scenario probability is 40% (100 percent - 60 percent = 40 percent).

Reference: *PMBOK® Guide* 6th Ed., page 435

186. A. Net path value for positive reviews = $200K - $120K = $80K; net path value for not so positive reviews = $90K - $120K = -$30K; expected monetary value for building a new mobile app = 0.60 ($80K) + 0.40 (-$30K) = $36K.

Reference: *PMBOK® Guide* 6th Ed., page 435

187. A. Taking ownership for the decisions we make or fail to make, the actions we take or fail to take, and the resulting consequences is defined as the responsibility of project managers. Respectability is not as defined. Confidentiality and consistency are not as described and are not values as defined in the code.

Reference: *Code of Ethics and Professional Conduct*, page 2

188. A. Building a new mobile app: net path value for positive reviews = $200K - $120K = $80K; net path value for not so positive reviews = $90K - $120K = -$30K; expected monetary value = 0.60 ($80K) + 0.40 (-$30K) = $36K.

Enhancing an existing mobile app: net path value for positive reviews = $120K - $50K = $70K; net path value for not so positive reviews = $60K - $50K = $10K; expected monetary value for building a new mobile app = 0.60 ($70K) + 0.40 ($10K) = $46K.

The decision expected monetary value is the larger of the two decision nodes which is $46K.

Reference: *PMBOK® Guide* 6th Ed., page 435

189. C. As project managers, showing high regard for ourselves, for others, and for the resources entrusted is respect. Honesty, responsibility and fairness are the other three values described in the code.

Reference: *Code of Ethics and Professional Conduct*, page 4

190. D. Taking time to listen to others' point of view, seeking to understand them, is aspirational respect.

Reference: *Code of Ethics and Professional Conduct*, page 4

191. B. Acting in a way that is abusive to another member of the team is a breach of the mandatory respect standard.

Reference: *Code of Ethics and Professional Conduct*, page 4

192. A. Making decisions and acting impartially and objectively is defined as the value of fairness.

Reference: *Code of Ethics and Professional Conduct*, page

193. B. Providing equal access to information to those who are authorized to have the information is an example of aspirational fairness.

Reference: *Code of Ethics and Professional Conduct*, page 5

194. C. Disclosure of potential conflict of interest is an example of mandatory fairness.

Reference: *Code of Ethics and Professional Conduct*, page 5

195. D. To try to understand the truth and act in a truthful manner in both communications and conduct is a definition of honesty.

Reference: *Code of Ethics and Professional Conduct*, page 6

196. A. Creating an environment in which others feel safe to tell the truth is an example of aspirational honesty.

Reference: *Code of Ethics and Professional Conduct*, page 6

197. B. Engaging in dishonest behavior for personal gain is a breach of the mandatory honesty code.

Reference: *Code of Ethics and Professional Conduct*, page 6

198. A. Conduct by a team member that results in others feeling humiliated is an example of abusive manner. This is not allowable behavior, and it is not permitted by any aspirational or mandatory standard.

Reference: *Code of Ethics and Professional Conduct*, page 8

199. A. Only one person must be held accountable for any one deliverable or task to avoid confusion of responsibility.

Reference: *PMBOK® Guide* 6th Ed., page 317

200. B. A project manager's responsibility, both legally and morally, to promote the best interests of the organization is known as the duty of loyalty. This is good practice and may be an aspirational standard as well, but it is described explicitly as the duty of loyalty. It is not aspirational respect as defined in the code.

Reference: *Code of Ethics and Professional Conduct*, page 8

Bonus Questions

201. A. The most commonly used dependency in precedence diagramming method is finish-to-start (FS).

Reference: *PMBOK® Guide* 6th Ed., pages 189-190

202. B. Precedence Diagramming Method (PDM) relationship types include finish-to-start (FS), finish-to-finish (FF), start-to-start (SS), and start-to-finish (SF). FS is the most commonly used. In contrast, the start-to-finish (SF) is rarely used.

Reference: *PMBOK® Guide* 6th Ed., page 190

203. B. The dependency is mandatory because the lawsuit must be resolved first before the project activity can start. The dependency is also external because the lawsuit resolution is a non-project activity.

Reference: *PMBOK® Guide* 6th Ed., pages 191-192

204. D. Communication technology is a tool and technique of the Plan Communications Management process. Inputs to the Plan Communications Management process include project management plan, stakeholder register, enterprise environmental factors, and organizational process assets.

Reference: *PMBOK® Guide* 6th Ed., pages 370-371

205. D. Avoid, transfer, mitigate, and accept are risk response strategies for negative risks or threats. Enhance, exploit and share are risk response strategies for positive risks or opportunities. Accept can be used for both threats and opportunities.

Reference: *PMBOK® Guide* 6th Ed., pages 442-444

Chapter 7: Practice Test C

1. Managing projects involves a number of project management process groups that are required to accomplish the project objectives. Without proper integration management, a project is likely to fail. What is the primary focus of project integration management?

   A. Integrating the project management plan with third-party plans
   B. Managing the integration of the benefits management plan and the project management plan
   C. Coordinating and ensuring alignment of the various processes within the project management process groups
   D. Integrating the project management plan with internal governance requirements within the organization

2. A critical role for a project manager is to manage the project integration activities. Integration is primarily concerned with effectively integrating processes among the project management process groups that are required to accomplish project objectives within an organization's procedures. Which one of the following is *not* part of integrative project management processes?

   A. Perform Integrated Change Control
   B. Develop Project Charter
   C. Estimate Costs
   D. Close Project or Phase

3. A project should not start without an authorized project charter. Projects are chartered and authorized as a result of one or more stimulants, which can be problems, opportunities, or business requirements. Examples of valid stimuli for chartering projects by a business enterprise include all the following *except* _____.

   A. A social need
   B. A political conflict
   C. A legal requirement
   D. A technological advance

4. In most enterprises, a project may not be formally chartered and initiated until the completion of a number of documents. The following are examples of these documents *except* _____.

   A. Business case
   B. Benefits management plan
   C. Agreements
   D. Assumption log

5. The project charter is a mandatory document that is required before a project is allowed to start. The project charter, either directly or by reference to other documents, should address a number of information items. The following items are part of the contents of the project charter *except* _____.

A. Project purpose or justification
B. Assigned project manager responsibility and authority level
C. Procurement management plan
D. Measurable project objectives and related success criteria

6. An important input to developing the project charter is the organizational process assets. The organizational process assets that can influence the Develop Project Charter include the following *except* _____.

A. Organizational theory
B. Monitoring and reporting methods
C. Templates
D. Historical information repository

7. Most organizations have an organizational knowledge base which is a part of the organizational process assets available for project management teams. When developing the project charter and subsequent project documentation, any or all of the assets that are used to influence the project's success can be drawn from organizational process assets. An important element of these assets is the organization's processes and procedures, which include all of the following *except* _____.

A. Project contracts
B. Project closure guidelines
C. Change control procedures
D. Procedure for issuing work authorizations

8. Your project has been authorized by management, and you are in the process of planning. From the following list, which item is *not* an output of the project planning processes?

A. How work will be executed to achieve the project objectives
B. The project management processes tailored by the project management team
C. The final products resulting from the project activities
D. The life cycle used for the project

9. The project management plan documents many of the outputs of the planning processes. It may contain all the following *except* _____.

A. How changes will be monitored and controlled
B. How work will be executed to accomplish project objectives
C. The needs and techniques for communications among stakeholders
D. Techniques for negotiating with subcontractors

10. The project manager and the project team must perform multiple actions to execute the project management plan in order to accomplish the work defined in the project scope statement. Which of the following tasks are *not* parts of project execution?

A. Staff, train, and manage team members assigned to the project
B. Develop and prepare a draft copy and get a sign-off on the project charter
C. Document Lessons Learned and implement process improvement activities
D. Perform activities to accomplish project objectives

11. Without effective change management, a project that you are managing has a limited chance of success. To avoid uncontrolled changes, you set up a change control process, which is primarily concerned with _____.

A. Maintaining the integrity of the baselines, integrating product and project scope, and coordinating change across knowledge areas
B. Managing the contingency and management reserves for the project
C. Establishing a change control board that oversees the overall project change environment
D. Influencing factors that cause change and determining change that has occurred

12. Most of the project's budget is consumed during _____.

A. Project management plan development
B. Project management plan execution
C. Overall change control
D. Project initiation

13. The main purpose of the Develop Project Management Plan process is to _____.

A. Promote communication among stakeholders
B. Document project assumptions and constraints
C. Define key project objectives
D. Create a document to guide project execution and control

14. Integration management includes characteristics of unification, consolidation, articulation, and integrative actions that are crucial to project completion. This is achieved through Project Integration Management processes, which have the main aim of ensuring that the _____.

A. Project is completed within the approved budget and schedule
B. Proper scope has been defined for the project
C. Various elements of the project are properly coordinated
D. Project will satisfy the needs for which it was undertaken

15. A project management information system (PMIS) is one of the tools and techniques used by the project management team. Which of the following statements is *most* relevant to the PMIS?

A. It is the software used for schedule development
B. It is the collection of reports generated to support the execution of the project
C. It consists of the tools and techniques used to gather, integrate, and disseminate project output
D. It supports all aspects of the project and includes software tools and interfaces to other systems

16. All approved changes that impact the project's scope, cost, schedule, and/or risks must be reflected in the _____.

A. Performance measurement baselines and change management plan
B. Project management plan and performance measurement baselines
C. Change management plan and quality assurance plan
D. Quality assurance plan and project management plan

17. When developing the project scope statement, project assumptions must be defined and documented. Assumptions generally involve some risk because _____.

A. Assumptions are based on the entries in the lessons learned registry
B. Assumptions are based on factors that may not be true, may not be accurate, or may not be available
C. Assumptions are based on constraints
D. Historical information may not be available

18. Which tool or technique is used in the Develop Project Management Plan process?

A. Data analysis
B. Alternatives generation
C. Expert judgment
D. Decision making

19. In the project management context, integration includes characteristics of unification, consolidation, articulation, and integrative actions that are crucial to the success of the project. Which of the following is the most effective way to reinforce and accelerate the project integration process?

A. Having the sponsor apply direct influence on the project team
B. Through frequent periodic meetings
C. Assigning specific responsibilities to each project employee
D. Balancing competing demands and examining alternative options

20. Which of the statements below best describes a project's change control board (CCB)?

A. It is required only on large projects.
B. It is headed by the project manager.
C. It is a subcommittee of the configuration management board.
D. It is responsible for approving or rejecting changes to the project baselines.

21. Each project is unique and has specific objectives to achieve, and products, services, or results to develop and deliver. In general, project processes fall into three categories: processes used at predefined points, processes performed continuously, and processes that are:

A. Used at the closing of every phase
B. Used as part of ongoing operations
C. Performed periodically as needed
D. At the beginning of each phase of the project

22. Which of the following tasks is *not* a function of change management?

A. Track changes and identify changes
B. Record and update configuration items
C. Identify changes and document changes
D. Decide on changes and track change

23. Which Project Integration Management knowledge area process produces work performance data?

A. Direct and Manage Project Work
B. Perform Integrated Change Control
C. Develop Project Management Plan
D. Close Project or Phase

24. The following items are outputs of the Perform Integrated Change Control *except* _____.

A. Approved change requests
B. Project management plan updates
C. Project documents updates
D. Organizational process assets updates

25. Which statement best describes the Collect Requirements process?

A. Collect Requirements is the process of performing the work defined in the project management plan to achieve the project's objectives.
B. The output of Collect Requirements describes, in detail, the project's deliverables and the work required to create those deliverables.
C. An important part of the Collect Requirements process is ensuring that the schedule is accurately planned to have all stakeholders available at defined times.
D. Collect Requirements is the process of determining, documenting, and managing stakeholder needs and requirements to meet the project's objectives.

26. Which of the following actions is a part of project execution?

A. Obtaining the sponsor's approval of the project budget
B. Identifying the project stakeholders
C. Implementing the planned methods and standards
D. Designing the project organizational structure

27. Which Project Integration Management knowledge area process has deliverables as an output?

A. Develop Project Management Plan
B. Monitor and Control Project Work
C. Perform Integrated Change Control
D. Direct and Manage Project Work

28. The following statements about collecting requirements are accurate *except* for _____.

A. Providing the basis for defining the project scope
B. Providing the basis for defining the product scope
C. Addressing product requirements regardless of industry
D. Documenting and managing stakeholder needs

29. Which one of the following is *not* an output of Direct and Manage Project Work process?

A. Change requests
B. Change log
C. Work performance data
D. Deliverables

30. Which one of the following is an output of the Direct and Manage Project Work process?

A. Lessons learned register
B. Project management plan updates
C. Advanced change requests
D. Deliverables

31. The following items are part of the data collected routinely to measure and monitor work performance *except* _____.

A. Costs incurred
B. Deliverable status
C. Schedule forecasts
D. Schedule progress

32. Which one of the following activities is completed as part of the Monitor and Control Project Work process?

A. Performing activities to accomplish project objectives
B. Monitoring project risks
C. Staffing management and resource planning
D. Collecting and documenting Lessons Learned

33. Which one of the following activities is *not* part of monitoring and controlling the project work?

A. Implementing approved changes into the project scope, plans, and environment
B. Monitoring implementation of approved changes when and as they occur
C. Comparing actual project performance against the project management plan
D. Providing forecasts to update current cost and current schedule information

34. Change requests can be accepted or rejected or deferred by a change control board, and then updated into the change log. Approved change requests are an output of which of the following project processes?

A. Develop Project Management Plan
B. Develop Project Charter
C. Perform Integrated Change Control
D. Direct and Manage Project Work

35. Which one of the following Perform Integrated Change Control activities best takes into consideration the overall project objectives in an integrated fashion?

A. Approving or rejecting all requests for changes or modifications to project documents, deliverables, or baselines
B. Reviewing high priority changes and forwarding them to the change control board for approval
C. Streamlining the prioritization and approval of changes that only affect the scope, time, and/or cost of the project
D. Considering undocumented changes that indicate a reduction in risk to the overall project

36. Configuration management is critical for project success and product integrity. Which one of the following statements reflects the main purpose of configuration status accounting?

A. It provides the basis from which the configuration of products is defined.
B. It establishes that performance and functional requirements have been met.
C. It documents the technical and financial impacts of requested changes.
D. It captures, sorts, and reports the configuration identification list, proposed changes status, and change implementation status.

37. Uncontrolled changes can lead to project failure. The Perform Integrated Change Control process is primarily concerned with managing and controlling changes to the project and the product. All of the following are outputs of Perform Integrated Change Control process *except* _____.

A. Work performance reports
B. Approved change requests
C. Project management plan updates
D. Project documents updates

38. As manager of a large project in a large organization under a contract with a customer, you created a multi-tiered structure of a number of change control boards (CCBs). The following statements are all true about the CCBs *except* _____.

A. A CCB is responsible for reviewing change requests and approving or rejecting those change requests.
B. The roles and responsibilities of the CCB are clearly defined and agreed upon by appropriate stakeholders.
C. The CCB may not necessarily record all of the decisions and recommendations that they made.
D. All CCB decisions are documented and communicated to the stakeholders for information and follow-up actions.

39. Which of the following statements is correct about change requests for projects with change control boards (CCB) in place?

A. Change requests are approved by the project's change control board (CCB)
B. Very few corrective actions, preventive actions, and defect repairs will be approved
C. Approved change requests will take longer to get implemented and they will cost more
D. Change requests will be given a higher priority relative to existing approved requirements

40. The Close Project or Phase process includes finalizing all activities across all of the project management process groups to formally complete the project or phase. The following activities are necessary for administrative closure *except* _____.

A. Satisfying completion or exit criteria
B. Transferring the project's products, services, or results
C. Deciding to accept or reject changes to the project or product
D. Collecting project or phase records

41. The procedures used in the Close Project or Phase process include all of the following activities *except* _____.

A. Reviewing all prior information to ensure that all project work is complete
B. Archiving project information for future use by the organization
C. Documenting the reasons for project termination
D. Verifying and deciding on all submitted change requests

42. Which of the following is *not* considered a part of organizational process assets?

A. Government or industry standards
B. Standardized guidelines and work instructions
C. Organization communication requirements
D. Process measurement databases

43. Closing a project or phase includes all of the following inputs *except* _____.

A. Project management plan
B. Accepted deliverables
C. Approved change requests
D. Organizational process assets

44. You are managing a two-year project that spans four different countries. As part of the requirements-gathering process, you have used virtual sessions to compile a list of product requirements. Two differing views remain on one major requirement. You consult with the project sponsor, who reviews the comments and makes a decision. She justifies this by stating it will have a greater benefit to most of the end users. What method of decision making is this?

A. Plurality
B. Dictatorship
C. Majority
D. Unanimity

45. Project administrative closure procedures involve all of the following actions and activities *except* _____.

A. Raising problem reports for nonperforming parts of the system
B. Archiving project information for future use
C. Gathering Lessons Learned
D. Validating that completion and exit criteria have been met

46. You are managing a complex technology project. Because of unclear requirements in some areas of functionality, the project team has decided to create a rudimentary working model. This will be used to help the stakeholders review their original requirements and refine them, so that the requirements can move to a finalized design. This is an example of which kind of Collect Requirements technique?

A. Focus group
B. Prototyping
C. Observations
D. Change request

47. Under which of the following conditions would the transfer of finished and unfinished deliverables take place?

A. End of a key deliverable
B. End of contract
C. Project termination
D. Legal dispute

48. An activity in the Close Project or Phase process is to collect and archive project or phase files, including all the documentation resulting from the project activities. These include all the following *except* _____.

A. Project files
B. Expired customer data
C. Project or phase closure documents
D. Historical information

49. Which one of these items is an input to the Define Scope process?

A. WBS dictionary
B. Project scope statement
C. Work breakdown structure (WBS)
D. Project charter

50. Which one of the following items is an input to the Create Work Breakdown Structure (WBS) process?

A. Project management plan
B. Project charter
C. Project risk register
D. Accepted deliverables

51. Within Project Scope Management, the Collect Requirements process defines and documents stakeholders' needs to meet the project objectives. Tools and techniques used within this process include all of the following *except* _____.

A. Interviewing stakeholders by talking to them directly, using prepared and/or spontaneous questions
B. Nominal group technique to help prioritize ideas through a voting process
C. Development of the schedule baseline in order to manage stakeholders' requirements and expectations
D. Focus groups that use prequalified stakeholders to learn about their expectations concerning the proposed product

52. From the following list, which one is a potential output of the Define Scope process?

A. Requested changes
B. Project document updates
C. Issue log
D. Communication management plan

53. Which one of the following is included in the project scope statement?

A. Project charter
B. List of stakeholders
C. Work breakdown structure
D. Product scope description

54. What is the lowest level of decomposition in a WBS?

A. Work package
B. Component
C. Deliverable
D. Work item

55. Which of the following information is *not* contained in the WBS dictionary?

A. Acceptance criteria
B. Agreement information
C. Accepted deliverables
D. Code of account identifier

56. What is the main difference between scope validation and quality control?

A. Scope validation is concerned with acceptance of the deliverables, whereas quality control is concerned with the correctness of the deliverables.
B. Quality control is concerned with acceptance of the deliverables, whereas scope validation is concerned with meeting the quality requirements for deliverables.
C. Scope validation is concerned with testing the required deliverables to ensure that they are feasible, whereas quality control is concerned with testing the final product.
D. Quality control is performed by groups external to the project, whereas scope validation is performed by the project management team.

57. Inspections can take all of the following forms *except* _____.

A. Audits
B. Reviews
C. Testing
D. Walkthroughs

58. The inputs to the Control Scope process include which of the following?

A. Requirements traceability matrix
B. Project budget
C. Project charter
D. Project organization charts

59. Which of the following is a tool or technique used in Control Scope process activities?

A. Product analysis
B. Expert judgment
C. Variance analysis
D. Stakeholder analysis

60. Which item of the following items is an output of the Control Scope process?

A. Accepted deliverables
B. Change requests
C. Trend analysis
D. Approved changes

61. An updated version of which of the following project documents is an output of the Control Scope process?

A. Work performance data
B. Work performance information
C. Change requests
D. Requirements traceability matrix

62. Which one of the following processes is part of the Project Schedule Management knowledge area?

A. Develop Project Charter
B. Develop Project Management Plan
C. Estimate Activity Durations
D. Monitor and Control Project Work

63. Which of the following processes does not use leads and lags as one of its tools and techniques?

A. Develop Schedule
B. Sequence Activities
C. Control Schedule
D. Define Activities

64. The project manager used the following tools and techniques: decomposition, rolling wave planning, and expert judgment. What Project Schedule Management outputs will be produced?

A. Project schedule network diagrams and project documents updates
B. Work performance information and data analysis
C. Activity duration estimates and project documents updates
D. Activity list, activity attributes, and milestone list

65. Which of the following statements is *not* true about the rolling wave planning technique?

A. It subdivides the project work packages into smaller components called activities.
B. It is a form of progressive elaboration in which future work is planned at a higher level of the WBS.
C. It decomposes work packages to a milestone level when information is less defined.
D. It decomposes work packages into activities as more becomes known about upcoming activities.

66. What is the shortest duration of the following project according to the critical path method (CPM)?

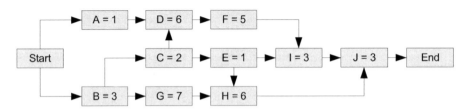

A. 18 units
B. 22 units
C. 19 units
D. 12 units

67. Referring to the following network diagram, what is the critical path?

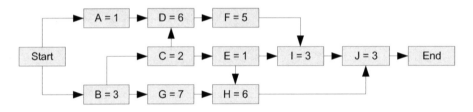

A. ADFIJ
B. BCEIJ
C. BCDFIJ
D. BGHJ

68. You have been assigned to manage a complex construction project. No one on your project team has deep knowledge or experience in the construction industry. You have hired a local consultant to deliver an awareness seminar for your project team to familiarize them with the local building codes and specialized construction techniques. Which process will this knowledge help you and your team to complete?

A. Estimate Activity Durations
B. Define Activities
C. Sequence Activities
D. Estimate Activity Resources

69. Which of the following terms about the project equipment and material resources is an input to the Estimate Activity Durations process?

A. Price
B. Availability
C. Make
D. Supplier

70. In activity duration estimating, three-point estimates are based on determining three types of estimates. Which one of the following is *not* one of the types of estimates used in the three-point estimating technique?

A. Most likely
B. Least likely
C. Optimistic
D. Pessimistic

71. Which schedule network analysis technique calculates the early start, early finish, late start, and late finish dates for all activities without regard for any resource limitations by performing a forward and backward pass analysis through the schedule network?

A. Resource leveling
B. Resource smoothing
C. Critical path method
D. Fast tracking

72. An assistant to the senior project manager produced an output that has specific start and end dates that have been agreed upon by key stakeholders and will be included in the project management plan. This particular output, reviewed and approved by the project management team, was developed using schedule network analysis. What is the name of this Develop Project Schedule Process output?

A. Schedule baseline
B. Activity list
C. Project schedule network diagrams
D. Activity duration estimates

73. From the following list, which is an input to the Control Schedule process?

A. Work performance information
B. Schedule forecasts
C. Work performance data
D. Change requests

74. From the following list, which is an item that could be found on a resource calendar when each specific resource is available?

A. Weekends
B. Resource skills
C. Vacation periods
D. Contract timelines

75. The following data analysis techniques are used when identifying risks *except* for _____.

A. Root cause analysis
B. SWOT analysis
C. Interviews
D. Document analysis

76. In your project, you share a skilled resource with other projects, and you must review your project schedule to reflect this resource's availability. You plan to do this through resource leveling. Resource leveling will often affect the project by making the schedule _____.

A. Shorter
B. Longer
C. More responsive to customer needs
D. Less flexible

77. In your project plan, you budgeted three weeks of effort for consultants, but the job was done in only two weeks. Calculate the percentage of variance.

A. 150%
B. 33%
C. 75%
D. 67%

78. On November 1, $1,000 worth of work on Task A was planned to be complete. The work performed at the planned rate was valued only at $850. Calculate the schedule variance.

A. −$100
B. $100
C. −$150
D. $150

79. Which of the following costs are *not* relevant during cost estimating?

A. Direct labor costs
B. Overhead costs
C. Material costs
D. Sunk costs

80. You are managing a project with a budget of $5 million. You are two months into the project, and the cost figures are shown in the following table:

Period	Actual Cost	Planned Value	Earned Value
Month 1	1,250,000	1,100,000	1,000,000
Month 2	500,000	600,000	750,000
Month 3	-	2,500,000	-
Month 4	-	800,000	-

What statement is *not* true about the project at the end of Month 1?

A. The project is behind schedule.
B. The project is over budget.
C. The cost performance index is 1.25.
D. The schedule variance is –$100,000.

81. You are managing a project with a budget of $5 million. You are two months into the project, and the cost figures are shows in the following table:

Period	Actual Cost	Planned Value	Earned Value
Month 1	1,250,000	1,100,000	1,000,000
Month 2	500,000	600,000	750,000
Month 3	-	2,500,000	-
Month 4	-	800,000	-

What statement is true about the project?

A. At the end of Month 2, the project is on budget.
B. At the end of Month 2, the project is behind schedule.
C. For Month 2, the cost performance index is 0.66.
D. For Month 2, the schedule variance is –$300,000.

82. A project consists of the three activities shown in the following table. Assuming that future work will be performed according to the budget, the estimate at completion (EAC) at this point in the project is _____.

Activity	% Complete	Planned Value	Earned Value	Actual Cost
A	100%	1,000	1,000	1,200
B	50%	1,000	500	700
C	0%	1,000	-	-

A. $3,400
B. $3,700
C. $3,200
D. $3,000

83. You were asked to prepare an estimate at completion (EAC) based on the work performed at the present cost performance index (CPI). Which EAC formula should you use?

A. EAC = AC + Bottom-Up ETC
B. EAC = BAC / CPI
C. EAC = AC + BAC - EV
D. EAC = AC + [(BAC - EV) / (CPI x SPI)]

84. Which of the following estimating techniques is the least accurate?

A. Analogous
B. Parametric
C. Three-point
D. Bottom-up

85. Given the following graphic report on a project, what can be said about the project performance at the point in time indicated as today's Date?

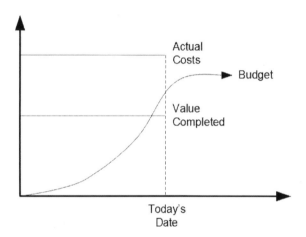

A. The project is over budget but ahead of schedule.
B. The project is over budget and behind schedule.
C. The project is under budget and ahead of schedule.
D. Additional information is needed before conclusions can be made about budget and schedule performance.

86. What is the difference between management reserves and contingency reserves?

A. There is no difference.
B. Management reserves are applied to schedule; contingency reserves are applied to cost.
C. Contingency reserves are included in the project's cost performance baseline and management reserves are not.
D. Management reserves are used for known unknowns, whereas contingency reserves are used for unknown unknowns.

87. Which of the following statements about quality and grade is correct?

A. High quality is always a problem and low grade in not a problem.
B. Low quality is always a problem and low grade is not a problem.
C. Both low quality and low grade are always a problem.
D. Low quality and high grade are always a problem.

88. The following are all direct advantages of continuous process improvement *except* _____.

A. It reduces waste
B. It reduces non-value-added activities
C. It increases process efficiency
D. It eliminates project risks

89. Which one of the following is *not* part of the quality costs?

A. Costs of investment made to prevent nonconformance to requirements
B. Costs incurred by appraising the product or service
C. Costs of productivity bonuses to the project team
D. Costs of services to ensure compliance with mandatory standards

90. Which of the following statements describes the Manage Quality process? It is:

A. The process of translating the quality management plan into executable quality activities
B. The execution of acceptance testing to ensure customer acceptance of the project
C. The application of verification techniques to ensure the correctness of the project's work products
D. The planning and implementing of inspections to ensure the correctness and functionality of deliverables in accordance with approved specifications

91. Modern quality management is an important component of successful project management in that both disciplines recognize the importance of all of the following trends *except* _____.

A. Customer satisfaction
B. Management responsibility
C. Additional tests and inspections
D. Continual improvement

92. The primary components of the quality management function are _____.

A. Quality planning, quality management, and quality control
B. Document and alternative analysis
C. Process and root cause analysis
D. Acceptance sampling and statistical process control

93. Manage quality _____.

A. Includes policing the conformance of the project team to specifications
B. Is a managerial process that defines the organization, design, resources, and objectives of quality management
C. Is concerned with the product design aspects and process improvements
D. Provides the project team and stakeholders with standards by which project performance is measured

94. The _____ has ultimate responsibility for quality on the project.

A. Project sponsor
B. Project manager
C. Functional manager
D. Quality manager

95. Project quality audits confirm the implementation all of the following *except* _____.

A. Approved change requests and defect repairs
B. Management reserves
C. Corrective actions
D. Preventive actions

96. Which one of the following is an output of Manage Quality?

A. Rejected change requests
B. Quality cost report
C. Quality testing plan
D. Change requests

97. The Plan Quality Management process uses a number of techniques for data representation. This includes all the following except:

A. Pareto diagram
B. Flowcharts
C. Matrix diagrams
D. Mind mapping

98. What technique is used to display the sequence of steps within a process that turns one or more inputs into one or more outputs?

A. Matrix diagrams
B. Histogram
C. Flowchart
D. Mind mapping

99. Which one of the following processes is *not* part of the project's resource related processes?

A. Acquire Resources
B. Plan Resource Management
C. Administer Resources
D. Manage Team

100. The RACI chart is an example of a Responsibility Assignment Matrix (RAM). Which of the following is *not* a correct description for describing roles and expectations?

A. Responsible
B. Assign
C. Consult
D. Inform

101. Project Resource Management includes which of the following processes?

A. Plan Resource Management, Estimate Activity Resources, Acquire Resources, Develop Team, Manage Team, and Control Resources
B. Hire Human Resources, Train Staff, Mentor Project Team, and Administer Payroll
C. Recruit Personnel, Maintain Labor Relations, and Administer Payroll
D. Build the Team, Communicate Roles, and Distribute Labor

102. Which one of the following is not an input to the Plan Resource Management process?

A. Project charter
B. Team charter
C. Enterprise environmental factors
D. Organizational process assets

103. The resource management plan addresses roles and responsibilities within the project. Which of the lists below captures the relevant details?

A. Role, authority, responsibility, and competence
B. Team values and communication guidelines
C. Decision-making criteria and process, and team agreements
D. Conflict resolution process and meeting guidelines

104. The Resource Management Plan component (which can be formal or informal) that describes when and how the project resource requirements will be met is called the _____.

A. Organizational breakdown structure
B. Responsibility assignment matrix
C. Resource management plan
D. Resource assignment chart

105. Project team members are drawn from all available sources, both internal and external. The following characteristics influence or direct the assignments of the project team members except _____.

A. Availability
B. Cost
C. Experience
D. Hobbies

106. All of the following tools and techniques are used in team development except _____.

A. Team-building activities
B. Recognition and rewards
C. Stakeholder analysis
D. Training

107. Which one of the following behaviors is not a behavior indicating effective teamwork?

A. Team members share information and resources
B. Team members socialize together after work hours
C. Team members assist one another when workloads are unbalanced
D. Team members communicate in ways that fit individual preferences

108. Unplanned training takes place as a result of all of the following except _____.

A. Observation
B. Conversation
C. Project performance appraisal
D. Resource management plan

109. Which of the following is not true about the Develop Project Team process?

A. Virtual teams always outperform co-located teams by about 20%
B. Team development occurs throughout the project life cycle
C. All project team members share responsibility for enforcing team ground rules
D. A team member's recognition and rewards system is a recommended approach for team development

110. Which of the following statements is not a characteristic of virtual teams?

A. Team communications tend to heavily leverage email and other electronic forms.
B. Teams tend to be groups of people with a shared goal who spend little time meeting face to face.
C. Team members are concerned with managing diverse stakeholder views and expectations.
D. It is possible to include people with mobility handicaps.

111. Interpersonal conflicts can be difficult to resolve in a project environment because _____.

A. The project manager does not have authority to resolve these conflicts
B. The limited time of the project does not allow for resolution of these types of conflicts
C. These conflicts often involve ethics, morals, and value systems
D. The organizational structure of the project hinders resolution

112. The indicators of team effectiveness include all of the following except _____.

A. Increased conflict between the project manager and the project personnel
B. Evident improvements in skills
C. Continuous improvements in competencies
D. Reduced staff turnover

113. In contrast to projectized organizations, which of the following interpersonal skills are not required of project managers in a functional organization?

A. Understanding compensation plans, benefits, and career paths
B. Developing a vision of the future and the necessary strategies to achieve it
C. Aligning people through focused communication
D. Helping people to energize themselves to overcome barriers to change

114. Which of the following factors contributes the most to more effective team communications?

A. Performance appraisals
B. External feedback
C. Conflict resolution
D. Colocation

115. In an organization with a primarily functional structure where human resources are typically managed by departments, the project management team performs the following activities except _____.

A. Managing conflicts affecting project performance
B. Resolving problems affecting project performance
C. Establishing salary levels of the team members
D. Appraising performance of team members

116. You are now in the stage of executing a project. Which one of the following tasks is not part of the Manage Team process?

A. Tracking team performance
B. Providing feedback
C. Resolving issues
D. Allocating pay raises

117. The purpose of developing the project team is to increase the effectiveness of the team through all of the following except _____.

A. Improving the skills of the team members through exchanging knowledge and experience
B. Running a productivity competition to see who can work more hours
C. Encouraging team members to share information and resources
D. Improving the feelings of trust and cohesion among team members

118. Which of the following beliefs about conflict is typically held within projectized organizations?

A. Conflict is inevitable.
B. Conflict is bad.
C. Conflict is determined by the structure of the system.
D. Conflict is caused by the relationships among components.

119. Which of the following statements is true about the nature of conflicts?

A. The overall level of conflict remains relatively constant over the project life cycle.
B. Scarce resources and scheduling priorities are common sources of project conflicts.
C. Interpersonal situations are the most common sources of project conflicts.
D. Project managers typically favor the compromise approach to handling conflicts.

120. The 360-degree feedback principle in overall project or team member performance includes all of the following except _____.

A. Feedback from the project manager on the performance of the project team member
B. Feedback from the project team member's family and friends
C. Feedback from the project team member's superiors, managers, and supervisors
D. Feedback from the project team member's superiors, peers, and subordinates

121. The major processes of the Project Communications Management knowledge area are _____.

A. Plan Communications Management, Manage Communications, and Monitor Communications
B. Identify Stakeholders, Plan Communications Management, and Manage Communications
C. Identify Stakeholders, Plan Communications Management, and Manage Stakeholder Engagement
D. Plan Communications Management, Manage Communications, and Control Stakeholder Engagement

122. Which one of the following Project Communications Management processes is part of the Monitoring and Controlling process group?

A. Plan Communications Management
B. Manage Stakeholder Engagement
C. Monitor Communications
D. Manage Communications

123. In the project's communication management, which one of the following is not a key component of the basic model of communication?

A. Decoding
B. Message
C. Encoding
D. Messenger

124. Which one of the following factors does not affect a communications management plan?

A. Geographical distribution of project staff
B. Project length
C. Executive requirements
D. Available technologies

125. Your client, with whom you have good relations, verbally requests that you include office supplies as part of your agreement. This action is not supported under your contract. Which medium would be best to use to initially respond to your client's request?

A. Presentation to management
B. Telephone call
C. Verbal request to add it to the contract
D. Written communication requesting a change to the contract

126. You were part of a team that worked on a complex systems integration project. The technical architect left the company during the project. Six months later, the technical architect contacts you and asks for an electronic copy of the project technical solution document because he has only a paper copy and is working on a similar project. You should _____.

A. Send him the details because he developed the original infrastructure and therefore knows all the information already
B. Not send him the details but invite him to dinner so he can review it with you
C. Not send him the files; he does not have a legitimate need to know
D. Send him the files along with a confidentiality agreement that he must sign

127. Which one of the following is not part of the communications management plan?

A. To whom information will be distributed
B. What, how, and how often information will be gathered
C. What methods will be used to distribute information
D. All memos, correspondence, and reports from project personnel

128. Which of the following techniques is used in the Manage Communications process?

A. Stakeholder buy-in
B. Executive interviews
C. Communication methods
D. Channel evaluation

129. The project sponsor requests a monthly meeting with the project manager to allow the project manager to present status information in person, rather than sending a report by email. This additional activity requires an update to _____.

A. The project charter
B. The communications management plan
C. The stakeholder management plan
D. The project's change control process

130. There are different methods of communications: verbal and written, formal and informal. Choice of the communication method depends on the situation. Formal written correspondence is mandated in which one of the following situations?

A. The product undergoes casual in-house testing.
B. The client requests additional work not covered under the contract.
C. The project manager calls a meeting.
D. A customer executive requests a review of the project.

131. Work performance reports can include all of the following except _____.

A. Results of the ISO audit
B. Results of cost control
C. Results of quality control
D. Results of schedule control

132. The outputs of the Monitor Communications process include all of the following except _____.

A. Project documents updates
B. Work performance information
C. Change requests
D. Work performance data

133. In which project management process group is the Identify Stakeholders process performed?

A. Initiating
B. Planning
C. Executing
D. Monitoring and Controlling

134. A formal written response is most suitable when _____.

A. Discussing work assignments
B. Directing the contractor to make changes
C. The interpreter has a short memory
D. Contacting the client is necessary

135. Which one of the following tools is not one of the tools and techniques used in the Monitor Communications process?

A. Project management Information system
B. Expert judgment
C. Project reporting
D. Meetings

136. Which of the following statements is not a true statement about actively managing stakeholder engagements in a project?

A. It increases the likelihood that the project will stay on track.
B. Project team members may spend unnecessary efforts in communicating with stakeholders.
C. The project manager is responsible for managing stakeholder engagement.
D. It helps limit disruption during the project by proactively managing issues.

137. As the project manager, you wish to impose a complex accounting method by which subordinates will calculate project costs. You have time for only one approach. Which type of communication would be most effective in communicating this method?

A. Verbal, face-to-face
B. Verbal, telephone
C. Written
D. Nonverbal

138. It is important for a project manager to assess the complexity of the communication requirements of the project by calculating the number of communication channels. If you are managing a project with seven stakeholders, what is the total number of potential communication channels?

A. 16
B. 36
C. 28
D. 56

139. The project you are managing has a variety of stakeholders, including a number of contractors. The project's issue log is an input to the _____ process.

A. Identify Stakeholders
B. Plan Stakeholder Management
C. Monitor Stakeholder Engagement
D. Manage Stakeholder Engagement

140. As stakeholder requirements are identified, issues will be logged for resolution. Once resolved, they will be documented with a number of information items. The following are examples of possible information items recorded in the issue log except _____.

A. Follow-up actions agreed upon by the relevant stakeholders
B. Root cause analysis of the issue
C. Results of negotiations with functional managers
D. Results of the project risk analysis

141. Which one of the following is the best way to prepare a response to unknown risks?

A. Disregard them until they are identified through the Identify Risks process
B. Prepare a risk response
C. Plan to address them the same way as the known risks
D. Leverage management reserve to address them

142. Which of the following statements is false about the risk management plan?

A. The risk management plan is a subset of the project management plan.
B. The Plan Risk Management process produces the risk management plan.
C. The risk management plan should be updated frequently.
D. Risk management plans may include budgeting, timing, and tracking details.

143. Which one of the following techniques is used in the Identify Risk process?

A. Regression analysis
B. Brainstorming
C. Decomposition
D. Structured analysis

144. A risk register typically contains the following except _____.

A. List of potential responses
B. Potential risk owners
C. Work breakdown structure identifier
D. List of identified risks

145. In a bubble chart that depicts the detectability, proximity, and impact values of various risks within a project, _____ bubbles with lower detectability and lower proximity are acceptable.

A. Small
B. Medium
C. Large
D. All

146. In quantitative risk analysis and modeling, sensitivity analysis will typically use a(n) _____ to compare the relative importance and impact of variables with a high degree of uncertainty against variables that are more stable.

A. Decision tree diagram
B. Tornado diagram
C. Expected monetary value
D. Control chart

147. In any project, risks can be negative (threats) or positive (opportunities). Which of the following is not a strategy for dealing with negative risks?

A. Exploit
B. Mitigate
C. Avoid
D. Transfer

148. In any project, risks can be negative (threats) or positive (opportunities). Which of the following is not a strategy for responding to positive risks?

A. Exploit
B. Enhance
C. Share
D. Increase

149. Which one of the following is an input to the Monitor Risks process?

A. Work performance information
B. Project management plan
C. Change requests
D. Project management plan updates

150. Which one of the following is not a tool or technique used in monitoring risk?

A. Meetings
B. Expert judgment
C. Reserve analysis
D. Technical performance measurement

151. Project Procurement Management deals with purchasing or acquiring products, services, or results from external providers to enable the project team to perform the project work. All of the following are procurement management processes except _____.

A. Plan Procurement Management
B. Conduct Procurements
C. Estimate Procurements
D. Control Procurements

152. Which of the following is not typically a component of the procurement management plan?

A. Timeline for procurement activities
B. How procurements will be coordinated with other aspects of the project
C. Constraints and assumptions
D. The selected sellers

153. Which of the following contract types has the lowest risk for the buyer?

A. Cost plus fixed fee
B. Firm fixed price
C. Cost plus incentive fee
D. Time and materials

154. Which one of the following is not a cost-reimbursable contract?

A. Cost plus fixed fee (CPFF)
B. Fixed price incentive fee (FPIF)
C. Cost plus incentive fee (CPIF)
D. Cost plus award fee (CPAF)

155. Which one of the following usually is not a likely source selection criterion used to evaluate seller proposals?

A. Sellers' management approach
B. Sellers' technical approach
C. Sellers' financial capacity
D. Sellers' stock price

156. Which of the following is not an output of the Conduct Procurements process?

A. Selected sellers
B. Agreements
C. The requested product
D. Project management plan updates

157. Which one of the following is not a tool or technique used in the Conduct Procurements process?

A. Expert judgment
B. Bidder conferences
C. Procurement negotiations
D. Claims administration

158. The agreement is an output of which of the following Project Procurement Management processes?

A. Control Procurements
B. Close Procurements
C. Plan Procurement Management
D. Conduct Procurements

159. Which one of the following is not an output of the Conduct Procurements process?

A. Procurement statement of work
B. Project documents updates
C. Bid documents
D. Change requests

160. Which one of the following in not part of the tools and techniques used in the Control Procurements process?

A. Claims administration
B. Inspections and audits
C. Data analysis
D. Advertising

161. Which one of the following items is generally not subject for discussion during procurement negotiations?

A. Responsibilities and authorities
B. Overall schedule, payment, and price
C. Technical solutions
D. Project personnel

162. Project documents are among the inputs for Control Procurements. All of the following are components except _____.

A. Assumption log
B. Milestone list
C. Payment system
D. Quality reports

163. You are managing a project that will involve third-party sellers. The bid documents have been released, and several questions and requests for clarifications have been submitted. To be fair, you and the procurement officer will hold a real-time meeting with all prospective sellers to answer their questions. This is known as _____.

A. Proposal evaluation techniques
B. A bidder conference
C. Procurement negotiations
D. Inspections and audits

164. Your company has signed a contract with a third party for your project. Late in the project, you and the third party believe that a contract change is necessary. Which of the following statements is true?

A. Contract change is not possible at this late stage of the project
B. You should refer to a neutral organization
C. Change is possible by following the agreed upon change control process defined in the contract
D. Trying to dissuade the third party from any changes is an appropriate action at this point

165. Which of the following is not a process of the Project Procurement Management knowledge area?

A. Plan Cost Management
B. Plan Procurement Management
C. Conduct Procurements
D. Control Procurements

166. There are several variations of an agreement document. However, most of them typically include the following except for _____.

A. Procurement statement of work or major deliverables
B. Interpersonal and team skills for negotiation
C. Schedule, milestones, or date by which a schedule is required
D. Performance reporting and change request handling

167. Contracts are legally binding documents between the buyer and the seller. Complete this sentence with one of out of the following clauses: Many organizations perform contract administration _____.

A. Separate from the project
B. As part of the project
C. As part of their personnel department
D. External to the organization

168. As part of your project, the team is investigating which, if any, work packages will be performed by third-party sellers and which will be performed internally by the project team, taking into account resource availabilities and skills. This is known as (a) _____.

A. Procurement statement of work
B. Requirements documentation
C. Procurement audit
D. Make-or-buy decision

169. Of these options, which one is not an input to the Conduct Procurements process?

A. Organizational process assets
B. Procurement management plan
C. Project organizational chart
D. Procurement documentation

170. Which of the following project management processes is not among those that directly interact with the Control Procurements process?

A. Direct and Manage Project Work
B. Initiate the Project
C. Monitor and Control Project Work
D. Perform Integrated Change Control

171. Of these options, which one is not an input to the Control Procurements process?

A. Work performance data
B. Risk management plan
C. Inspections and audits
D. Approved change requests

172. Data analysis is one of the tools and techniques used in the Control Procurements process. It includes all of the following *except* _____.

A. Performance reviews
B. Earned value analysis
C. Trend analysis
D. Audit analysis

173. The following are administrative activities for Control Procurements process *except* _____.

A. Payment of invoices
B. Reviewing seller proposals
C. Refinement of procurement plans
D. Monitoring the procurement environment

174. The enterprise environmental factors that can influence the Control Procurement process include the following *except* _____.

A. Seller organization's code of ethics
B. Contract change control system
C. Market conditions
D. Financial management

175. Organizational process assets updates resulting from the Control Procurement process could include all of the following *except* _____.

A. Procurement files
B. Payment schedule and requests
C. Gathering of lessons learned
D. Changing the contract

176. Contested changes are those requested changes for which the buyer and seller cannot agree on compensation for the change or whether a change has occurred. Which one of the following terms is not a term used to refer to contested changes?

A. Claims
B. Disputes
C. Refund requests
D. Appeals

177. What documentation includes the procurement contract, seller-developed technical documentation, seller performance reports, and results of contract-related inspections?

A. Procurement management plan
B. Procurement contract award
C. Closed procurements
D. Procurement documentation

178. Which one of the following is not a tool or technique in the Control Procurements process?

A. Inspections
B. Trend analysis
C. Procurement audits
D. Manage budget

179. Which of the following statements is not true about the Control Procurements process?

A. Tools and techniques include expert judgment, market research, and meetings
B. Tools and techniques include procurement audits, claims administration, and inspection
C. Inputs include project management plan and procurement documentation
D. Outputs include closed procurements and organizational process assets updates

180. The outputs of Control Procurements process include the following expect _____.

A. Lessons learned register updates
B. Cost baseline updates
C. Schedule baseline updates
D. Work performance data

181. The requirements for contract closure usually are included in which of the following documents?

A. Configuration management plan
B. Requirements documentation
C. Change management
D. Procurement management plan

182. How does the buyer inform the seller that the deliverables have been accepted or rejected?

A. Verbal confirmation
B. Written communication
C. Formal written notice
D. Change request

183. Professional project managers are expected to align their daily performance with four values that have been identified as the most important to the project management community. Which of the following is not part of those four values?

A. Responsibility
B. Hard work
C. Respect
D. Honesty

184. A project manager is systematically gathering and analyzing information to determine whose interests should be taken into account throughout the project. He is also working to determine their expectations and initial requirements. What process output is he trying to produce?

A. Project charter
B. Stakeholder management plan
C. Stakeholder register
D. Organizational process assets

185. If a project manager uses expert judgment, meetings, and data analysis when planning stakeholder engagement, what output will be produced?

A. Project management plan
B. Organizational process assets
C. Stakeholder engagement plan
D. Enterprise environmental factors

186. Which of the following is not a valid classification for analyzing the engagement level of stakeholders?

A. Unaware
B. Interested
C. Resistant
D. Neutral

187. A project sponsor has a high authority and high interest on the project. If he engages actively to ensure the success of the project, his engagement level can be classified as _____.

A. Leading
B. Supportive
C. Neutral
D. Unaware

188. You notice that a European team leader on one of your projects has been communicating with an Asian member of the team in an abusive manner. Your duty as a project manager is to _____.

A. Ignore this behavior to keep the project going smoothly
B. Ask the team leader to stop this behavior
C. Ignore this behavior to keep your good relationship with the team intact
D. Record the facts regarding this to substantiate the team leader's behavior and report the team leader to his or her functional manager

189. As a project manager, in which of the following situations would you pursue disciplinary action?

A. A member of the project team reports non-ethical behavior of another team member
B. A member of the project team complains that he or she is the subject of unethical abuse by another member of the team
C. A member of the project team retaliates against a colleague who raised an ethical complaint against him or her
D. A member of the project team files an ethics-related complaint without substantiating it with facts

190. You have been asked by the program manager to manage a highly sensitive project related to building a nuclear reactor. The project requires specialized knowledge about the nuclear industry. You have never worked in that industry before, although you managed a number of defense projects in other conventional areas. Which of the following is the most appropriate action for you to consider?

A. Take on the project and start self-learning about the nuclear industry
B. Inform the program manager that you do not have experience in working in the nuclear industry and that you are prepared to learn on the job
C. Tell your manager that you will learn on the job and ask him or her not to inform the customer that you do not have the right knowledge, so your company will not lose the opportunity
D. Refuse the project because you do not have the right experience

191. You completed an advanced technology project for one customer. You moved on to manage a related project for another customer, and you wanted to copy some of the work products to use in the second project without telling the first customer. What should you do?

A. Copy the work products and ask your management not to tell the first customer
B. Copy the work products without telling your management or the customer
C. Do not copy the work products before asking the first customer for permission
D. Ask a member of the first project team to copy the work products for you without informing anyone else

192. You are reading a document that was produced by the previous project manager. The document listed the current and desired engagement levels of key stakeholders, information to be distributed to stakeholders, and time frame and frequency for the distribution. What document are you reading?

A. Stakeholder engagement assessment matrix
B. Communications management plan
C. Project management plan
D. Stakeholder engagement plan

193. The Management Stakeholder Engagement process updates the project management plan and the project documents. Through change requests, the same process directly interacts with the _____ process.

A. Perform Integrated Change Control
B. Control Procurements
C. Plan Communications Management
D. Plan Stakeholder Management

194. You are managing a large international project that pays well. Your uncle asked you to hire his son in the project, even though that cousin does not have the necessary skills. Hiring the cousin would constitute which type of conflict of interest?

A. Fairness/mandatory
B. Responsibility/aspirational
C. Honesty/mandatory
D. Respect/mandatory

195. Which statement is true about managing stakeholder engagement?

A. The project issue log documents the changes that occur during a project
B. The communications management plan provides guidance on how the various stakeholders can be best involved in the project
C. The stakeholder management plan provides guidance and information on managing stakeholder expectations
D. The communications management plan provides guidance and information on managing stakeholder expectations

196. Several accidents in a nuclear energy project led to safety issues on a number of occasions, under the same project managers. Which of the following values did the project managers betray?

A. Fairness
B. Responsibility
C. Respect
D. Honesty

197. A newly assigned project manager discovered a discrepancy in the budget that was prepared by the previous project manager. If he communicates the discrepancy to the project sponsor, the project will most likely be canceled immediately and his contract will be terminated prematurely. Which value would he be violating the most if he delays the disclosure of the budget discrepancy until he can find a replacement contract?

A. Responsibility
B. Respect
C. Fairness
D. Honesty

198. As a professional project manager, you were faced with a decision involving potential conflicts of interest. You believe that your decision was correct and advantageous for the project. All of the following statements are necessary preconditions for engaging in this decision-making process except _____.

A. Making full disclosure to the affected stakeholders
B. Having an approved mitigation plan
C. Obtaining the consent of the stakeholders to proceed
D. Reporting the situation to the PMI®

199. A project manager promised project team members bonuses that he never intended to deliver. Which type of value does this behavior represent?

A. Responsibility/aspirational
B. Responsibility/mandatory
C. Fairness/aspirational
D. Honesty/aspirational

200. As manager of a large project, you needed to recruit a junior project manager with specific skills. After the new junior project manager had a few months on the job, you realized that he did not have all the skills he claimed to have. Which of the following value standards did his behavior violate?

A. Fairness/mandatory
B. Responsibility/mandatory
C. Respect/aspirational
D. Responsibility/aspirational

Bonus Questions

201. Thomas is managing an international project that will span many years. Although the raw materials are sourced from one country, he is anticipating that inflation will impact the labor costs in at least two other countries where the project will be implemented. The price of fuel, a key component in the project, may fluctuate as well. What would be the most appropriate contract given the nature of his project?

A. Cos plus incentive fee (CPIF)
B. Firm fixed price (FFP)
C. Fixed price incentive fee (FPIF)
D. Fixed price with economic price adjustment (FP-EPA)

202. If the procurement decision will be based primarily on price, which bid document would be most appropriate?

A. Invitation for bid (IFB) or request for quotation (RFQ)
B. Request for proposal (RFP) or request for information (RFI)
C. Request for information (RFI) or invitation for bid (IFB)
D. Invitation for bid (IFB) or request for proposal (RFP)

203. Which of the following is not an input of the Direct and Manage Project Work process?

A. Project charter
B. Project management plan
C. Approved change requests
D. Enterprise environmental factors

204. Pre-assignment, negotiation, decision making, and virtual teams are tools and techniques of the _____ process.

A. Build Project Team
B. Acquire Project Team
C. Develop Project Team
D. Manage Project Team

205. During the contract life cycle, the buyer may view the seller as _____.

A. Forming, norming, storming, and adjourning
B. Pre-assignment, negotiation, acquisition, and payment
C. Bidder, selected source, and contracted supplier or vendor
D. Plan, assure, control, and close

Chapter 8: Answers to Practice Test C

1. **C.** Managing a project involves managing multiple processes across multiple process groups. Without effective integration of the project processes across different groups, the project is likely to fail. Project integration management is about coordinating the various processes within the project management process groups.

Reference: *PMBOK® Guide* 6th Ed., pages 69-70

2. **C.** Perform Integrated Change Control, Develop Project Charter, and Close Project or Phase are all process that belong to the Project Integration Management knowledge area. Other processes that belong to this knowledge area include Develop Project Management Plan, Direct and Manage Project Work, Manage Project Knowledge, and Monitor and Control Project Work. Estimate Costs is a process of the Cost Management knowledge area.

Reference: *PMBOK® Guide* 6th Ed., pages 69, 71

3. **B.** A social need, a legal requirement, or a technological advance can be a valid stimulant for chartering a project. Additional stimuli can be market demand, organizational need, and ecological impacts. Although a political conflict could affect the business of the enterprise, a response to it is usually achieved through business and management strategies, rather than at a project level.

Reference: *PMBOK® Guide* 6th Ed., pages 77-78

4. **D.** Inputs of the Develop Project Charter process include business documents (business case and benefits management plan), agreements, enterprise environmental factors, and organizational process assets. Assumption log, along with the project charter, are outputs of the Develop Project Charter process.

Reference: *PMBOK® Guide* 6th Ed., page 75

5. **C.** Project purpose or justification, assigned project manager responsibility and authority level, and measurable project objectives and related success criteria are common items addressed within the project charter, which produced as part of the Develop Project Charter process. The procurement management plan is part of the project management plan and is produced at later stages of the project.

Reference: *PMBOK® Guide* 6th Ed., page 81

6. A. The organizational process assets that can influence the Develop Project Charter include organizational standard policies, processes, procedures, portfolio, program, project governance framework, monitoring and reporting methods, templates, historical information, and lessons learned repository

Reference: *PMBOK® Guide* 6th Ed., page 79

7. A. Project closure guidelines, change control procedures, and work authorization procedures are all considered to be parts of the organization's processes and procedures. They are usable across all projects. The Project Contract, which is a specific document relating to a specific project, is neither a process nor a procedure.

Reference: *PMBOK® Guide* 6th Ed., page 84

8. C. The outputs of the planning process include how work will be executed to achieve the project objectives, the project management processes tailored by the project management team, and the project life cycle. The final product resulting from the project activities is an output of the executing process of Direct and Manage Project Work.

Reference: *PMBOK® Guide* 6th Ed., pages 86-89

9. D. Outputs of the project planning processes include how changes will be monitored and controlled, how work will be executed to accomplish project objectives, and the need and techniques for communications among stakeholders. Techniques for negotiating with subcontractors are relevant across many projects. However, these techniques are not included in the project management plan.

Reference: *PMBOK® Guide* 6th Ed., pages 86-89

10. B. Except for the development of the project charter, all of the other options are part of project execution. Because no project should start without an authorized project charter, developing and preparing a draft copy and getting a sign-off on the project charter precede project execution.

Reference: *PMBOK® Guide* 6th Ed., page 91

11. A. Managing the contingency and management reserves is associated with cost and risk management. Establishing a change control board that oversees the overall project change environment is an activity of change control, as is influencing factors that cause change and determining a change has occurred. The primary objectives of the Perform Integrated Change Control process are to maintain the integrity of baselines, integrate product and project scope, and coordinate changes across knowledge area.

Reference: *PMBOK® Guide* 6th Ed., page 113

12. B. Project management plan development, overall change control, and project initiation are activities that cover limited aspects of the overall project. They do not involve the whole development team, and they do not consume the majority of the project budget. Project plan execution requires the project manager and the project team perform multiple actions to execute the project management plan to accomplish the work defined in the scope baseline.

Reference: *PMBOK® Guide* 6th Ed., page 549

13. D. Defining key project objectives and documenting project assumptions and constraints are completed prior to developing the project management plan. However, because the planning process is iterative, approved adjustments may be made later on in the project. Promoting communications among stakeholders is done throughout project execution. The main purpose of developing the project management plan is to create a document to guide project execution and control.

Reference: *PMBOK® Guide* 6th Ed., page 82

14. C. Completing the project within approved budget and schedule, and ensuring that it satisfies the needs for which it was undertaken, are among the overarching objectives for project success. Defining proper scope for the project is a primary focus of Scope Management. The collective aim of Project Integration Management processes is to ensure the proper coordination of the various elements of the project.

Reference: *PMBOK® Guide* 6th Ed., pages 69-70

15. D. Schedule development, collection of reports, or tools and techniques to gather, integrate, and disseminate project output are all individual aspects of the PMIS. Therefore, the most relevant option is that one that includes all of them and interfaces to other systems.

Reference: *PMBOK® Guide* 6th Ed., page 95

16. B. The change management plan and quality assurance plan do not reflect approved changes. The project's change control procedures detail the steps by which official company standards, policies, plans, and procedures, or any project documents, will be modified and how any changes will be approved and validated. For approved changes to be implemented and delivered by the project, they have to be reflected in the project management plan and in the performance measurement baselines. These documents must be modified to reflect the activities and resources required to implement the approved changes.

Reference: *PMBOK® Guide* 6th Ed., page 115

17. B. Assumptions are factors that are considered to be true for planning purposes, whereas constraints are factors that will limit the project management team's options. Assumptions are specific to individual projects, and they are not necessarily dependent on either historical information or lessons learned registry. Assumptions are based on factors that may not be true, may not be accurate, or may not be available.

Reference: *PMBOK® Guide* 6th Ed., pages 81, 155

18. C. Expert judgment, data analysis, decision making, interpersonal and team skills, and product analysis are tools and techniques of the Define Scope process. Only expert judgment is a tool or technique of the Develop Project Management Plan process.

Reference: *PMBOK® Guide* 6th Ed., pages 76, 106

19. D. The integration effort involves making trade-offs among competing objectives and alternatives, which requires communications and negotiation with a variety of stakeholders throughout the project. The sponsor may choose not to have direct communications with the project team. Frequent periodic meetings do not necessarily accelerate the project integration process. Assigning responsibilities to the project team members is an activity for planning the project.

Although integration occurs throughout the project cycle, project integration can be reinforced and accelerated when balancing competing demands and examining any alternative approaches.

Reference: *PMBOK® Guide* 6th Ed., page 69

20. D. A CCB may be used on any project, large and small. A CCB is not typically headed by the project manager, and it is not a subcommittee of a configuration management board. The CCB is a formally chartered group responsible for evaluating, approving, escalating, deferring or rejecting changes to the project baselines.

Reference: *PMBOK® Guide* 6th Ed., page 115

21. C. Project processes fall into three categories: processes used at predefined points, processes performed continuously and Performed periodically as needed.

Reference: *PMBOK® Guide* 6th Ed., page 22

22. B. Change management activities include identifying, documenting, deciding on, and tracking changes. Configuration management records and updates information about project items.

Reference: *PMBOK® Guide* 6th Ed., pages 88, 119

23. A. Outputs of the Direct and Management Work process include deliverables, work performance data, issue log, change requests, project management plan updates, organizational process assets updates and project documents updates.

Reference: *PMBOK® Guide* 6th Ed., page 71

24. D. Approved change requests, project management plan updates, and project documents updates are outputs of the Perform Integrated Change Control process. Organizational process assets updates are outputs of the Close Project or Phase process and other processes, but not the Perform Integrated Change Control process.

Reference: *PMBOK® Guide* 6th Ed., page 71

25. D. The Collect Requirements process is the process of determining, documenting, and managing stakeholders' needs to meet the project's objectives.

Reference: *PMBOK® Guide* 6th Ed., pages 138-140

26. C. Sponsor's approval of the project budget, stakeholder identification, and designing the project organization are all activities associated with initiating and planning processes. As part of directing and managing project execution, the project team performs the work as outlined in the project management plan. That work includes implementing the planned methods and standards.

Reference: *PMBOK® Guide* 6th Ed., page 595, 670

27. D. Developing the project management plan, monitoring and controlling project work, and performing integrated change control do not produce deliverables. Deliverables, work performance data, issue log, change requests, project management plan updates, project documents updates, and organizational process assets updates are outputs of the Direct and Manage Project Work process.

Reference: *PMBOK® Guide* 6th Ed., pages 71

28. C. The Collect Requirements process determines, documents, and manages stakeholder needs and the corresponding requirements to meet the stakeholders' objectives. It also provides the basis for defining the project scope and product scope. Although the product scope provides the basis for requirements, product requirements are industry-specific and are therefore not part of the Collect Requirements process.

Reference: *PMBOK® Guide* 6th Ed., pages 139-140

29. B. Outputs of the Direct and Manage Project Work process include deliverables, work performance data, issue log, change requests, project management plan updates, project documents updates, and organizational process assets updates.

Reference: *PMBOK® Guide* 6th Ed., page 90

30. D. Lessons learned register is an output of the Manage Project Knowledge process but *not* the Direct and Management Project Work process. The Perform Integrated Change Control process includes project management plan updates and approved change requests as outputs. Deliverables are an output of the Direct and Manage Project Work process.

Reference: *PMBOK® Guide* 6th Ed., page 71

31. C. Work performance data, an output of the Direct and Manage Project Work process, includes costs incurred, deliverable status, and schedule progress are part of the data collected routinely to measure and monitor work performance. The Monitor and Control Project Work process uses schedule forecasts as one of its inputs.

Reference: *PMBOK® Guide* 6th Ed., pages 95, 105, 107-108

32. B. Performing activities to accomplish project objectives is completed in the Direct and Manage Project Work process. Collecting and documenting the Lessons Learned is part of the Manage Knowledge process, and staffing management and resource planning is part of developing the project management plan. Monitoring project risks is included in the Monitoring and Controlling process group.

Reference: *PMBOK® Guide* 6th Ed., pages 107-108

33. A. Monitoring implementations of approved changes when and as they occur, comparing actual project performance against the project management plan, and providing forecasts to update current cost and performance against the project management plan are activities in monitoring and controlling the project work. Implementing approved changes into the project scope, plans, and environments is part of directing and managing project execution, not monitoring and controlling activities.

Reference: *PMBOK® Guide* 6th Ed., pages 107-108

34. C. Approved change requests are an output of the Perform Integrated Change Control process.

Reference: *PMBOK® Guide* 6th Ed., pages 118-120

35. A. Reviewing high priority changes and forwarding them to the change control board for approval, streamlining the prioritization and approval of changes that only affect the scope, time, and/or cost of the project, and considering undocumented changes that indicate a reduction in risk to the overall project do not take into consideration the overall project objectives in an integrated fashion. The best answer is approving or rejecting all requests for changes or modifications to project documents, deliverables, or baselines.

Reference: *PMBOK® Guide* 6th Ed., page 113

36. D. The main purpose of configuration status accounting it to capture, sort, and report configuration identification list, proposed changes status, and change implementation status. The basis from which the configuration of products is defined is provided through configuration identification. Establishing that performance and functional requirements have been met is provided through configuration audits, and documenting the technical and functional impacts of requested changes is achieved through configuration control.

Reference: *PMBOK® Guide* 6th Ed., pages 118-119

37. A. Approved change request updates, change log, project management plan updates, and project documents updates are all outputs of the Perform Integrated Change Control process. Work performance reports are an input to, and not an output of, the Perform Integrated Change Control process.

Reference: *PMBOK® Guide* 6th Ed., page 120

38. C. It true that a CCB is responsible for reviewing change requests and approving or rejecting them, and it is true that the roles and responsibilities of the CCB are clearly defined and agreed by appropriate stakeholders. It is also true that all CCB decisions are documented and communicated to the stakeholders for information and follow-up actions. The statement that the CCB may not necessarily record all of the decisions and recommendations that they have made is incorrect. It is imperative that the CCB accurately and completely document and communicate their work to the appropriate stakeholders.

Reference: *PMBOK® Guide* 6th Ed., page 115

39. A. Of the available options, the only correct statement is the fact that change requests are approved by the project's CCB. The other options are not true.

Reference: *PMBOK® Guide* 6th Ed., page 115

40. C. The statements are correct *except* for deciding whether to accept or reject product or project updates. These changes should occur prior to closing the project not during the Close Project or Phase process.

Reference: *PMBOK® Guide* 6th Ed., pages 121-123

41. D. Closing project or phase includes reviewing all prior information to ensure that all project work is complete, archiving project information for future use by the organization, and documenting reasons for the project termination. Verifying and deciding on all submitted change requests is done through the Perform Integrated Change Control process.

Reference: *PMBOK® Guide* 6th Ed., pages 121-123

42. A. The two main categories of organizational process assets (OPAs) are processes and procedures, and organizational knowledge bases. Standardized guidelines and work instructions, as well as organization communication requirements, are part of the processes and procedures; process measurement databases can be a part of the organizational knowledge base. Government or industry standards are enterprise environmental factors, and therefore are not considered a part of the organizational process assets.

Reference: *PMBOK® Guide* 6th Ed., page 126

43. C. The project management plan, accepted deliverables, and organizational process assets, such as closure guidelines, are inputs into the Close Project or Phase process. Approved change requests are inputs of the Direct and Manage Project Work process.

Reference: *PMBOK® Guide* 6th Ed., pages 90, 121

44. B. This is not an example of the majority decision-making method, even though the sponsor believes the majority of end users would benefit. The majority decision method requires that more than 50% of the group approving the decision. It is not an example of unanimity wherein all stakeholders agree. Nor it is a plurality, wherein one choice is preferred by the largest number of votes. Dictatorship is the correct option because the sponsor made the decision by herself.

Reference: *PMBOK® Guide* 6th Ed., page 144

45. A. As part of the Closing process group, project administrative closure procedures involve archiving project information for future use, gathering Lessons Learned, and validating that completion and exit criteria have been met. Raising problem reports for nonperforming parts of the system is part of the Perform Integrated Change Control process, which belongs to the Monitoring and Controlling process group.

Reference: *PMBOK® Guide* 6th Ed., page 123

46. B. Prototyping allows stakeholders to experiment with a model of the final product and refine requirements. Prototyping also supports the concept of progressive elaboration because stakeholders use iterations of working models, experimentation, feedback, and revision.

Reference: *PMBOK® Guide* 6th Ed., pages 142, 147

47. C. Transfer of finished and unfinished deliverables does not take place at the end of key deliverable, at the end of contract, or as a result of a legal dispute. If the project was terminated prior to completion, the formal documentation indicates why the project was terminated and formalizes procedures for the transfer of the finished and unfinished deliverables of the cancelled project.

Reference: *PMBOK® Guide* 6th Ed., page 128

48. B. As part of the Close Project or Phase process, organizational process assets may be updated including project files, project or phase closure documents, and historical information. Customer data beyond the required retention period are considered expired and should be destroyed.

Reference: *PMBOK® Guide* 6th Ed., page 128

49. D. Project charter, project management plan, project documents, enterprise environmental factors, and organizational process assets are inputs to the Define Scope process.

Reference: *PMBOK® Guide* 6th Ed., page 130

50. A. Inputs to the Create WBS process include project management plan, project documents, enterprise environmental factors, and organizational process assets. The other options are incorrect.

Reference: *PMBOK® Guide* 6th Ed., page 127

51. C. Interviews, nominal group technique and focus groups are some of the techniques used in the Collect Requirements process. These tools and techniques and others help elicit, analyze, and record the requirements in enough detail to be measured once project execution begins. The schedule baseline is established following the creation of the work breakdown structure (WBS).

Reference: *PMBOK® Guide* 6th Ed., page 138

52. B. Outputs of the Define Scope process include the project scope statement and project documents updates. Requested changes, the issue log, and communication management plan are not outputs of the Define Scope process.

Reference: *PMBOK® Guide* 6th Ed., page 150

53. D. The project charter, a list of stakeholders, and the work breakdown structure are not included in the detailed project scope statement. The product scope description is included in the project scope statement, together with product acceptance criteria, deliverables, and exclusions.

Reference: *PMBOK® Guide* 6th Ed., page 154

54. A. Component, deliverable, and work item are terms that can be used when creating a WBS. A work package is at the lowest level of the WBS represents a manageable work effort.

Reference: *PMBOK® Guide* 6th Ed., page 158-161

55. C. Acceptance criteria, agreement information, and code of account identifier are some of the information contained in the WBS dictionary. Accepted deliverables is an output of the Validate Scope process.

Reference: *PMBOK® Guide* 6th Ed., pages 162-163

56. A. Scope validation formalizes the acceptance of completed project deliverables, whereas quality control monitors and records the results of quality activities to ensure that the project products, services, and results meet the defined quality standards.

Reference: *PMBOK® Guide* 6th Ed., pages 163, 298-300

57. C. Inspections can take the form of any of the verification techniques: audits, reviews, or walkthroughs. Testing is a validation technique, as opposed to a verification technique.

Reference: *PMBOK® Guide* 6th Ed., page 166

58. A. Inputs to the Control Scope process include project management plan, requirements documentation, requirements traceability matrix, work performance data, and organizational process assets. Although the performance measurement baseline is an input, the project budget includes the Management Reserve, which is outside of the cost baseline. Therefore the project budget, project charter, and project organization charts are not correct.

Reference: *PMBOK® Guide* 6th Ed., page 167

59. C. Product analysis, expert judgment, and stakeholder analysis are not used in the Control Scope process. The Control Scope process includes determining the cause of variance relative to the scope baseline and deciding whether corrective action is required. This is achieved through variance and trend analysis techniques.

Reference: *PMBOK® Guide* 6th Ed., page 167

60. B. Control Scope does not produce outputs of accepted deliverables, trend analysis or approved changes. The Control Scope process can generate change requests, which are processed for review and disposition in to the Perform Integrated Change Control process.

Reference: *PMBOK® Guide* 6th Ed., pages 167

61. D. Work performance data is an output of the Control Scope process. Outputs include work performance information, change requests, project management plan, and project documents. Updated project documents comprise of lessons learned register, requirements documentation, and requirements traceability matrix.

Reference: *PMBOK® Guide* 6th Ed., page 167

62. C. The Project Schedule Management knowledge area includes the following six processes: Plan Schedule Management, Define Activities, Sequence Activities, Estimate Activity Durations, Develop Schedule, and Control Schedule. Develop Project Charter, Develop Project Management Plan, and Monitor and Control Project Work are processes in the Project Integration Management knowledge area.

Reference: *PMBOK® Guide* 6th Ed., pages 174, 70

63. D. Develop Schedule, Control Schedule, and Sequence Activities include leads and lags as a tools and technique. The Sequence Activities process does not.

Reference: *PMBOK® Guide* 6th Ed., page 174

64. D. The Define Activities process in the Project Schedule Management knowledge area uses decomposition, rolling wave planning, meetings and expert judgment to produce the activity list, activity attributes, and milestone list as outputs.

Reference: *PMBOK® Guide* 6th Ed., page 174

65. A. Rolling wave planning is a form of progressive elaboration in which the work to be accomplished in the near term is planned in detail and future work is planned at a higher level until more information becomes known.

Reference: *PMBOK® Guide* 6th Ed., page 185

66. B. Using the critical path method (CPM), the maximum or critical path is 22 units (B, C, D, F, I, and J). The critical path determines the shortest duration in which a project can be completed because the project cannot be finished until all of the tasks in the critical path have been completed.

Reference: *PMBOK® Guide* 6th Ed., pages 189-190, 210-211

67. C. The critical path is the longest duration path within the project therefore it is BCDFIJ with a duration of 25.

Reference: *PMBOK® Guide* 6th Ed., pages 189-190, 210-211

68. D. Estimating activity resources involves determining what resources (persons, equipment, or material) and what quantities of each resource are to be used. Such information is potentially generic and can be delivered by a local industry consultant. The local knowledge of specialized techniques is useful for activity resource estimating, particularly when using expert judgment, alternatives analysis, and published estimating data tools and technique to produce outputs.

Reference: *PMBOK® Guide* 6th Ed., pages 320-322

69. B. Estimate Activity Duration is the process of approximating the number of work periods needed to complete individual activities with estimated resources. One of the inputs to this process is resource calendars that capture the characteristics (type, quantity, availability, and capability) of both equipment and material resources.

Reference: *PMBOK® Guide* 6th Ed., page 199

70. B. The types of estimates used in the three-point estimating technique are most likely, optimistic, and pessimistic. Least likely is not a type of estimate used in the three-point estimates.

Reference: *PMBOK® Guide* 6th Ed., pages 201

71. C. The critical path method calculates the early start, early finish, late start, and late finish dates for all activities without regard for any resource limitations by performing a forward and backward pass analysis through the schedule network.

Reference: *PMBOK® Guide* 6th Ed., page 210

72. A. The schedule baseline, a component of the project management plan, uses schedule network analysis to determine the planned start and end dates, which are then subsequently reviewed and approved by the project management team and key stakeholders. The other options are inputs, not outputs, of the Develop Schedule process.

Reference: *PMBOK® Guide* 6th Ed., page 217

73. C. Inputs to the Control Schedule process include the project management plan, work performance data, resource calendars, schedule data, and organizational process assets. Work performance information, schedule forecasts, change requests, project management plan updates, and project documents updates are outputs of the Control Schedule process.

Reference: *PMBOK® Guide* 6th Ed., page 222

74. B. The correct option is resource skills. The resource calendar includes availability, capabilities, and skills of human resources. Resource calendars also specify when and for how long project resources will be available during the project, and it may include attributes such as resource experience and/or skill level. All the other answers are not correct.

Reference: *PMBOK® Guide* 6th Ed., page 323

75. C. The Identify Risks process uses the following data analysis techniques: root cause analysis, assumption and constraint analysis, SWOT analysis, and document analysis. Interview is a data gathering, not data analysis, technique.

Reference: *PMBOK® Guide* 6th Ed., pages 414-415

76. B. Resource leveling is used to address when sheared resources or critical resources are available only at certain times, or are available only in limited quantities; or to keep selected resource usage at a constant level during specific time periods during the project work. This leveling of resource usage can cause the original critical path to change, usually making the schedule longer.

Reference: *PMBOK® Guide* 6th Ed., page 211

77. B. In the question PV (planned value) equals 3 weeks and EV (earned value) equals 2 weeks. SV (schedule variance) is calculated as SV = EV − PV. Therefore, 2 weeks of work are complete (EV) and you budgeted for 3 weeks (PV) so the SV (schedule variance) is 1 week

The percentage of the variance would be SV (schedule variance) / PV (planned value) which equals 1 / 3 or the correct answer of 33%.

Reference: *PMBOK® Guide* 6th Ed., pages 261-265

78. C. SV (schedule variance) = EV (earned value) − PV (planned value). The EV = $850 and PV = $1,000, so the SV equals −$150.

Reference: *PMBOK® Guide* 6th Ed., pages 261-265

79. D. Direct labor costs, overhead costs, and material costs may all be taken into consideration based on what costs would be attributed to the project as defined in the Cost Management Plan. Sunk costs are costs that have already been incurred and that cannot be recovered; therefore, they are not part of the cost estimating process.

Reference: *PMBOK® Guide* 6th Ed., page 241

80. A. For month 1, the Cost Performance Index (CPI) = Earned Value / Actual Cost which is 1,000,000 / 1,250.000 = 0.88 therefore the statement that CPI at the end of month 1 is 1.25 is not true. A CPI value less than 1.0 indicates a cost overrun, and a CPI value more than 1.0 indicates a cost under run; hence, at the end on Month 1, the project is behind schedule and over budget.

Reference: *PMBOK® Guide* 6th Ed., pages 261-265

81. A. At the end of Month 2, EV is $1,750,000 and AC for the same period is $1,750,000. Therefore at the end of Month 2 the project is on budget.

Reference: *PMBOK® Guide* 6th Ed., pages 261-265

82. A. Because we are assuming that future work will be completed at the rate originally budgeted, the correct formula to use is EAC = AC + (BAC − EV). EAC = $1,900 (AC) + [3000 (BAC) - $1,500 (EV)]. Therefore, EAC = $1900 + $1500 or $3400.

Reference: *PMBOK® Guide* 6th Ed., pages 261-265

83. A. There are several ways to calculate the Estimate at Completion (EAC) depending on the approach that the project team defined in the Cost Management Plan. To calculate the EAC with the assumption that the remaining work will be performed at the same rate of performance as what's happened to date from a cost perspective (CPI) you would use the equation EAC = BAC / CPI.

Reference: *PMBOK® Guide* 6th Ed., pages 261-265

84. A. Analogous cost estimating uses the actual cost of previous, similar projects as the basis for estimating the cost of the current project. It is generally less accurate because there is a limited amount of detailed information about the project (for example, in the early phases). Parametric estimating technique provides better estimates compared to analogous especially if the statistical model and the underlying historical data are robust; the three-point estimating technique considers uncertainty and risk by using optimistic, most likely, and pessimistic estimates; and bottom-up estimates are considered to be the most accurate because work is estimated at the lowest level and then "rolled-up" for higher level estimates.

Reference: *PMBOK® Guide* 6th Ed., pages 244-245

85. B. The curve illustrates that the value of the work completed is less than the planned value (i.e., budget) so the project is behind schedule, and the actual cost is more than the planned cost, so the project is over budget.

Reference: *PMBOK® Guide* 6th Ed., pages 263-264

86. C. Contingency reserves are allowances for unplanned but potential risks that may occur. They are included in the cost performance baseline. Management reserves are budgets reserved for unknown, unknowns, or risks that couldn't have logically been foreseen. They are not part of the project cost performance baseline but are included in the overall budget for the project.

Reference: *PMBOK® Guide* 6th Ed., page 245

87. B. Quality is the degree to which a set of inherent characteristics of a product or service are measured to determine whether the requirements were met. Grade is a category assigned to products or services having the same functional use but different technical characteristics. A level of quality that fails to meet quality requirements is always a problem, low grade is not.

Reference: *PMBOK® Guide* 6th Ed., page 274

88. D. Continuous process improvement can lead to reducing waste, reducing non-value-added activities, and increasing the project efficiency. Continuous process improvement doesn't necessarily eliminate all project risk.

Reference: *PMBOK® Guide* 6th Ed., pages 289-290

89. C. Quality costs are the total cost of the activities to achieve quality. This includes the cost of preventing nonconformance to requirements, cost of appraising the product or service, and cost of ensuring compliance with mandatory standards. Costs of productivity bonuses are not part of the quality costs.

Reference: *PMBOK® Guide* 6th Ed., pages 282-283

90. A. The Manage Quality process translates the quality management plan into executable quality activities.

Reference: *PMBOK® Guide* 6th Ed., page 288

91. C. Trends in modern quality management include customer satisfaction (meeting customer expectations), mutually beneficial partnership with suppliers (relationships based on partnership and cooperation with the supplier), continual improvement (always looking for a better way to do things), and management responsibility (management must provide the resources to succeed).

Reference: *PMBOK® Guide* 6th Ed., page 275

92. A. Document and alternative analysis, and process and root cause analysis are tools and techniques of Manage Quality. Acceptance sampling and statistical process control are associated with the Validate Scope and Control Quality respectively. Quality management consists of quality planning, quality management, and quality control.

Reference: *PMBOK® Guide* 6th Ed., pages 272, 292

93. C. The Manage Quality process is concerned with the product design aspects and process improvements. Control Quality is focused on assuring deliverables conform to specifications.

Reference: *PMBOK® Guide* 6th Ed., page 289

94. B. All aspects of quality, including ensuring deliverables meet requirements through the Control Quality process, are the ultimate responsibility of the project manager.

Reference: *PMBOK® Guide* 6th Ed., pages 299-300

95. B. Project quality audits confirm the implementation of approved change requests and defect repairs, corrective actions, and preventive actions. Management reserves are not part of the cost performance baseline and are outside the scope of a project quality audit.

Reference: *PMBOK® Guide* 6th Ed., pages 294-295

96. D. The Manage Quality process outputs include quality reports, testing and evaluation documents, change requests, project management plan updates, and project documents updates.

Reference: *PMBOK® Guide* 6th Ed., page 288

97. A. Plan Quality Management uses a number of techniques for data representation which include flowcharts, matrix diagrams, mind mapping, and logical data model.

Reference: *PMBOK® Guide* 6th Ed., page 284

98. C. A flowchart displays the sequence of steps within a process that turns one or more inputs into one or more outputs.

Reference: *PMBOK® Guide* 6th Ed., page 284

99. C. The Project Resource Management knowledge area includes the following processes: Plan Resource Management, Estimate Activity Resources, Acquire Resources, Develop Team, Manage Team, and Control Resources. Administer Resources is not a Resource Management process.

Reference: *PMBOK® Guide* 6th Ed., page 308

100. B. Project managers use the RACI chart to communicate roles and expectations within the project. RACI stands for responsible, accountable, consult, and inform. There can only be one resource assigned to the "Accountable" role.

Reference: *PMBOK® Guide* 6th Ed., page 317

101. A. There are six processes in the Project Resource Management knowledge area: Plan Resource Management, Estimate Activity Resources, Acquire Resources, Develop Team, Manage Team, and Control Resources.

Reference: *PMBOK® Guide* 6th Ed., page 308

102. B. Inputs to the Plan Resource Management process includes the project charter, project management plan, project documents, enterprise environmental factors, and organizational process assets. Team charter is one of the outputs of the Plan Resource Management process.

Reference: *PMBOK® Guide* 6th Ed., page 308

103. A. The roles and responsibilities section of the resource management plan captures the role, authority, responsibility, and competence details. The other options describe the elements associated with a team charter, not specifically roles and responsibilities.

Reference: *PMBOK® Guide* 6th Ed., pages 318-319

104. C. The resource management plan describes when and how the project resource requirements will be met by incorporating details such as acquiring resources, roles and responsibilities, identification of resources, organization charts, team resource management, training needs, resource control, and recognition plan.

Reference: *PMBOK® Guide* 6th Ed., pages 318-320

105. D. Availability, cost, and experience influence the assignment of project team members. Hobbies should not influence the assignment of the project team members.

Reference: *PMBOK® Guide* 6th Ed., pages 318-319, 328-330

106. C. Team-building activities, recognition and rewards, and training are all used in team development, which takes place through the Develop Team process. Stakeholder analysis is a tool and technique of the Identify Stakeholders process, not the Develop Team process.

Reference: *PMBOK® Guide* 6th Ed., pages 341-342, 507

107. B. The fact that team members socialize after work hours does not mean that they will work more effectively on the project. The other options describe behaviors that indicate effective teamwork.

Reference: *PMBOK® Guide* 6th Ed., pages 337-339

108. D. Observation, conversation, and project performance appraisals are means for gaining project knowledge in an unplanned training environment. The resource management plan captures scheduled training for the project team, which is a planned training event.

Reference: *PMBOK® Guide* 6th Ed., page 342

109. A. The statement about virtual and co-located teams are simply false. The other options are true about project team development.

Reference: *PMBOK® Guide* 6th Ed., pages 341-342

110. C. Email communication, a shared goal, and possible inclusion of people with mobility handicaps are all characteristics of virtual teams. Virtual team members are not concerned with managing diverse stakeholder views and expectations. This is the job of the project manager.

Reference: *PMBOK® Guide* 6th Ed., page 311

111. C. Conflicts often involve ethics, morals, and value systems because many project teams include people from different cultures, with different ethics, morals, and value systems. Interpersonal conflicts produced by these factors are the most difficult to resolve in a project environment.

Reference: *PMBOK® Guide* 6th Ed., pages 348-349

112. A. Evident improvements in skills, continuous improvements in competencies, and reduced staff turnover are all indicators of the team effectiveness. Increased conflict between the project manager and the project personnel is not an indicator of project team effectiveness.

Reference: *PMBOK® Guide* 6th Ed., pages 336-339

113. A. Understanding compensation plans, benefits, and career paths are the responsibility of functional and personnel managers rather than project managers. The other options describe interpersonal skills necessary for project managers.

Reference: *PMBOK® Guide* 6th Ed., pages 341, 348-349, 527

114. D. Colocation involves placing many or all of the project team members in the same physical location to enhance their performance as a team. It encourages face-to-face communication, which reduces noise and misunderstandings of the messages communicated.

Reference: *PMBOK® Guide* 6th Ed., page 340

115. C. Establishing the salary levels of team members is not normally the responsibility of the project manager. Salaries and pay raises are the responsibility of functional and personnel managers, rather than project managers. The other options indicate responsibilities of project managers.

Reference: *PMBOK® Guide* 6th Ed., page 343

116. D. Tracking team performance, providing feedback, and resolving conflict are all part of the Manage Team process. Allocating pay raises is usually the responsibility of a functional manager and not part of project team management.

Reference: *PMBOK® Guide* 6th Ed., page 345

117. B. Teams will more likely increase effectiveness if they exchange knowledge and experience, share information and resources, and have improved feelings of trust and cohesion among other team members. Running a productivity competition to see who can work more hours will not sustainably increase the effectiveness of the project team.

Reference: *PMBOK® Guide* 6th Ed., pages 336-339

118. A. In projectized organizations, the project manager has full authority over the project resources. Project managers typically hold the view that conflict is inevitable, but managing it properly and resolving it in a constructive manner could lead to positive results for the project.

Reference: *PMBOK® Guide* 6th Ed., pages 348

119. B. The overall level of conflict does not remain constant over the project lifecycle, and interpersonal situations are not among the most common sources of project conflicts. The most preferred approach for handing conflict is collaborate/problem solve which typically leads to consensus and commitment.

Reference: *PMBOK® Guide* 6th Ed., pages 348-349

120. B. Feedback from project team member's family and friends is not part of 360-degree feedback.

Reference: *PMBOK® Guide* 6th Ed., page 343

121. A. The Project Communications Management knowledge area includes the following processes: Plan Communications Management, Manage Communications, and Monitor Communications. The Project Stakeholder Management knowledge area includes the following processes: Identify Stakeholders, Plan Stakeholder Management, Manage Stakeholder Engagement, and Control Stakeholder Engagement.

Reference: *PMBOK® Guide* 6th Ed., page 360

122. C. Only the Monitor Communications process in the Project Communications Management knowledge is in the Monitoring and Controlling process group. The Manage Stakeholder Engagement process is part of the Project Stakeholder Management knowledge area and is part of the Executing process group.

Reference: *PMBOK® Guide* 6th Ed., page 25

123. D. Noise, message, and encoding are all key components of the basic model of communications. The correct option is messenger because the basic model of communication demonstrates how an idea or information is sent and received between two parties, defined as the sender and receiver. It does not have a messenger as a component of the model.

Reference: *PMBOK® Guide* 6th Ed., page 371

124. B. Geographical distribution of project staff and available technology affect the choice of the communication method and media. Executive requirements affect the contents and frequency of communications. Project length does not directly affect the project communications plan.

Reference: *PMBOK® Guide* 6th Ed., pages 369-376

125. D. Presentations, telephone calls, and verbal requests are not the best medium for initial response to the client request because they do not formally record the request. Your client's request represents a change to the contract, so the response must come in a formal written request, which should turn into a change request to the contract.

Reference: *PMBOK® Guide* 6th Ed., pages 369-376

126. C. The correct answer is not to send him the files because he does not have a legitimate need to know. Information distribution is only to current project stakeholders. Once a member of the team leaves the project, he or she is no long a stakeholder or member of the project team.

Reference: *PMBOK® Guide* 6th Ed., pages 379-381

127. D. The communication plan includes identifying to whom information will be distributed; what, how, and how often information will be gathered; and what methods will be used to distribute information. Memos, correspondence, and reports from project personnel are actual communication deliverables, not part of the project communication management plan itself.

Reference: *PMBOK® Guide* 6th Ed., pages 377-378

128. C. Stakeholder buy-in, executive interviews, and channel evaluations are not tools and techniques of the Manage Communications process. Communication methods define the techniques used in the Manage Communications process to ensure the creation and distribution of information.

Reference: *PMBOK® Guide* 6th Ed., page 379, 383

129. B. This activity does not require an update in the project charter, the stakeholder management plan, or the project change control process. The method of information distribution to stakeholders is defined in the communications management plan for the project. This change in information presentation media and frequency must be reflected in updates to the project's communications management plan.

Reference: *PMBOK® Guide* 6th Ed., pages 377-378

130. B. A request for additional work is effectively a request for change, which should be formally submitted in writing before it is submitted for assessment and decision by the appropriate change control authority.

Reference: *PMBOK® Guide* 6th Ed., pages 366-367

131.   A. Work performance reports are the integrated output of the results of the knowledge area control processes and are created in the Monitor and Control Project process. . The results of the ISO audit will not be typically included in a work performance report unless it was included within the overall Quality Management work performance information.

Reference: *PMBOK® Guide* 6th Ed., pages 112, 382

132. D. Outputs of the Monitor Communications process include work performance information, change requests, project management plan updates, and project documents updates. Work performance data is an input to the Monitor Communications process.

Reference: *PMBOK® Guide* 6th Ed., page 388

133.A. The Identify Stakeholders process is part of the Initiating process group in which the project charter is also created. Identifying stakeholders is performed early in the project life cycle, before the processes in the Planning, Executing, and Monitoring and Controlling process groups.

Reference: *PMBOK® Guide* 6th Ed., page 25

134. B. Any request for change should be submitted in written form because a change may have a financial impact and impact the contract. There must be formal written documentation of it.

Reference: *PMBOK® Guide* 6th Ed., pages 359, 388

135. C. Project reporting is a tool and technique of the Manage Communications process. Tools and techniques of the Control Communications process include information management systems, expert judgment, and meetings.

Reference: *PMBOK® Guide* 6th Ed., page 388

136. B. Proper management of stakeholder engagement ensures that the communication needs and expectations of various stakeholders are met by proactively soliciting feedback, addressing issues, and clarifying requirements. These are the responsibilities of the project manager. If implemented correctly, project stakeholder management will increase the likelihood of project success and limit the disruptions in the project.

Reference: *PMBOK® Guide* 6th Ed., pages 523-524

137. A. Unlike telephone conversations and written or non-verbal communications, verbal face-to-face is the most effective method of communicating complex situations because it allows for immediate feedback and clarification. The sender and receiver of the message can also take advantage of both verbal and nonverbal (tone of voice, gestures, and so forth) elements of the communication.

Reference: *PMBOK® Guide* 6th Ed., pages 360-365

138. C. The formula for calculating the total number of potential communication channels is [n (n -1)] / 2, where *n* is the number of individuals involved in the communications. Seven stakeholders and you total eight people. Therefore the correct answer is 8 (8-1) / 2 which gives us 56/2 or a total of 28 communication channels or paths.

Reference: *PMBOK® Guide* 6th Ed., pages 370

139. C. The issue log, along with project management plan, work performance data, organizational process assets, enterprise environmental factors, and project documents are inputs to the Monitor Stakeholder Engagement process.

Reference: *PMBOK® Guide* 6th Ed., page 530

140. D. The issue log may contain the follow-up action agreed on, the root cause analysis of the issue, and the results of any negotiations with functional managers to resolve the issues. The correct option is the results of the project risk analysis because they are not recorded in the issue log but are recorded in the project risk register and risk report.

Reference: *PMBOK® Guide* 6th Ed., pages 96, 417, 532

141. D. Project risks are either known or unknown. Known risks are those that can be identified, analyzed, and planned for. Although it is difficult to plan for unknown risks, they should not be disregarded. Unknown risks are harder to manage proactively and they cannot be treated as known risks. The project manager should work with management to leverage management reserve as needed.

Reference: *PMBOK® Guide* 6th Ed., page 245

142. C. Except for the statement that a risk management plan should be updated frequently, the other options are valid statements about risk management plans. The risk register should be updated frequently. The risk management plan should only be updated as changes are made to the project.

Reference: *PMBOK® Guide* 6th Ed., pages 405-408

143. B. Regression analysis, decomposition, and structured analysis are not techniques of the Identify Risks process. Brainstorming is used when identifying risks as a way to generate multiple ideas.

Reference: *PMBOK® Guide* 6th Ed., page 414

144. C. The risk register is an output of the Identify Risks process. It typically contains a list of identified risks, a list of potential responses, and potential risk owners. The work breakdown structure is not contained in the risk register.

Reference: *PMBOK® Guide* 6th Ed., page 417

145. A. Small bubbles with lower detectability and lower proximity, where the bubble size represents the impact value, are acceptable risks.

Reference: *PMBOK® Guide* 6th Ed., page 426

146. B. Sensitivity analysis, a technique used for event and project-oriented quantitative risk analysis and modeling, typically uses tornado diagrams to compare the relative importance and impact of variables with a high degree of uncertainty against variables that are more stable. Expected monetary value (EMV) analysis uses data and probability to calculate the average outcome of scenarios that may or may not happen. Decision tree diagrams are commonly used in EMV analysis. Control charts are used in project quality management, not project risk management.

Reference: *PMBOK® Guide* 6th Ed., pages 304, 434

147. A. Strategies for dealing with negatives risks include escalate, mitigate, avoid, accept, and transfer. Exploit is a strategy for dealing with positive risks (opportunities), and not with negative risks (threats).

Reference: *PMBOK® Guide* 6th Ed., pages 442-443

148. D. Strategies for responding to positive risks include escalate, exploit, share, enhance, and accept. Increase is not a risk response strategy.

Reference: *PMBOK® Guide* 6th Ed., pages 444

149. B. Inputs to the Monitor Risk process are project management plan, risk register, work performance data, and work performance reports. The other options are outputs of the Monitor Risks process.

Reference: *PMBOK® Guide* 6th Ed., page 453

150. B. Expert judgment is a tool or technique of five Project Risk Management processes but not for monitoring risks. Tools and techniques of the Monitor Risk process include risk assessment, risk audits, variance and trend analysis, technical performance measurement, reserve analysis, and meetings.

Reference: *PMBOK® Guide* 6th Ed., page 453

151. C. Project Procurement Management knowledge area processes include Plan Procurement Management, Conduct Procurements, and Control Procurements. There is no Estimate Procurements process.

Reference: *PMBOK® Guide* 6th Ed., page 459

152. D. The procurement management plan, an output of the Plan Procurement Management process, typically contains among other things, the timeline for procurement activities, how procurements will be coordinated with other project aspects, and constraints and assumptions. Selected sellers are an output of the Conduct Procurements process, which occurs after the completion of the procurement management plan.

Reference: *PMBOK® Guide* 6th Ed., page 475

153. B. The firm fixed price contract has the lowest risk for the buyer because the amount to be paid is known and agreed upon before the work starts, regardless of how the seller will produce the deliverables.

Reference: *PMBOK® Guide* 6th Ed., pages 471-472

154. B. All legal contractual relationships fall into one of two broad contract types, either fixed-price contracts or cost-reimbursable contracts. Time and material contracts is a hybrid approach. Fixed-price incentive fee is not a cost-reimbursable contract.

Reference: *PMBOK® Guide* 6th Ed., pages 471-472

155. D. Stock price is not a reliable predictor of a seller's ability to deliver the needs of the project. Additionally, if one of the providers is a not-for-profit or private company, this criterion cannot be used. Valid sellers' evaluation criteria may include understanding of the need, price, technical capability, management approach, technical approach, financial capacity, and other factors.

Reference: *PMBOK® Guide* 6th Ed., pages 478-479

156. C. Outputs of the Conduct Procurements process include selected sellers, agreements, resource calendars, change requests, project management plan updates, and project documents updates. The requested product is not an output of the Conduct Procurements process.

Reference: *PMBOK® Guide* 6th Ed., page 482

157. D. Expert judgment advertising, bidder conferences, data analysis, and procurement negotiations are all tools and techniques used during the Conduct Procurements process. Claims administration takes place during the Control Procurements process and not during the Conduct Procurements process.

Reference: *PMBOK® Guide* 6th Ed., pages 487-488

158. D. Agreements, along with selected sellers, resource calendars, change requests, project management plan updates, and project documents updates are outputs of the Conduct Procurements process.

Reference: *PMBOK® Guide* 6th Ed., page 482

159. A. Selected sellers, agreements, change requests, project management plan updates, project documents updates, and organizational process assets updates are outputs of the Conduct Procurements process. Procurement statement of work is an output of the Plan Procurement Management process.

Reference: *PMBOK® Guide* 6th Ed., pages 466, 482

160. D. Expert judgment, claims administration, data analysis, inspection, and audits are tools and techniques of the Control Procurement process. Advertising is used in the Conduct Procurements process.

Reference: *PMBOK® Guide* 6th Ed., page 460

161. D. Contract discussion during procurement negotiations covers responsibilities and authorities, overall schedule, payment and price, as well as technical solutions. Project personnel are generally not included during procurement negotiations.

Reference: *PMBOK® Guide* 6th Ed., page 488

162. C. Project documents are among the inputs for Control Procurements. These may include assumption log, lessons learned, milestone list, quality reports, requirements documentation, requirements traceability matrix, risk register, and stakeholder register.

Reference: *PMBOK® Guide* 6th Ed., pages 495-496

163. B. Bidder conferences are meetings used to ensure that all prospective buyers have a clear and shared understanding of the procurement process and so that there is no preferential treatment. Proposal evaluation techniques and procurement negotiations are other tools and techniques in the Conduct Procurement process. Inspections and audits are used in the Control Procurements process.

Reference: *PMBOK® Guide* 6th Ed., page 487

164. C. As long as the defined change control process is followed and both parties agree on the contract amendments, changes can be introduced at any point during the execution of an agreement.

Reference: *PMBOK® Guide* 6th Ed., page 494

165. A. Processes within the Project Procurement Management knowledge area comprise of Plan Procurement Management, Conduct Procurements, and Control Procurements. The Plan Cost Management process belongs to the Project Cost Management knowledge area.

Reference: *PMBOK® Guide* 6th Ed., page 460

166. B. Interpersonal and team skills are tools and techniques of the Conduct Procurements process. Agreements include major components such as procurement statement of work or major deliverables; schedule, milestones, or date by which a schedule is required; performance reporting; and change request handling.

Reference: *PMBOK® Guide* 6th Ed., pages 488-489

167. A. Because of the legal aspect, many organizations treat contract administration as an organizational function that is separate from the project. While a procurement administrator may be on the project team, this individual typically reports to a supervisor from a different department.

Reference: *PMBOK® Guide* 6th Ed., page 494

168. D. A make-or-buy decision is used to determine if particular work can be done by the project team or must be purchased from other sources. The Procurement statement of work outlines the work that the buyer is requesting from the seller. Requirements documentation is not a decision process. Procurement audit is a structured review of the procurement process.

Reference: *PMBOK® Guide* 6th Ed., pages 498-499

169. C. Project organization chart is not an input to the Conduct Procurements process. Inputs to the Conduct Procurements process include procurement management plan, project documents, procurement documentation, seller proposals, enterprise environmental factors, and organizational process assets.

Reference: *PMBOK® Guide* 6th Ed., page 482

170. B. The Control Procurements process is about managing procurement relationships, monitoring performance, and making changes and corrections as necessary. These activities interact directly with the following processes: Direct and Manage Project Work, Monitor and Control Project Work, and Perform Integrated Change Control. Initiate the project is not a process.

Reference: *PMBOK® Guide* 6th Ed., page 494

171. C. Inspections and audits are tools and techniques of the Control Procurements process, not inputs. Inputs to the Control Procurements process include the risk management plan, procurement documentation, agreements, procurement documentation, approved change requests, work performance data, enterprise environmental factors, and organizational process assets.

Reference: *PMBOK® Guide* 6th Ed., page 492

172. D. Data analysis is one of the tools and techniques for Control Procurements process and includes performance reviews, earned value analysis, and trend analysis.

Reference: *PMBOK® Guide* 6th Ed., page 498

173. B. The Control Procurements process administrative activities include collection of data and mapping project records, refinement of procurement plans, set up for gathering, analyzing, and reporting procurement-related data, monitoring the procurement environment, and payment of invoices. Reviewing seller proposals is conducted as a part of the Conduct Procurements process.

Reference: *PMBOK® Guide* 6th Ed., page 494

174. A. The enterprise environmental factors that can influence the Control Procurement process include contract change control system, market conditions, financial management and accounts payable, buying organization's code of ethics. Seller organization's code of ethics is incorrect. .

Reference: *PMBOK® Guide* 6th Ed., page 497

175. D. Archiving the procurement files, payment schedule and requests, lessons learned, seller performance evaluation documentation, prequalified seller lists updates are all organizational process assets that could be updated in the Control Procurement process.

Reference: *PMBOK® Guide* 6th Ed., page 501

176. C. Contested changes are referred to as claims, disputes, or appeals. The correct answer is refund requests because that term is not typically used to refer to contested changes.

Reference: *PMBOK® Guide* 6th Ed., page 498

177. D. Procurement documentation includes the contract with all supporting schedules, requested unapproved contract changes, and approved change requests. Procurement documentation also includes any seller-developed technical documentation and other work performance information such as deliverables, seller performance reports and warranties, financial documents including invoices and payment records, and the results of contract-related inspections.

Reference: *PMBOK® Guide* 6th Ed., page 499

178. D. Tools and techniques for the Control Procurements process include procurement audits, procurement inspections, expert judgment, claims administration, data analysis, and audits. Project budget is not a tool or technique of the Control Procurements process.

Reference: *PMBOK® Guide* 6th Ed., page 492

179. A. Expert judgment, market research, and meetings are tools and techniques of the Plan Procurement Management process, not the Control Procurements process.

Reference: *PMBOK® Guide* 6th Ed., page 492

180. D. Control Procurements process outputs include closed procurements, work performance information, procurement documentation updates, change requests, project management plan updates, updates to the project documents listed above and organizational process assets updates.

Reference: *PMBOK® Guide* 6th Ed., page 492

181. D. The configuration management plan, requirements documentation, and change management plan do not contain the requirements for contract closure. The procurement management plan describes how the procurement process will be managed from developing the procurement documents through contract closure.

Reference: *PMBOK® Guide* 6th Ed., page 499

182. C. Written communication may be formal or information so it not a necessarily reliable evidence of deliverables being accepted or rejected. Change requests do not reflect evidence of acceptance or rejection. Formal written notice is provided by the buyer to the seller as evidence of acceptance or rejection.

Reference: *PMBOK® Guide* 6th Ed., page 499

183. B. Responsibility, respect, and honesty are not correct options because along with fairness, they are the four values identified by PMI. Although hard work is a desirable trait, it is not one of those values.

Reference: *Code of Ethics and Professional Conduct*, pages 2-6

184. C. Stakeholder analysis systematically gathers and analyzes information to determine whose interests should be taken into account throughout the project. Stakeholder analysis is a tool and techniques of the Identify Stakeholders process. Therefore, the project manager is trying to produce a stakeholder register, an output of the Identify Stakeholders process. The project charter, business documents, project management plan, project documents, agreements, enterprise environmental factors, and organizational process assets are inputs used by the Identify Stakeholders process to produce the stakeholder register.

Reference: *PMBOK® Guide* 6th Ed., pages 504, 511-514

185. C. Tools and techniques of the Plan Stakeholder Engagement process include expert judgment, data gathering, data analysis, decision making, data representation, and meetings. Stakeholder engagement plan is an output of the Plan Stakeholder Engagement process. The other options are inputs to this process.

Reference: *PMBOK® Guide* 6th Ed., page 504

186. B. The engagement level of stakeholders can be classified as unaware, resistant, neutral, supportive, and leading. Interested is not one of the valid classifications for analyzing the engagement level of stakeholders.

Reference: *PMBOK® Guide* 6th Ed., pages 521-522

187. A. A stakeholder is considered leading if he is aware of the project and its potential outcomes and is actively engaged in ensuring the project's success. Supportive is a stakeholder who aware of the project and its potential outcomes and is supportive of the project, but not as actively engaged in its success. Neutral is aware of the project yet neither supportive nor resistant. Unaware is unaware of the project and its potential impacts.

Reference: *PMBOK® Guide* 6th Ed., pages 521-522

188. D. Ignoring this behavior can lead to negative effect on the project. Asking the team leader to stop this behavior is an ineffective resolution and ignoring this behavior will lead to deterioration of the relationship with the team. Abusive behavior should be recorded and substantiated so that it can be reported in a factual manner to the appropriate functional manager.

Reference: *Code of Ethics and Professional Conduct*, pages 3-4, 8

189. C. A member of the project team reporting unethical behavior of another team member or complaining of unethical abuse should not automatically trigger disciplinary action before further investigation. A member of the project team filing an ethics-related complaint without substantiating it with facts does not trigger a disciplinary action without further investigation. When a member of the project retaliates against a colleague who raised an ethical complaint against him or her, a disciplinary action is justified.

Reference: *Code of Ethics and Professional Conduct*, page 3

190. B. The options on taking on the project and starting self-learning without letting anyone know, or asking your manager not to inform the customer that you do not have the right knowledge are both unethical behavior. Refusing the project without informing your program manager could lead to lost opportunity. Inform the program manager that you do not have experience working in the nuclear industry and that you are prepared to learn on the job is correct. By doing this you fulfill your ethnical obligation and leave him or her to make the decision concerning how to proceed.

Reference: *Code of Ethics and Professional Conduct*, page 2

191. C. The correct answer to the question is to ask for permission before copying work products. This corresponds to guidelines on intellectual property rights. All the other answers contradict the aspirational standard on responsibility that states we protect proprietary or confidential information that has been entrusted to us.

Reference: *Code of Ethics and Professional Conduct*, page 3

192. D. The stakeholder engagement assessment matrix classifies the stakeholders based on their engagement levels such as unaware, resistant, neutral, supportive, and leading. Both the communications management plan and stakeholder management plans are subsets of the project management plan. The stakeholder engagement plan specifically identifies the strategies to effectively engage the stakeholders.

Reference: *PMBOK® Guide* 6th Ed., page 522

193. A. Through change requests, the Management Stakeholder Engagement process directly interacts with the Perform Integrated Change Control process.

Reference: *PMBOK® Guide* 6th Ed., page 524

194. A. Responsibility/aspirational deals with basing our decisions and actions that are in the best interests of society, public safety, and the environment, and our acceptance of assignments consistent with our background, experience, skills, and qualifications. Honesty/mandatory deals with not engaging in behaviors designed to deceive others, or in dishonest behaviors. Respect/mandatory deals with negotiating in good faith, seeking to understand others, and conducting ourselves in a professional manner. The fairness/mandatory value standard states that "When we realize that we have a real or potential conflict of interest, we refrain from engaging in the decision-making process." Conflicts of interest must be avoided out of the principle of fairness to all parties involved.

Reference: *Code of Ethics and Professional Conduct*, pages 4-5

195. D. The change log, not the issue log, documents the changes that occur during a project. The stakeholder management plan provides guidance on the best way to get the stakeholders involved in the project. In contrast, the communications management plan provides guidance and information on managing stakeholder expectations.

Reference: *PMBOK® Guide* 6th Ed., page 525

196. C. Fairness is about acting impartially and objectively. Responsibility is about taking ownership for the decisions we make. Honesty is about understanding the truth and acting in a truthful manner both in our communications and in our conduct. Project managers are expected to uphold the value of respect, that is, to show high regard for one's self, others, and the people who are working on the project directly and indirectly. Safety of others is part of the resources entrusted to us.

Reference: *Code of Ethics and Professional Conduct*, page 4

197. D. Responsibility includes taking ownership of our decisions; respect encompasses how we treat ourselves, others, and those people who work in the project; and fairness deals with being impartial in our actions. The correct option is honesty because one of its aspirational standards entails providing information in a timely manner.

Reference: *Code of Ethics and Professional Conduct*, page 6

198. D. We need to proactively and fully disclose any real or potential conflicts of interest to the appropriate stakeholders. As a professional project manager, before any decisions involving potential conflict of interest you should make a full disclosure to the affected stakeholders, have an approved mitigation plan, and obtain the consent of the stakeholders to proceed. It is not necessary to report such a situation to the PMI®.

Reference: *Code of Ethics and Professional Conduct*, page 8

199. A. The responsibility/aspirational standard states that "We fulfill commitments that we undertake—we do what we say we will do." Responsibility/mandatory deals with upholding the policies, rules, regulations, and laws, and reporting unethical or illegal conduct to appropriate management. Fairness/aspirational deals with transparency in our decision-making process and objectivity in our actions. Honesty/aspirational deals with seeking to understand the truth, being truthful in our communications and our conduct, and providing accurate information in a timely manner.

Reference: *Code of Ethics and Professional Conduct*, pages 2-3

200. B. The responsibility/mandatory standard states that we should only accept assignments where we have the proper background, experience, skills, and qualifications. Fairness/mandatory deals with fully disclosing any real or potential conflict of interest to the appropriate stakeholders, and refraining from attempting to influence outcomes. Respect/aspirational deals with our behaviors and attitudes toward others. Responsibility/aspirational deals with basing our decisions and actions on the best interests of society, public safety, and the environment, and our acceptance of assignments consistent with our background, experience, skills and qualifications.

Reference: *Code of Ethics and Professional Conduct*, pages 2-3

Bonus Questions

201. D. Given the long duration and the international nature of the project, FP-EPA is the most appropriate contract because it can address the economic fluctuations that may occur during the execution of the project.

Reference: *PMBOK® Guide* 6th Ed., page 471

202. A. Bid or quotation often applies to procurement where the primary consideration is price. As a result, invitation for bid (IFB) or request for quotation (RFQ) is the correct option.

Reference: *PMBOK® Guide* 6th Ed., pages 477, 709, 714

203. A. Project management plan, project documents, approved change requests, enterprise environment factors, and organization process assets are the four inputs of the Direct and Manage Project Work process.

Reference: *PMBOK® Guide* 6th Ed., page 90

204. B. Pre-assignment, negotiation, decision making, and virtual teams are tools and techniques of the Acquire Project Team process.

Reference: *PMBOK® Guide* 6th Ed., page 328

205. C. "The seller can be viewed during the contract life cycle first as a bidder, then as the selected source, and then as the contracted supplier or vendor.

Reference: *PMBOK® Guide* 6th Ed., page 461

Chapter 9: Practice Test D

1. Project Integration Management combines and unifies processes and activities across all knowledge areas. In an agile environment who is responsible for engaging the project team in project integration activities?

A. Project management office
B. Project manager
C. Project manager and the project team members
D. Project management office and the project manager

2. As a project manager, you are handling a project in an adaptive environment with high risk, uncertainty, and changing requirements. In this case, when do you define the project scope?

A. At the beginning of the project and any changes to the scope are progressively elaborated
B. Scope is defined, developed, and refined iteratively through the lifecycle of the project
C. Scope is defined for the highest priority items first; remaining items are defined over time
D. Scope is never defined, the processes are updated using integrated change control if needed

3. In an agile or adaptive environment, within Project Scope Management, what are the two processes that are repeated for each iteration to ensure that the project deliverables within the product backlog meet the current needs?

A. Plan Scope Management and Validate Scope
B. Collect Requirements and Define Scope
C. Define Scope and Control Scope
D. Validate Scope and Control Scope

4. Within Project Schedule Management which tool and technique can be used by both agile and waterfall approaches to deliver incremental value to the customer?

A. Decomposition
B. Schedule management plan
C. Milestone list
D. Rolling wave planning

5. What is the method that is used in a Kanban system to limit the team's work in progress in order to balance the demand against team's delivery output?

A. Iterative scheduling
B. On-demand scheduling
C. Rolling wave planning
D. Schedule compression

6. When an agile approach is used, how is the current status of the project schedule determined?

A. Reprioritizing the remaining work plan against the total time remaining on the project
B. Determining total amount of work delivered and accepted against the elapsed time cycle
C. Comparing estimated amount of work against work remaining to complete the project
D. Comparing the rate of deliverables against estimated work planned for the project

7. The Project Procurement Management processes involve agreements between the two parties—a buyer and a seller. For large projects that may use an adaptive approach, the two parties need to sign one of the following:

A. Strategic partnership agreement
B. Non-disclosure agreement
C. Memorandum of understanding
D. Master services agreement

8. Which of the below types of team compositions would be best suited to deliver an IT project with highly volatile requirements?

A. Virtual team
B. Distributed team
C. Self-organizing team
D. Subject matter experts

9. In high-variability environments using an adaptive or agile approach how are risks best mitigated?

A. Risks are identified during the initial project planning and are managed progressively
B. Risks are addressed during the execution of the project as they are identified and defined
C. Have the project risk exposure within an acceptable range pre-defined for the project
D. Risks are identified and addressed at the beginning and execution of each iteration

10. When an agile or adaptive approach used to deliver a highly-volatile project, within Project Scope Management, how can you refine and bridge the gap between the real business requirements and the originally stated business requirements?

A. Build and review prototypes
B. Use expert judgement
C. Conduct product analysis
D. Document detailed Requirements

11. You are working on an agile/adaptive project with a cross-functional team. What common reflective practice can you adopt to help your team be more efficient when delivering future iterations of the current project?

A. Lessons learned
B. Integration
C. Retrospectives
D. Continuous improvement

12. Which one of the following statements is *not* true when considering team composition on an agile project?

A. Team composition can have a positive or negative impact on team productivity
B. Team composition is directly related to one of the four core agile values
C. Team productivity is independent of team composition and has no impact either way
D. The best architecture, requirements, and design emerge from self-organizing teams

13. One of the agile principles state: "simplicity—the art of maximizing the amount of work not done is essential". Which of the following processes directly support this agile principle?

A. Backlog Preparation and Backlog Refinement
B. Progressive Elaboration and Rolling Wave Planning
C. Data Analysis and Backlog Refinement
D. Prototyping and Rolling Wave Planning

14. Bill has been working on an agile project and he is trying to determine how he can showcase the progress the team has made to his project stakeholders. In an agile/adaptive project what is the primary measure of progress?

A. Working software
B. Team velocity
C. Team composition
D. Benefits realization

15. Ben is leading a new team of generalized-specialists, what advice would you give Ben with regards to the efficient and effective method of conveying information within an agile development team on an ongoing and regular basis?

A. Promote face-to-face conversation
B. Facilitate weekly project status meetings
C. Conduct regular retrospectives
D. Facilitate daily stand-up meeting

16. What is the most common leadership style advocated within agile and adaptive project management practices?

A. Autocratic leadership style
B. Servant leadership style
C. Situational leadership style
D. Transformational leadership style

17. Which one of the following is *not* one of the four values of the *Agile Manifesto*?

A. Customer collaboration over contract negotiation
B. Working software over comprehensive documentation
C. Following a plan over responding to change
D. Individuals and interactions over processes and tools

18. Which of the following characteristics would be true for activities within an iterative or agile project life cycle? Select the most correct answer:

A. Activities are performed once for the entire project
B. Activities are repeated until correct or accepted
C. Activities are performed once for a given product increment
D. Activities are progressively elaborated through the project

19. Bill has been traditionally working in predictive project delivery project. Recently Bill was asked to lead an agile project for a new software release for his company. What is one of the key goals Bill needs to consider in agile project delivery?

A. Manage to the budget of the project
B. Manage to project schedule established
C. Ensure speed of delivery of the new release
D. Deliver value to the customer in frequent intervals

20. The primary difference between iteration-based agile life cycle and a flow-based agile life cycle is:

A. In iteration-based agile life cycle, iterations are time-boxed to a predefined length of time; in a flow-based agile life cycle the iterations are not time-boxed to a predefined duration.
B. Iterations are time-boxed to a predefined length of time for both iteration-based agile life cycle and a flow-based agile life cycle.
C. In iteration-based agile life cycle, the iterations are not time-boxed to a pre-defined duration; in a flow-based agile life cycle the iterations are time-boxed to a predefined length of time.
D. Iterations are not time-boxed to a predefined length of time for both iteration-based agile life cycle and a flow-based agile life cycle.

21. You have been appointed as the program manager of a large and complex e-commerce software development and end-to-end roll-out program for a financial institution. Due to the number of stakeholders and complexity of the program, the initial requirements are not clearly understood. Upon further discussions with the key stakeholders, you determine that the customer has a strong preference to follow a predictive project delivery method. As part of this program there is a roll-out of the services to over a 1,000 retail banks nationwide. Understanding this complexity, you are concerned that you may not be able to deliver the entire project in a predictive way. You ask for a meeting with the project sponsor to convince the sponsor to run the projects within this program in one of the following ways:

A. Largely predictive approach with agile components
B. Agile development followed by a predictive rollout
C. Combine agile and predictive approaches simultaneously
D. Largely agile approach with predictive components

22. Jane is leading a complex project and is demonstrating the following characters: active listening, coaching, and promoting the energy and intelligence of others as well as a safety, respect, and trust. What leadership style is Jane demonstrating?

A. Collaborative leadership
B. Servant leadership
C. Consensus based leadership
D. Distributed leadership

23. Agile/adaptive principles promote the building teams of motivated individuals and advocate giving them the environment and support they need to work as a team to get the job done. Which one of the following statements is not a benefit of agile/adaptive teams focused on optimizing the flow of value?

A. Team members are most likely to collaborate when focused on optimizing the flow of value
B. Teams finish valuable and quality work faster when focused on optimizing the flow of value
C. Teams waste less time as they are dedicated to the project and they do have to multitask
D. Team members focus on their own subject matter expertise to optimize the flow of value

24. Susan is responsible for interfacing with the customer and key stakeholders, managing customer requirements and expectations, and helping the customer determine the work that is of most value to them. What role is Susan playing?

A. Project sponsor
B. Product owner
C. Team facilitator
D. Project manager

25. In a flow-based agile lifecycle, the team pulls features from the backlog based on its capacity to start work rather than on an iteration-based schedule. Which one of the following statements is true with regards to the cycle time required to complete project work? Select the most correct answer.

A. Discussed and agreed by the dedicated and cross-functional project team
B. Can change depending on the time required to build a product feature
C. Determined by the product owner ensuring value is delivered to the customer
D. Time-boxed to the same length of time for each iteration until project completion

26. You have been recently hired as an agile coach in a new company wanting to adopt agile and adaptive project management practices. You observe that some of the functional managers are having a challenge understanding the concept of dedicated teams. In building your case to provide an explanation, which one of the following statements is not true about dedicated team members working in an agile or adaptive project environment?

A. Multitasking reduces the throughput of the team's ability to produce work products
B. Team members can make mistakes when working on multiple priorities simultaneously
C. Dedicated teams can be productive if less than 20% of their time is allocated to other activities
D. Team members assigned to two projects of equal weight cannot work 50% on each project

27. You are working on a new agile project where half the team members are located in New York and the other of the team is based in Sao Paulo, Brazil. What is one of the techniques that can be used to bridge the gap of physical distance for agile teams working from multiple locations with overlapping time zones?

A. Fishbowl windows
B. Team collaboration
C. Continuous integration
D. Pair programming

28. It is highly recommended that every project has a project charter. Among many benefits this document articulates the relevance and objectives of the project for the project team members. When considering an agile project, which one of the following is not one of the key questions a project team would be able to garner from the project charter?

A. Who is the product owner?
B. Why are we doing this project?
C. Who benefits and how?
D. How are we going to work together?

29. You are working on an agile project with very stringent deadlines and it requires the team members to be collaborating with each other on an ongoing basis. Most of the team members happen to be located in the same geographic area. In order to maximize success and ease communication among team members, you decide to promote the idea of the team work in a collocated manner. Which of the following is not a benefit of a co-located team?

A. Better communication
B. Improved team dynamics
C. Better control of teams
D. Reduce cost of learning

30. The team facilitator in an agile or adaptive project is also the servant leader. This role is designed to remove impediments, support the team, and provide a stable work environment among other responsibilities. This role may also be referred any one of the following *except*:

A. Project manager
B. Product owner
C. Scrum master
D. Team coach

31. Retrospectives are an important element of agile project practices as it allows the teams to reflect and make improvements to the product and as well as team processes. The following statement are true about retrospectives *except*?

A. Retrospectives can occur when the team completes a release
B. Retrospectives are mainly facilitated by the product owner
C. Retrospectives can occur when the team appears to be stuck
D. Retrospectives help the team when work is not flowing through

32. The daily standups are a critical success factor to teams working in an agile project. All of the following statements are true about the daily standup meeting in a iteration-based agile project *except*:

A. The daily standups are time-boxed to 15 mins and are typically held at the same time each day
B. The daily standups are a forum where the team can quickly solve identified problems
C. Anyone of the team members including the team facilitator can facilitate a daily stand-up
D. One of the questions that is answered in a daily stand-up is: "what are my impediments?"

33. You are working on creating a new web application in an iteration based-agile project. Once the product features are created they need to be demonstrated to and accepted by one of the following roles:

A. Project sponsor
B. End customer
C. Product owner
D. Team facilitator

34. Bob is working on an agile project. His team is constantly coming up with inaccurate estimates. What is one of the following tactics can Bob suggest to his team in order to alleviate this problem?

A. Try to get more senior members to the team who have experience with agile projects
B. Split larger user stories into smaller ones that are more manageable in a single iteration
C. Ask the product owner to provide better explanations of the requirements to the team
D. Ask the team facilitator to hold a planning meeting to discuss the product requirements

35. In an iteration-based agile project using a Scrum framework, the team develops the items with the highest business value first by collaborating with each other to accomplish the work. The length of time for each iteration is:

A. Time-boxed to a pre-defined duration for each iteration
B. Can change depending on the time required to build each feature
C. Progressively elaborated to fit the needs of the a agile life cycle
D. Determined by the product owner who is representing the customer

36. The project team defined the detailed scope and received approval before the start of the next iteration. They have been repeating this process every month for the past six months now. Whenever they encounter changes, they do their best to incorporate them into the next iteration's detailed scope. This project team is likely following a/an _____ life cycle.

A. Predictive
B. Iterative
C. Incremental
D. Adaptive

37. As part of Project Integration Management knowledge area, what can be expected for a project manager working in an agile/adaptive environment?

A. The expectations from a project manager will not change but the control of the detailed product planning and delivery is delegated to the team.
B. The expectations from a project manager will not change and the control of the detailed product planning and delivery is delegated to the product owner.
C. The expectations from a project manager will change as he/she will not be involved in the teams' day to day work activities.
D. The expectations from a project manager will change as he/she will relinquish all project integration activities to the development team.

38. You are working on a Scrum project to deliver a new electronic card access system and you are responsible for maximizing the business value of the product of the project. In this case what role are you playing?

A. Scrum master
B. Project sponsor
C. Product owner
D. Development team

39. You are working on an agile project that has adopted the Extreme Programming (XP) practices. Within XP there are 12 primary practices that are grouped into four key practice areas (themes). What are the four key practice areas (themes) in XP?

A. Organizational, technical, planning, and integration
B. Technical, integration, communication, and feedback
C. Feedback, technical, planning, and organizational
D. Communication, technical, planning, and integration

40. The Kanban Method may be best used when a team or organization is in need of the following conditions *except*

A. Flexibility – teams are not bound by time-boxes and will work on the highest priority item in a backlog
B. Focus on continuous delivery – teams are focused on flowing work through the system to completion
C. Increased productivity and quality – productivity and quality are increased by limiting work in progress
D. Timeboxing – team can plan, execute, and review the work in increments of predefined time scales

41. Which one of the following project management methods are you practicing if you are visualizing the workflow, limiting work in progress, managing work, and implementing feedback loops?

A. Scrum
B. Extreme Programming (XP)
C. Kanban
D. Crystal Methods

42. If you are working on an agile/adaptive project and you are able to take one or more roles what agile/adaptive method are you practicing? The roles are product manager, chief architect, development manager, chief programmer, domain expert, and class owner?

A. Scrum
B. Extreme Programming (XP)
C. Kanban
D. Feature Driven Development (FDD)

43. You are working on an agile project delivery framework where the emphasis is placed on constraint-driven delivery. You are working on the _____ framework.

A. Kanban
B. Dynamics Systems Development Method (DSDM)
C. Crystal
D. Extreme Programming (XP)

44. You are working for a large telco company and they have just announced that they will be adopting the Scaled Agile Framework (SAFe) for their enterprise level projects. SAFe focuses on providing a knowledge base of patterns for scaling development work across all levels of the enterprise. The SAFe framework is practicing all but one of the following principles:

A. Take an economic view
B. Centralize decision making
C. Apply systems thinking
D. Visualize and limit work in progress

45. Which one of the following statements would be true about the Large Scale Scrum (LeSS) framework?

A. LeSS promotes the use of principles such as systems thinking, whole product focus, and transparency
B. LeSS promotes single team retrospectives that are shared with the larger cross-functional team
C. LeSS promotes multiple product backlogs to be maintained for each team working on the project
D. LeSS promotes the team to work in silos in order to gain focus and efficiency of work completion

46. Disciplined Agile (DA) is a process decision framework that integrates several agile best practices into a comprehensive model. Which one of the following principle is *not* true about DA?

A. People-first
B. Learning-oriented
C. Plan-driven
D. Scalable

47. You are working on an agile method that realizes that each project may require a slightly tailored set of policies, practices, and processes in order to meet the project's unique characteristics. Its core values include: people, interaction, community, skills, talents; and communication. In this case you are practicing the _____ framework.

A. Kanban
B. Dynamics Systems Development Method (DSDM)
C. Crystal
D. Extreme Programming (XP)

48. Which of the frameworks below produce the following artefacts: product backlog, sprint backlog, and product increments?

A. Scrum
B. Dynamics Systems Development Method (DSDM)
C. Crystal
D. Extreme Programming (XP)

49. As it relates to project procurement management in agile/adaptive projects, many vendor relationships are governed by fixed milestones, "phase gates" focused on intermediate artifacts, rather than full deliverable of incremental business value. Payment terms can be structured based on _____ deliverables in order to enhance the project's agility.

A. Value-driven
B. Goal-based
C. Time-based
D. Cost-based

50. Some iteration-based projects use burndown charts to see how the project is progressing over time. Burndown chart show all of the following *except*:

A. Work remaining
B. Rate of completion
C. Work completed
D. Time remaining

51. Tim is new to the role of the product owner. He is trying to grasp various metrics he has available to him. He understands that the sum of the total story points for a feature completed in the past iteration allows the team to plan its next capacity more accurately. This historical performance information is called _____.

A. Throughput
B. Velocity
C. Capacity
D. Burndown

52. Lead time is one of the measurements used by used by flow-based agile teams. Lead time can be defined as:

A. Time it took to deliver an item from the time it was added to the board to the time it was delivered
B. The time required to process an item and response time it took for the team to complete the item
C. The time that an item waits on the prioritized product backlog until work is commenced on the item
D. Cycle time it took to complete the item from the time the customer requested the item until release

53. Jim is a product owner working on an iteration-based agile project. He regularly works with the development team to prepare some stories for the upcoming iteration. He does this during one or more sessions in the middle of the iteration. This process is called _____.

A. Backlog preparation
B. Backlog refinement
C. User story creation
D. Value based prioritization

54. Flow-based agile has a different approach to stand-ups where they focus on team's throughput. During the stand-up meetings the team addresses all *but one* of the following questions:

A. What do we need to do to advance this piece of work?
B. What do we need to complete our individual work?
C. Is anyone working on anything that is not on the board?
D. Are there any bottlenecks or blockers for the flow of work?

55. A short time interval within a project which is usually of a fixed length where a team conducts research or creates a prototype of a solution to provide its validly is called a _____.

A. Sprint
B. Spike
C. Race
D. Pivot

56. A service request manager is equivalent to a product owner and he/she is the person responsible for ordering service requests to maximize value in a continuous flow environment. Which one of the following frameworks typically uses such a role?

A. Scrum
B. DSDM
C. XP
D. Kanban

57. A lean enterprise technique used to document, analyze, and improve the flow of information of materials required to produce a product or service for a customer is called _____.

A. Value based prioritization
B. Value stream mapping
C. Smoke testing
D. Continuous integration

58. You are working on an adaptive/agile project and you and your teammates are collectively working on resolving a specific impediment that is preventing the team from moving forward. This technique is called _____.

A. Collaborating
B. Swarming
C. Mobbing
D. Refactoring

59. An organization structure that is set up in such a way that it only manages to contribute to a subset of the aspects required for delivering value to the customer is called a _____.

A. Hierarchal organization
B. Value based organization
C. Siloed organization
D. Flat organization

60. An information radiator is a visible physical display that provides information to the rest of the organization enabling up-to-the-minute knowledge sharing without having to disturb the team. All *but one* of the following are typical examples of information radiators in agile/adaptive projects:

A. Burndown chart
B. Scrum board
C. Kanban board
D. User story

61. Scrumban is a hybrid agile framework where teams use Scrum as a project management framework and Kanban for process improvement. All but one are characteristics of Scrumban:

A. The work on a Scrumban project is organized into small "sprints"
B. Scrumban uses kanban boards to visualize and monitor the work
C. The work on a Scrumban project is managed by using work-in-progress limits
D. There are unique predefined roles specific to the Scrumban framework

62. A contract structure that allows a level of flexibility by describing different aspects in documents where the fixed items can be locked into a master agreement and dynamic items such as scope, schedule, and budget can be formalized in a lightweight state of work is called a _____.

A. Multi-tiered structure
B. Fixed-price contract
C. Time and materials contract
D. Master services agreement

63. Project agility has many organizational considerations. Business practices that allow agile/adaptive teams to be successful include all *but one* of the following:

A. Procurement teams need to change contracts that allow frequent delivery of value
B. Internal management processes and policies may require greater flexibility
C. The human resources teams may need to employ more individual incentives
D. Finance departments may need to capitalize the product(s) in different ways

64. The process of enhancing the user experience by focusing on improving the usability and accessibility to be found in the interaction between the user and the product it called _____.

A. UAT
B. UX design
C. Beta testing
D. Value streaming

65. The practice of attempting to solve organizational problems by only using specific predefined methods, without challenging the methods in light of experience is called _____.

A. Smoke testing
B. Single loop learning
C. Continuous Improvement
D. Double loop learning

66. One of the four main reasons a project can be initiated is to create, improve, or fix products, processes, or services. Within this umbrella, as it relates to business process improvements, an organization can implement a project resulting for a lean six sigma value stream mapping exercise. Value stream mapping can be defined as a technique that is:

A. Used to document, analyze, and improve the flow of information of materials required to produce a product or service for a customer.
B. A visual practice of organizing work into a useful model to help understand the sets of high-value features to be created over time.
C. A set of guidelines based on achieving quality, speed, and customer alignment thereby delivering business value to the customer.
D. A strategic planning technique that acts as a roadmap to the organization while building new products and services.

67. You are working as part of an agile team and you have come upon a blocker; an issue that is preventing you from proceeding to the next step in the development process. This issue or blocker is more commonly known as a/an_____.

A. Dispute
B. Impediment
C. Concern
D. Obstruction

68. Every project exists in an organizational context where the cultures, structure, and policies can influence both the direction and the outcome of any project. These dynamics can challenge the most experienced project leaders. The preferences of an organization on a set of scales characterized by the following core values: exploration versus execution, speed versus stability, quantity versus quality, and flexibility versus predictability relates to _____.

A. Organizational culture
B. Organizational practices
C. Organizational biases
D. Organizational principles

69. You are working on an adaptive project where you are documenting system or application performance requirements. These requirements are better known as _____.

A. User requirements
B. Functional specifications
C. User stories
D. Impact mapping

70. When working on an adaptive project, it is important for the development team to be able to visualize the end users of the product of the project. A description of the end users, their goals, motivations, and representative personal characteristics can be defined as
_____.

A. User groups
B. Personas
C. Customers
D. Characters

71. What is a commonly known term that can apply to both predictive as well as adaptive projects that describes the iterative process of increasing the level of detail in a project management plan as greater amounts of information and more accurate estimates become available
_____.

A. Backlog refinement
B. Progressive elaboration
C. Refactoring analysis
D. Rolling wave planning

72. When selecting team members to work on an agile project it is important to assemble a team of cross-functional experts. It is advisable to avoid having team members who only have a deep specialization in one specific area, and no other skills or interest in other areas of the project. Which one of the following describes people who only have a deep specialization in one area?

A. Cross-domain experts
B. T-shaped people
C. I-shaped people
D. Generalists-specialists

73. You have been asked to engage in leading an agile transformation project for an insurance company. One of the first things you do is to assess the organization's readiness for this change. You realize that in order to be successful there needs to be executive management's support and willingness to change. The list below identifies some additional attributes required for success. Which would you not be looking for as a characteristic of the organizations' willing to shift the way it views, reviews, and assesses employees?

A. Talent management maturity and capabilities inherent within the organization
B. Focus on short-term budgeting and metrics versus long-term organizational goals
C. Leaders rewarded for local efficiencies rather than end-to-end flow of project delivery
D. Centralization or decentralization of project, program and portfolio management functions

74. The organization's culture is known to be its DNA. When considering an agile transformation journey, it is important to understand how the organization's culture will influence the use of agile approaches. Although organization culture is difficult to change, all but one of the following can influence employees' willing to be open to change:

A. A safe and open work environment
B. Transparency with team members
C. Individual achievements are rewarded
D. An environment that promotes honesty

75. Bob is new to agile approaches. He has been asked to work on an agile project team to re-engineer processes within the organization with a mandate to achieve a 5% efficiency improvement. Jim is an experienced agile coach working in the same organization. Bob decides to seek out some advice from Jim regarding his new project and embracing an agile mindset. All but one of the following questions will help Bob in embracing an agile mindset:

A. How can I help the project team embrace the agile or adaptive practices?
B. What can the team deliver quickly to obtain early feedback and benefit the next delivery cycle?
C. What controls can be put in place to ensure the team delivers the 5% efficiency mandate?
D. How can the servant-leadership approach benefit the achievement of the team's goals?

76. You are working on an agile team focused on a rapid product development project. In order to gain maximum efficiencies, your ideal team size should fall within the following ranges:

A. 15 to 20 team members
B. 3 to 9 team members
C. 12 to 15 team members
D. 9 to 18 team members

77. Rob is a seasoned product owner working on an intense agile project for a new product launch. In order to ensure the project remains as efficient as possible, Rob uses several tactics for product backlog refinement. All but one of the following are ways in which Rob can conduct backlog preparation and refinement:

A. Encourage the team to work as triads of developer, tester, and business analyst to discuss and write user stories that delivery business value to the customer
B. Present the overall story concept to the development team and allow the team the opportunity to discuss and refines the concepts into user stories
C. Work hand-in-hand with the team to find various ways to explore and write the stories together, making sure all the stories are small enough for the team to produce a steady flow work
D. Delegate the story creation process to the role of the team facilitator also known as the servant leader and have them work with the team to create the stories

78. You have been appointed as the team facilitator for a new agile project. Your project sponsor has asked you to work with the product owner to assemble a team of experts to deliver your project. What is the ideal compilation of an agile project team?

A. Cross-functional and co-located
B. Distributed and disbursed
C. Cross-functional and distributed
D. Disbursed and dedicated

79. Adherence to quality norms is vital for successful agile project delivery. There are many technical practices that help the team to deliver at their maximum speed while adhering to quality. Acceptance Test-Driven Development (ATDD) is a technical practice where:

A. The team writes automated tests before creating the product increments for the project
B. The entire team gets together and discusses the acceptance criteria for a work product
C. The team employs system-level testing for end-to-end unit testing building blocks
D. Work is frequently incorporated and retested to determine the product works as intended

80. An agile project team working on a new service deployment project is constantly struggling with being able to remove obstacles and barriers, what might be the possible cause for this condition?

A. Absent product owner
B. Absent project sponsor
C. Absent team facilitator
D. Unclear project expectations

81. Accruing technical debt or design debt refers to deferred cost of work not done at an earlier point in the product life cycle. In an agile project, it is recommended that technical debt be cleared at the end of an iterative cycle or through the progression of the project. All but one of the following are ways in which to avoid or minimize technical debt:

A. Refactoring
B. Defining "done" criteria
C. Agile modeling
D. Swarming

82. You are working on an agile project using a Kanban project management framework. Your team is measuring story points completed versus actual stories completed. Which one of the agile principles do you think the team is violating by only measuring story points?

A. Continuous attention to technical excellence and good design enhances agility
B. The primary measure of progress is working software [working service or product]
C. The best architectures, requirements, and designs emerge from self-organizing teams
D. Business people and developers must work together daily throughout the project

83. The term "lightweight" is commonly used in agile practices. Which one of the following statements is *not* true regarding "lightweight" agile practices?

A. Projects with high-degree of uncertainty can use "lightweight" estimation methods to generate high-level costs for the project
B. Crystal, Kanban, Scrum, FDD, and XP can be considered "lightweight" project management methods within the agile umbrella
C. Colocation and frequent business conversations allow for "lightweight" requirements as gaps in understanding can be easily resolved
D. Detailed requirements need to be provided in order for agile projects to be able to sustain "lightweight" development practices

84. You are working on a hyper-competitive project in the pharmaceutical industry. There are safety critical product components that require additional documentation and conformance checked beyond what the general agile project management frameworks suggest. Given the criticality of the successful outcome your project, which one of the following project management frameworks/approaches might be best suited for your project?

A. Waterfall Approach
B. Scrum Framework
C. Kanban Framework
D. Hybrid Approach

85. In agile projects with a fixed budget contract the supplier may offer the customer the option to vary the project scope at specific predefined points in the project. The customer is given the option to adjust features to fit the capacity and needs of the project. Then the customer can leverage innovation opportunities while limiting the suppliers' risk of over commitment. This contracting technique is called:

A. Early cancellation option
B. Team augmentation
C. Dynamic scope option
D. Fixed price increments

86. As organizations continue to adopt agile practices the traditional role of the project management office (PMO) is also continuing to change and evolve. Which one of the following statements is *not* true about the changing role of the agile PMO?

A. An agile PMO is value-driven
B. An agile PMO is invitation-oriented
C. An agile PMO is multidisciplinary
D. An agile PMO is scope-driven

87. Producing quality products or services is a key defining factor in successful project delivery. Agile methods call for frequent quality reviews through built in steps throughout the project rather than toward the end of the project. Which one of the following statements is *not* true with regards to adherence of quality processes in an agile project?

A. Focus on small batches of work with the aim to uncover inconsistencies and quality issues early
B. Recurring retrospectives regularly check on the effectiveness of the quality processes
C. When considering speed and quality; speed to market is more important than adherence to quality
D. Look for root cause of issues and suggest trials of new approaches as a means to improve quality

88. Team collaboration through dedicated, cross-functional teams is intended to boost productivity and facilitate innovative problem solving. Which one of the following roles provides the team with a platform and work environment conducive to successful team collaboration in an agile/adaptive project?

A. Executive sponsor/functional leader
B. Product owner/service request manager
C. Project sponsor/business owner
D. Team facilitator/servant leader

89. You are developing frequently, providing feedback, and delivering value. What role are you playing in an agile or adaptive project environment?

A. Cross-functional team member/developer
B. Product owner/Service request manager
C. Team facilitator/servant leader
D. Project sponsor/business owner

90. Monitoring and controlling processes are required to track, review and regulate the progress and performance of the project; identify any areas in which changes to plan are required; and initiate the corresponding changes. When working on agile and adaptive projects, which one of the following statements is *not* true with regards to the monitoring and controlling process group on an agile/adaptive project?

A. Sampling progress frequently via short iterative cycles
B. Measuring the number of change impacts and defect remediation
C. Requests for change and defect reports are evaluated by the servant leader
D. Track, review, and regulate progress by maintaining a prioritized backlog

91. The executing processes are performed to complete the work defined in the project management plan to satisfy the project requirements. In most agile, iterative, and adaptive life cycle the work is executed iterations. Which one of following statements is *not* true with regards to the executing process group when working on an agile, iterative, and adaptive life cycle?

A. Each iteration is short, fixed time period to undertake work executed
B. Relevant stakeholders and the team conduct regular retroactive reviews
C. Team members are empowered to self-organize the work executed
D. Only senior team members are included on such projects due to volatility

92. Closing processes are the processes performed to formally complete or close a project, phase, or contract. The work on iterative, adaptive, and agile projects is prioritized to understand the highest business value items first. Which one of the following statement is *true* regarding the iterative, adaptive, and agile projects and the closing process group?

A. If the closing process group prematurely closes a project or phase, there is a high chance that some useful business value will have been realized
B. There is no correlation between the benefits realized and the closing process group in iterative, adaptive, and agile projects
C. An iterative, adaptive, or agile project should never be closed until all the benefits are realized and the full business value is delivered to the customer
D. If the closing process group prematurely closes a project or phase, the project will end and no business value will have been realized

93. Successful agile teams work together and collaborate in a variety ways. A technique in which multiple team members focus simultaneously and coordinate their contribution on a particular work item is called _____.

A. Pairing
B. Mobbing
C. Swarming
D. Teeming

94. A collective approach to defining requirements and business-oriented functional tests for software products based on capturing and illustrating requirement using realistic examples instead of abstract statements is called _____.

A. Prototyping
B. Specification by example
C. Random sampling
D. Impact mapping

95. When two or more agile frameworks, methods, elements, practices are used together such as Scrum in combination with Kanban, or Scrum in combination is extreme programming (XP). This is commonly referred to as:

A. Hybrid approach
B. Blended agile
C. Hybrid agile
D. Mixed methods

96. Projects experiencing a high degree of change require active engagement and participation with stakeholders. The regular interactions with the stakeholder community will help mitigate risk, build trust, and likely increase the success of the project. All but one are tactics for engaging stakeholders actively and regularly:

A. Promote aggressive transparency with all key stakeholders
B. Post project artefacts publically to surface issues quickly
C. Only communicate with stakeholders via the product owner
D. Include stakeholders in project meetings as appropriate

97. Your team is using extreme programming inspired engineering practices. XP advocates a product quality technique whereby the design of a product is improved by enhancing its maintainability and other desired attributes without altering its expected behavior. This practice is commonly referred to as _____.

A. Smoke Testing
B. Pair Programming
C. Refactoring
D. Pair work

98. In agile or adaptive project practices, a unit-less of measure used in relative user story estimation technique is called _____.

A. Affinity estimation
B. Story point
C. User story
D. Relative sizing

99. In an agile or an adaptive project, a project acceleration and collaboration technique whereby any team member is authorized to modify any project work, product, or deliverable, thus emphasizing team-wide accountability is called _____.

A. Collective code ownership
B. Refactoring methods
C. Specification by example
D. Team collaboration

100. A visual practice of organizing work into a useful model to help understand the sets of high-value features to be created over time is called _____.

A. User story mapping
B. User story creation
C. Value stream mapping
D. Rolling wave planning

101. The project charter serves as a document that formally authorizes the existence of a project, and it establishes the partnership between the requestor and the organization performing the work. When working in an adaptive environment, which one of the following statements is true with regards to the project charter?

A. It is a contract between the parties that define the project deliverables
B. It provides details that will need to be included in the release schedule
C. It is a document that is revisited and revalidated on a frequent basis
D. It details the project approach and milestone dates for the project

102. When considering an agile project, a charter alone might not be sufficient to align a project team when initiating the project. To establish standards and norms for the project, an agile team might also utilize one of the following:

A. Collaborative workspace
B. Team charter
C. Documented business case
D. Project vision statement

103. Projects can be established for a number of reasons and they can be undertaken in a variety of ways. Which of the statements below best describes an agile life cycle approach?

A. An approach that allows for feedback to be incorporated so that improvements can be made prior to completion
B. An approach that focuses on defining and planning the work up front, and execution in a sequential process
C. An approach that is both iterative and incremental to refine work items and delivery of output frequently to the customer
D. An approach that delivers finished products or increments to the customer for use immediately after release

104. The fundamental delineation between an iterative life cycle and an incremental life cycle can be best described as:

A. An iterative life cycle allows for feedback of unfinished work whereas an incremental life cycle provides deliverables that the customer may use immediately
B. Both iterative and incremental life cycles allows for continuous feedback throughout the project so that unfinished work can be refined
C. An incremental life cycle allows for feedback of unfinished work whereas an iterative life cycle provides deliverables that the customer may use immediately
D. Both iterative and incremental approaches provide deliverables that the customer may use immediately after release

105. A project life cycle provides the basic framework for managing the project through a series of phases that a project passes through from its inception to its completion. Which of the following statements most accurately describes a hybrid life cycle:

A. A change driven life cycle with multiple phases of project delivery from inception to completion
B. Determines the project budget in the initial phase, but modifies it frequently as changes occur
C. Successively adds functionality to product as the phases of the project continue to evolve and change
D. Known elements of the project are managed predictively, and evolving elements are managed adaptively

106. When developing the project integration management plan, one consideration for an agile or adaptive environment is:

A. That the team members determine how plans and components should integrate
B. The role of the servant leader should ensure the deliverable due dates are aligned
C. Each phase of the project should be completed before the next phase begins
D. The links among the project management process groups may be iterative

107. Managing a project using an agile approach requires the entire team to adopt an agile mindset. In this endeavor many roles will change from established predictive methods. The traditional role of the project manager within an agile environment:

A. Complements the role of the team facilitator by focusing on project documentation and artifacts, while the project manager focuses on the team
B. Changes to put a stronger emphasis on coaching and facilitating the team as well, clears barriers for the team as impediments arise
C. Replaces the role of the product owner to gather and maintain all product-related project requirements from the customer
D. Tracks and manages the status of the agile team's deliverables directs the project work and communicates with all project stakeholders

108. Within Project Cost Management, agile favors empirical and value-based measurements. What would be considered more of a traditional measurement that can also be applied to agile projects?

A. Team velocity
B. Story points remaining
C. Earned value analysis
D. Features delivered

109. Project Quality Management supports continuous process improvement activities as undertaken on behalf of the performing organization. Agile methods call for frequent quality review steps to be built in throughout the project life cycle. These are called:

A. Stage gates reviews
B. Recurring retrospectives
C. Quality checklists
D. Quality audits

110. Project Resource Management practices are changing and evolving. Project with high variability and uncertainty benefit from team structures that maximize focus and collaboration. When considering an adaptive project, the preference is to:

A. Set-up a dedicated, cross-functional, self-organizing team
B. Obtain external resources utilizing the procurement process
C. Utilize highly specialized subject matter experts
D. Leverage functional managers in a matrix environment

111. Product scope is the features and functions that characterize a product, service, or result. When considering an agile environment, who is responsible for defining the scope of the product deliverables?

A. The team facilitator
B. The product owner
C. The project sponsor
D. The customer

112. High variability environments by nature incur more project risk. In order to manage and mitigate these risks, what strategies can be embraced within an environment that has adopted an agile method? Select the most correct answer.

A. Develop a risk mitigation plan with identified risks
B. Re-prioritize risks as they become more probable
C. Frequently review incremental work products
D. Prioritize risks with the greatest potential impact

113. Earned value management (EVM) integrates the scope baseline with the cost baseline and schedule baseline to form the performance measurement baseline. Which of the following traditional EVM metric's can be translated into agile terms for measuring costs?

A. Cost variance
B. Cost performance index
C. Cost baseline
D. Cost trend analysis

114. Changes are inevitable in any project. High-uncertainty projects have high rates of change, complexity, and risks. Agile approaches can explore feasibility in short cycles and quickly adapt based on evaluation and feedback. In an agile project, changes are:

A. Assessed, approved, and communicated to all stakeholders
B. Reviewed, rejected, or deferred by the project manager
C. Embraced for the customer's competitive advantage
D. Are reviewed and added to the next working sprint

115. Successful projects require leaders with strong interpersonal and leadership skills. Leadership is described as the ability to lead a team and inspire them to do their jobs well. In project management, there are multiple leadership theories defining leadership styles that should be incorporated as needed for each situation or team. Which one of the following leadership styles are best suited for an agile project?

A. Laissez-faire
B. Interactional
C. Transactional
D. Servant leader

116. When considering a flow-based agile method, the cumulative flow diagram (CFD) is a great tool for tracking and forecasting project work. When reviewing a CFD, all *but* one are indications that a team has trouble with accumulating work:

A. As the number of tasks starts to increase, the work completed band will also increase
B. A sudden rise within one of the bands can indicate a delay in completing those tasks
C. As the number of completed tasks start to increase, the work in progress starts to increase
D. All bands except work completed should be rising at more or less an even rate

117. David is working on a project that will develop vehicle safety software that will be utilized by fleet management companies. He is responsible for ranking the project work based on its business value to his customer. What role is David playing?

A. Project sponsor
B. Team facilitator
C. Product owner
D. The customer

118. John is working on an agile team that isn't fully utilized at all times and finds that there is an uneven flow of incoming work. He is often waiting for things to work on, and then is rushed to complete assignments. What is one thing that would make a difference during planning to ensure the team is being utilized effectively?

A. Measure work in progress during the start of the project
B. Ask the product owner to clearly define user stories
C. Plan to the team's actual capacity and not to more
D. Shorten iteration cycles to ensure efficiency

119. Teams use daily standup meetings to uncover problems, barriers, issues, and to report status of what each member is working on. This process ensures the team members stay connected with each other and open the lines of communication among each other in a consistent manner. Which of the following questions is *not* asked during the daily standup meetings?

A. What work did I complete?
B. What are the risks or impediments in my way?
C. What new work has come up since the last standup?
D. What am I planning to complete before the next standup?

120. The term "velocity" is commonly used in agile practices. Which one of the following statements best describes velocity?

A. Equals the average number of story points or stories completed in an iteration
B. Average cycle time required to complete a user stories in a given iteration
C. The length of time it takes to release a set of features to a customer
D. Total number of stories completed in each iteration of the project or project phase

121. In Project Resource Management, within the executing process group you are acquiring resources, and developing and managing the team. In order to optimize delivery, agile teams are made up of _____?

A. I-shaped people
B. Generalist-specialists
C. B-shaped people
D. Domain experts

122. An iteration burndown chart improves transparency and visibility and should be displayed in the agile team working area. An iteration burndown chart can provide valuable data at a glance, but does *not* include:

A. The amount of work remaining
B. The amount of work completed
C. A diagonal line representing ideal time
D. A trend line to calculate forecast completion

123. A newly formed agile team is working together for the first time. At the beginning of the project, the team estimated that they could complete 26 story points per iteration. Each iteration is two weeks in duration, and they have planned to complete 16 iterations. At the end of the first iteration, the team completed 23 story points. What is their SPI (schedule performance index)?

A. 88%
B. 80%
C. 12%
D. 40%

124. If an agile team has a total fixed budget of $3.5M and they have spent $2.8M to date and have completed 90% of the project deliverables within 22 of the 30 iterations planned, what is their CPI (cost performance index)?

A. 85 cents on the dollar
B. 80 cents on the dollar
C. 95 cents on the dollar
D. 91 cents on the dollar

125. The various agile approaches practiced today share common roots with the agile mindset, values, and principles. Which of the following statements is true in an agile environment?

A. Agile processes promote sustainable development maintaining a constant pace
B. Maintaining organizational assets and documentation is the responsibility of the team
C. Comprehensive documentation is essential for completing the project deliverables
D. Project scope, time, and costs are defined by at the beginning by the product owner

126. Julie is the product owner at a marketing company. Her project is launching a new social media platform that is being customized for internal use. A key feature is not working as intended, and Julie has declined to accept the product increment created by the team. In what forum would this occur?

A. A retrospective meeting
B. A backlog planning session
C. A demonstration/review meeting
D. A project close-out meeting

127. Agile methods are based on the premise that it is better to deliver small batches of work frequently. This allows teams to identify any issues or inconsistencies early in the project. This is particularly useful when monitoring and controlling _____?

A. Project schedule
B. Project quality
C. Project risk
D. Project resources

128. Linda works for an organization that is complementing its existing product line to introduce a new add-on product that already has some competition in the market. She wants to release something quickly, as there is a noticeable drop in sales revenue as customers opt to select a single vendor that meets their needs. Linda is very familiar with the top three features the competition offers, and wants to release something comparable, but also has plans to introduce supplementary features that differentiate Linda's company from the rest. Linda has managed to get one of her existing customers to agree to participate in a pilot program and provide real-time feedback. Because requirements are still evolving, the team is taking an iterative and agile approach to the scope of the project. A key benefit to this approach is that:

A. Agile methods build and review prototypes and in order to refine the requirements
B. Agile methods allow you to release product faster in order to boost sales revenues
C. An agile approach is more competitive than other more traditional methods
D. Agile methods utilize cross-functional teams which have broader market experience

129. Integrated change control is the process of reviewing, approving, and managing all change requests. In an agile environment changes are primarily evaluated based on _____?

A. Alternatives analysis
B. Multicriteria decisions
C. Business value
D. Cost-benefit analysis

130. When addressing the improvement opportunities/items that were identified during the retrospective, the following guideline should be taken into consideration:

A. The items should be reviewed and prioritized by the product owner
B. The team should complete all items that were identified prior to the iteration
C. The number of action items should be limited to the teams' capacity
D. Items identified through qualitative measures should be discarded

131. Acceptance criteria are considered to be a set of conditions that are required to be met before deliverables are accepted. Which of the following statements is true with regards to acceptance criteria?

A. Acceptance criteria is defined by the team
B. Every user story has unique acceptance criteria
C. Acceptance criteria is only used in agile projects
D. "Done" criteria is the same as acceptance criteria

132. Business value can be defined as the net quantifiable benefit derived from a business endeavor. That benefit may be tangible and/or intangible. Predictive projects typically deliver business value at the end of the project. Which of the statements below best describe the delivery of business value in an agile or adaptive project?

A. Business value is delivered upon validation of the scope of the project
B. Team can maximize business value through successive prototypes
C. Business value is delivered once the product backlog has been prioritized
D. Agile or adaptive projects deliver business value at the end of project

133. Lucy is a new tester who has recently joined your iteration based agile project. As the servant leader, you are helping Lucy get acclimated to the terminology and processes of iteration based agile. All but one of the statements below describe time-boxing in iteration based agile practices:

A. Pre-agreed, consistent duration that aids with scheduling of project meetings
B. Daily-stand-ups, iteration planning, retrospectives, and demos are time-boxed
C. Daily stand-ups are time-boxed to no longer than 15 mins of duration each day
D. Kanban Method uses time-boxing to plan for work capacity and throughput

134. Which one of the following best describes the "definition of done"?

A. Team checklist of the criteria that needs to be met in order for a deliverable to be considered complete
B. A unique set of criteria for each user story required to be defined when the user story is created
C. A team checklist of for a user-centric requirement that has all the information the team requires
D. Set of team best practices and generally accepted norms for a successful project outcome

135. Requirements that describe the environmental conditions or qualities required for the product to be effective including reliability, security, performance, safety, level of service supportability and retention are known as:

A. Functional requirements
B. Non-functional requirements
C. Business requirements
D. Stakeholder requirements

136. _____ provides a high-level summary schedule which determines the features to be developed and shipped to the customer at predefined intervals of time considering blackout windows, seasonality, and customer requirements among other factors.

A. Iteration planning
B. Schedule baseline
C. Agile release planning
D. Schedule compression

137. You are working on a large scale agile project and portions of the project work is being contracted to a third party service provider. In this case, due to the adaptive nature of your project, how do you ensure the work is progressing and the schedule is under control?

A. Assign someone from your project team to monitor and control the 3rd party's work schedule
B. Only contract portions of the work that can be easily managed, executed, monitored, and controlled
C. Ensure regular milestone status updates are provided by the 3rd party contractors and suppliers
D. Include members of the 3rd party contractor to participate in all meetings related to the project

138. Jim is working on a new iteration based agile project. How would Jim ensure his team captures the best practices or lessons learned?

A. Conducting retrospectives
B. Conducting JAD sessions
C. Conducting project reviews
D. Conducting status meetings

139. In an iteration based agile environment, which is one of the following tools and techniques can be used in the control schedule process?

A. Critical path method
B. Burndown chart
C. Expert judgment
D. Performance reviews

140. You are working on a high-variability agile project with a strict budget. In this case, which of the following statements is true with regards to project cost management?

A. The cost of resources is the factor with the highest degree of variability
B. Limiting the number of design reviews may increase the project cost
C. The scope and schedule are often adjusted to stay within cost constraints
D. Cost management planning is done once at the beginning of the project

141. When working on an adaptive project where functionality of the product of the project will be required to be ready for the customer at varying time intervals based on business needs, dependencies and other variables, which one of the following provides a high-level summary timeline, typically three to six months ahead for the project team to know what specific functionality needs to be ready and by when?

A. Project schedule
B. Release plan
C. Product roadmap
D. Program schedule

142. You have been recently hired as an agile coach for an organization that is transitioning from predictive project methods to more hybrid and agile approaches. Which one of the following techniques would you recommend the project teams use to generate project labor forecasts for a project with a high degree of variability?

A. Detailed estimation
B. Lightweight estimation
C. Funding limit reconciliation
D. Cost aggregation

143. _____ gauge the root-cause of the issues and improve the effectiveness of the quality process in an adaptive environment.

A. Quality management plans
B. Recurring retrospectives
C. Project quality audits
D. Quality metrics and reviews

144. In an iteration based adaptive project, validate scope and control scope are the two processes repeated for each iteration. What two key roles are typically engaged in these processes?

A. Project sponsor and product owner
B. Stakeholders and project team members
C. Project sponsor and customer representatives
D. Project team members and servant leader

145. When considering an unpredictable, fast-paced, and highly competitive environment where the long-term scope if difficult to define, iterative and on-demand scheduling are the approaches adapted to provide feedback and suitability of deliverables. Which is the primary knowledge area that can provide guidance to such issues?

A. Project integration management
B. Project risk management
C. Project schedule management
D. Project scope management

146. Agile release planning provides a high-level summary timeline of the release schedule based on the product roadmap, its vision, and evolution. What is the average length of time typically considered for a high-level summary timeline of a release schedule?

A. 2 to 5 months
B. 3 to 6 months
C. 1 to 6 months
D. 2 to 6 months

147. What is the practice in modern project quality management that creates value, optimizes costs, and resources and meets the customer's needs and expectations?

A. Management ownership and accountability
B. Continual improvement such as PDCA
C. Mutually beneficial partnership with suppliers
D. Customer satisfaction and delivery of value

148. Modern quality management approaches seek to minimize variation and to deliver results that meet the requirements. In agile environments, customer satisfaction is maintained throughout the project by engagement of the team and _____.

A. Project owner
B. Project sponsor
C. Stakeholders
D. End users

149. Jim is opening a new restaurant. One of Jim's friends who works in the mobile app industry advises Jim that he should consider launching a mobile app to help customers place take out-orders ahead of coming to the store. Jim thinks that a mobile app would be a great idea, but he is concerned as he is operating on a very tight budget. Jim's friend introduces Jim to a senior product owner in his company for an introductory meeting. How best to you think this senior product owner should best advise Jim?

A. Advise Jim that the scope and schedule for the app can be adjusted to stay within cost constraints to launch an app with basic functionality
B. Explain to Jim that the project can only be initiated once the appropriate budget can be set aside for the full functionality of the mobile app
C. Due to the cost constraints, advise Jim that a project of this nature can only be initiated once the full scope of the project can be determined
D. Explain to Jim that a cost management plan needs to be derived, therefore, Jim needs to decide on the functionality of the app

150. Project Quality Management includes the processes to identify, acquire, and manage the resources needed for the successful completion of the project. When working on an agile or adaptive project, when should the quality reviews be conducted?

A. Prior to the product being released
B. Towards the end of the project
C. At the beginning and end of project
D. Throughout the project life cycle

151. One of the 12 agile principles states that "simplicity-the art of maximizing the amount of work not done-is essential." All but one of the following statements support this principle.

A. Work on only what is essential and valuable to the customer
B. Avoid duplicating effort by multiple team members
C. Complete all committed work to ensure success of the project
D. Large number of features developed are rarely used by the customer

152. Agile principles encourage you to build projects around motivated individuals and give them the environment and support they need as well trust them to get the ~~job~~ done. All *but* one of the following supports this principle:

A. Encourage the team to self-organize the work
B. Promote open communication via daily stand-ups
C. Help the team by directing the project work
D. Provide colocated team workspaces

153. When considering a project where there is very limited opportunity for interim deliverables, what is the most suitable project life cycle the team should select?

A. Predictive life cycle
B. Iterative life cycle
C. Incremental life cycle
D. Agile life cycle

154. How best can one describe the relationship between lean, agile, and the Kanban Method?

A. Lean, agile, and Kanban are disparate methods
B. Agile and Kanban are descendants of lean thinking
C. Kanban is not considered an agile method
D. Kanban is more prescriptive than some agile approaches

155. All *but* one of the following are true with regards to prototypes.

A. Prototypes encourage feedback and understanding of requirements
B. Progressive elaboration can occur through the use of prototyping
C. Prototypes provide the opportunity for obtaining early feedback
D. Prototyping is most often used in projects that use agile methods

156. When a team transitions from traditional predictive methods to more agile methods, the measurements used to track progress will also change. Which one of the following statements is true with regards to predictive measurements?

A. You can easily compare the progress of multiple agile teams
B. They often do not reflect the real state of the project
C. Valuable information such as % complete are provided
D. Provides ample time on warnings when a project is in trouble

157. The Agile Manifesto values "customer collaboration over contract negotiation." When negotiating procurements and contracts, it may be a good idea to take a more collaborative approach with vendors, and decompose the scope into micro deliverables to limit the financial risk of over-commitment to a single deliverable. This type of contracting technique is called _____.

A. A multi-tiered structure
B. Fixed-price increments
C. Graduated time and materials
D. Dynamic scope option

158. Agile team experience productivity losses between 20% and 40% when they are_____.

A. Task switching
B. Multitasking
C. Being blocked
D. Swarming

159. You are the new vice president of the e-commerce division for your company. After careful consideration, you would like to make a recommendation that your business group adopts using agile and adaptive project practices. You realize that you have a very limited number of resources who are trained in agile methods. To support this transformation effort, you decide to bring in an external agile coach. All *but* one of the following is true with regards to inviting an external agile coach into your organization.

A. When the coaching capability is not yet developed within the organization, an external coach may be required
B. External coaches have the advantage of experience and knowledge from working in a variety of organizations
C. If the role of the servant leader has yet to be established, an external coach can replace the need for this role
D. External coaches can provide unbiased and impartial views of the issues and challenges that may arise

160. An agile team charter may include items such as working agreements, meeting ground rules, and what the definition of done means to the team. The team charter can also be referred to as the _____.

A. Acceptance criteria
B. Social contract
C. Resource management plan
D. Team manifesto

161. In order to ensure relevant project information is shared with the right people at the right time across the organization, agile principles promote:

A. Adjustments to the project life cycle
B. Team empowerment
C. Aggressive transparency
D. Enterprise awareness

162. A fundamental for agile projects is to deliver working product frequently. When considering an iteration based agile project, which one of the below statements is *not* true?

A. The team demonstrates completed work items at the end of the iteration
B. The product owner reviews the product increments for acceptance/rejection
C. Only the fully completed items are demonstrated to the product owner
D. The demonstration reviews are generally scheduled in four to six week cycles

163. When implementing agile delivery, there are often impacts to the organization that should be taken into consideration. Which one of the following is *not* an impact on agile or accelerated delivery?

A. Customer acceptance of the project outputs becomes more prevalent
B. There may be more frequent handoffs between teams, departments, or vendors
C. Traditional project management methodologies will become obsolete
D. Iterative prototypes that involve re-work might be perceived as negative

164. The Kanban Method can be used in a variety of settings and is considered to be less prescriptive than other agile approaches. Unlike other agile methods Kanban does *not* promote the notion of _____.

A. Continuous delivery
B. Time-boxing
C. Flexibility
D. Just-in-time delivery

165. In iterative agile projects, the product owner will often work with the team to prepare user stories for the upcoming iteration in a backlog refinement session. Which one of the following is not a characteristic of a backlog refinement?

A. The overall story concept is presented to the team by the product owner
B. The product owner works with the team to write the stories together
C. Teams discusses and refines the concepts into as many stories as required
D. The product owner will provide rough estimate on all stories in the backlog

166. During the monitoring and controlling phase of the project, a project manager is monitoring the process of ensuring project information is shared with the project team and stakeholders. The preferred method for communicating in an agile environment is_____.

A. Informal communication
B. Push communications
C. Pull communications
D. Face-to-face communication

167. In high variability projects, lean methods and agreements for fast supply are important to control costs and achieve the project schedule. Which knowledge area does this relate to?

A. Project schedule management
B. Project cost management
C. Project scope management
D. Project resource management

168. All projects are risky since they are unique undertakings with varying degree of complexity that aim to deliver benefits hence organizations take a pragmatic approach to managing risks in a controlled and intentional manner to create value while balancing risk and reward. How are risks managed and understood in high-variability agile projects?

A. Frequent reviews of deliverables at the end of the project
B. Promoting knowledge sharing among the team members
C. Project manager assesses risks at the beginning of the project
D. A risk specialist manages the risks in high-variability agile projects

169. Although adaptive projects promote face-to-face communication, this is not always possible when considering global teams. Which of the following are key considerations related to project communication management for a global team using adaptive project practices?

A. Gain agreement on the use of spoken and written language
B. Review options for the use of communication technology
C. Evaluate the use of knowledge management repositories
D. Estimate the cost of setting up global versus local teams

170. Earned schedule (ES) is an emerging trend in project cost management. All *but* one of the statements below are true with regards to earned schedule (ES):

A. Earned schedule theory replaces the schedule variance measures used in traditional EVM
B. If the amount if earned schedule is greater than 0, then the project is considered ahead of schedule
C. The schedule performance index (SPI) using earned schedule metrics can be noted as ES/AT (actual time)
D. Earned schedule (ES)/actual time (AT) indicates the efficiency with which the work is being planned

171. Susan is working on an agile project. The project sponsor is looking for detailed estimates for her project. What should Susan say to her project sponsor?

A. Detailed estimates are reserved for short-term planning horizon in a just-in-time fashion
B. Detailed estimates cannot be provided for projects being executed in an agile environment
C. Detailed estimates can only be provided once the full scope of the project has been defined
D. Detailed estimates are subject to change as the requirements of the project change and evolve

172. In project integration management, one of the key considerations given is the selection of the development life cycle and approach that is most appropriate for the product, service, or result being created. All *but* one of the following are true with regards hybrid approaches:

A. Ideal when there is a high degree of uncertainty early in the project life cycle followed by predictive execution
B. Can be used as an interim approach when an organization is transitioning from traditional to agile methods
C. Well known elements can be executed predictively; evolving requirements executed iteratively
D. Only appropriate for projects incorporating one or more agile approaches such as Scrum and Kanban

173. One of the agile principles states that "business people and developers must work together daily throughout the project." All *but* one of the following practices supports this agile principle:

A. Product owner works to prepare and refine the backlog
B. Servant leader works to clear barriers and issues for the team
C. The customer attends all meetings to support the agile team
D. Product owner works with the team to create the user stories

174. When considering an agile mindset, what are the three critical factors in delivering value to the customer?

A. Inspection, adaption, and transparency
B. Transparency, communication, and collaboration
C. Communication, collaboration, and adaption
D. Collaboration, inspection, and communication

175. Implementing _____ is important to maintaining effective relationships with the stakeholders in an adaptive project.

A. A stakeholder engagement plan
B. Automated tools
C. A project charter
D. Communication strategies

176. All *but* one of the following statements are emerging trends and practices in project communications management.

A. Inclusion of stakeholders in project and review meetings
B. Taking a multifaceted approach to project communication
C. Increased use of social computing and social media
D. Engaging with stakeholders who are most affected

177. When considering project risk management, most projects focus only on risks that are uncertain future events that may or may not occur. As project management practices evolve and the focus of risk management broadens, non-event risks now need to be considered. Which of the following two are considered non-event risks?

A. Variability risks and ambiguity risks
B. Technical risks and management risks
C. Commercial risks and technical risks
D. Ambiguity risks and external risks

178. Emotional intelligence is described as the ability to identify, assess, and manage the personal emotions of oneself and other people, as well as the collective emotions of groups of people. When one has invested in personal emotional intelligence (EI), they display all *but* one of the following characteristics:

A. Increased self-awareness and self-management
B. Advanced relationship management skills
C. Ability to perceive and manage others' feelings
D. Politically astute and able to make things happen

179. Planning for physical and human resources is much less predictable in high variability projects. Concepts such as just-in-time (JIT), Kaizen, total productive maintenance (TPM), the theory of constraints (TOC) is based on one of the following and can be embraced for fast supply and better cost management:

A. Agile practices
B. Lean management
C. Agile Manifesto
D. Kanban

180. Some projects may be referred to as complex and difficult to manage. Complex can also be described as intricate or complicated. The three dimensions of complexity can be defined as:

A. System behavior, human behavior, and ambiguity
B. Organizational behavior, ambiguity, and system behavior
C. Human behavior, organizational behavior, and lack of strategy
D. Lack of strategy, organizational behavior, and system behavior

181. Emerging trends and practices in modern project quality management seek to minimize variation and deliver results that meet defined stakeholder requirements. What is the practice in modern project quality management that creates value, optimizes costs and resources and meets the customer's needs and expectations through joint relationships?

A. Management accountability and responsibility
B. Continual improvement such as PDCA
C. Mutually Beneficial partnership with suppliers
D. Customer satisfaction by meeting expectations

182. The role of the servant leader or team facilitator is typically responsible for creating and promoting a stable work environment for a team working on an agile project. All *but* one are goals of achieving a stable work environment:

A. The team can depend on each other to deliver the committed work
B. Intellectual capability is preserved and expanded as necessary
C. Team members with specialized skills are gathered for the project
D. A common understanding is developed for the approach to the work

183. Transparency and open collaboration are critical success factors in agile or adaptive projects. Team members are encouraged to discuss and share their work throughout the project. All *but* one of the following statements are true with regards to transparency in agile/adaptive projects:

A. Transparency requires courage to be able to openly communicate issues, challenges, and failures
B. Leading by example is a great way to ensure team members also feel comfortable to be transparent
C. Fear of failure is one of the main reasons that prevent team members from being open and transparent
D. Aggressive transparency is openly sharing issues, regardless of impact with senior management for support

184. A basic system or structure of ideas or facts that support an approach is called a
_____.

A. Framework
B. Methodology
C. Practice
D. Principle

185. Which of the following is *not* true about agile release planning in Project Schedule Management?

A. It provides a detailed summary timeline of the release schedule
B. Product owner and the team decide on release planning schedule
C. It helps in determining the number of sprints in the release
D. Helps the team determine the timeline for a releasable product

186. Which one of the following statements is *not* true with regards to an agile practitioner?

A. An agile practitioner is similar to the role of a servant leader who leads by serving their team
B. People who embrace the agile mindset and collaborate with like-minded colleagues
C. Agile practitioners evaluate and select the most appropriate agile practices for their projects
D. Some agile practitioners feel the role of the project manager is not needed as teams are self-organizing

187. All but one of the following statements are true with regards to distributed and dispersed teams.

A. Use of tools such as instant messaging, video conferencing, and electronic team boards can bridge the gap of physical distance among team members
B. When team members are disbursed, consider using iteration-based agile approaches in groups of two or three people working together more frequently
C. Dispersed teams may have each team member working in a completely different location, either in an office, or any other location
D. Distributed and dispersed teams are not recommended for agile and adaptive projects due to issues of physical distance among team members

188. Which one of the following statements is true with regards to "methodology"?

A. A system of practices, techniques, procedures, and rules used by those who work in a discipline
B. A basic system or structure of ideas or facts that support an approach
C. Appropriate combination of processes, inputs, tools, techniques, outputs, and life cycle phases
D. A document established by an authority, custom, or general consent as a model for example

189. Disciplined Agile (DA) is a process decision framework that integrates several agile best practices into a comprehensive model. Which one of the statements is *not* true with regards to Disciplined Agile (DA)?

A. DA was designed to offer a balance between those popular agile methods that are too narrow in focus
B. DA is specific to a particular set of business processes and is not scalable across the enterprise
C. DA tailors processes to achieve specific outcomes and offers guidance on cross-departmental governance
D. DA puts people first enumerating roles and organization elements at various levels

190. Enterprise Scrum is a framework designed to apply the Scrum method on more holistic organizational level rather than a single product development effort. Which of the following *not* true with regards to enterprise Scrum?

A. Extends the use of Scrum across all aspects of the organization
B. Generalizes the Scrum techniques to be applied across various scenarios
C. Most suitable for use in small to medium size organizations only
D. Scales the Scrum method with supplemental techniques as necessary

191. All but one of the below statements are true with regards to a team charter:

A. Establishes team values, agreements, and operating guidelines and principles for the team
B. It is prepared by the project manager or the role of a servant leader in agile projects
C. Outlines clear expectations regarding acceptable behavior by the project team members
D. It should be reviewed periodically to ensure a continued understand by all team members

192. All *but* one are true with regards to multi-project management within agile and adaptive projects:

A. Coordinates between agile/adaptive teams by communicating among multiple projects
B. Supports the sharing of information such as progress, issues, and retrospective findings
C. Sets the direction and guidance for the project team on how to proceed with the project
D. Helps manage major customer releases at the program level and portfolio level investments

193. When considering an agile or adaptive approach in an organization that is procurement-heavy, all but one of the following would be concerns that should be considered, addressed, and managed:

A. Although contracts govern the two parties, vendors typically look after their own financial viability
B. Once a project has been completed all the knowledge also exits as the vendor completes the project
C. Using a vendor limits the internal competencies needed for sustained flexibility and speed of delivery
D. Using vendors in an agile or adaptive projects is not recommended and should be limited where possible

194. Which one of the following agile practices embrace osmotic communications?

A. Scrum
B. Kanban
C. DSDM
D. Crystal

195. Scrum of Scrums is a technique that is used when two more Scrum teams consisting of three to nine members each need to coordinate their work instead of establishing one large Scrum team which can be inefficient. In Scrum of Scrums, a representative from each team attends a meeting with other team representatives with the goal of ensuring the teams are coordinating work and removing impediments to optimize the efficiency of all the teams. What is another term that can be used to describe Scrum of Scrums?

A. Macro Scrum
B. Meta Scrum
C. Mega Scrum
D. Scaled Scrum

196. Which one of the following agile methods uses the role of a flow master?

A. Scrum
B. Kanban
C. Extreme programming
D. Feature Driven Development

197. The continuum of project life cycles can be defined as:

A. The series of phases that a project passes through from its start to its completion
B. A form of project life cycle in which the project scope, time and cost are determined
C. An approach that is both iterative and incremental to refine work items and delivery frequently
D. A life cycle that provides finished deliverables to the customer may be able to use immediately

198. Your organization has been tagged to deliver a service improvement project that touches many internal business groups. You are considering using an adaptive method, however, due to the sheer size and scale of the project you are not sure if this would be a viable option. When considering a large project which one of the following tailoring considerations would you make?

A. Learn about agile program management and then craft an approach that fits the project context
B. Consider kicking off the project discovery using adaptive approaches and then move to a predictive delivery
C. Combine the most appropriate adaptive and predictive methods and be open making changes along the way
D. Due to the size of the project and complexity, it is best to use a predictive approach to ensure project success

199. The role of a service request manager is closely aligned to which of the following roles?

A. Servant leader
B. Project sponsor
C. Product owner
D. Project manager

200. Agile projects often deal with high rates of change or uncertainty. If you are finding that you need to ask the team to check in more frequently, visibly track impediments on an impediment board, and you are trying to visualize the flow of work in progress, you are most likely experiencing:

A. Impossible stakeholder demands
B. Unexpected or unforeseen delays
C. Siloed teams, rather that cross-functional teams
D. Unclear work assignments

Bonus Questions

201. The following are trends and emerging practices in Project Integration Management process *except* _____ .

A. Identify business needs
B. Use of automated tools
C. Use of visual management tools
D. Expanding the project manager's responsibilities

202. Which of the following factors should be considered when tailoring the application of Project Scope Management processes?

A. Management approaches
B. Knowledge and requirements management
C. Development life cycle
D. Lessons learned

203. Which of the following are trends and emerging practices in Project Schedule Management knowledge area?

A. Use of automated tools and use of visual management tools
B. Project knowledge management and hybrid methodologies
C. Iterative scheduling with a backlog and on-demand scheduling
D. Inclusion of earned schedule (ES) into earned value management (EVM)

204. General financial management techniques include _____ which are key concepts for Project Cost Management.

A. Deliverables alignment, knowledge creation and management, and data collection
B. Adaptive life cycles, predictive approaches, product backlog, and scope baseline
C. Defining activities, sequencing activities, and estimating activity durations
D. Return on investment, discounted cash flow, and investment payback analysis

205. Which of the following is *not* considered a trend or emerging practice in Project Quality Management?

A. Emotional intelligence
B. Customer satisfaction
C. Continual improvement
D. Management responsibility

Chapter 10: Answers to Practice Test D

1. **C.** The agile approach promotes the engagement of team members and the team is encouraged to determine how plans and components must integrate. The project manager focuses on building an environment that promotes collaborative decision-making and provides a platform where the team is able to respond to the changes.

    Reference: *PMBOK® Guide*, 6th Ed., page 74

2. **B**. In an adaptive or agile life cycle where projects have evolving requirements and high risk, the scope may not be fully defined or understood at the beginning of the project. According to the *PMBOK® Guide*, "There is often a gap between the real business requirements and the business requirements that were originally stated." Therefore, the deliverables are developed over multiple iterations where a detailed scope is defined and approved for each iteration before it begins.
    Reference: *PMBOK® Guide*, 6th Ed., page 133

3. **D**. In an agile or adaptive environment, Validate Scope and Control Scope are the two processes within the Monitoring and Controlling process group that are repeated for each iteration to ensure the project deliverables meet the current needs. These processes are supported by the sponsor and customer representatives through their continuous engagement by providing feedback on deliverables to ensure the product backlog reflects the current needs. Collect Requirements, Define Scope, and Create WBS processes are also repeated in an agile or adaptive environment, however, those processes are part of the Planning Progress Group.

    Reference: *PMBOK® Guide*, 6th Ed., page 131

4. **D.** Rolling wave planning is an iterative planning tool and technique where value can be delivered to the customer incrementally. The work that needs to be delivered near term is planned in detail, whereas the work in future is planned at a higher level. Decomposition is a tool and technique used for dividing and subdividing the project scope and project deliverables into smaller, more manageable parts. The schedule management plan is an input into Define Activities process and the milestone list is an output.

    Reference: *PMBOK® Guide*, 6th Ed., page 185

5. **B.** "On-demand scheduling is based on the theory-of-constraints and pull-based scheduling concepts from lean manufacturing." This method pulls work from a queue to be done on a priority basis as the resources become available to optimize the team's throughput. Iterative scheduling is a form of rolling wave planning where the requirements are documented and prioritized and refined prior to construction. Schedule compression is a technique used to shorten or accelerate the schedule duration without impacting the scope of the project.

    Reference: *PMBOK® Guide*, 6th Ed., page 177

6. B. When an agile approach is used in the Control Schedule process, the status of project schedule can be determined by comparing the total amount of work delivered and accepted against the estimates of work completed for elapsed time cycle as work is time-boxed in iterations.

Reference: *PMBOK® Guide*, 6th Ed., page 224

7. D. When an adaptive approach is used on large scale projects where the scope cannot be fully defined in the beginning of the project, a master services agreement (MSA) can be put in place to serve as the governing agreement between two parties. According to the *PMBOK® Guide*, "this allows changes to occur on the scope of the project without impacting the overall contract." The adaptive work can be defined in an appendix or supplementary document. Strategic partnership agreement and a non-disclosure agreement are not terms defined in the *PMBOK® Guide*. A memorandum of understanding is an agreement (verbal or written) that defines the initial intentions of a project.

Reference: *PMBOK® Guide*, 6th Ed., page 465

8. C. IT projects with highly volatile requirements can use an agile approach with a self-organizing team of generalized specialists rather than a team of subject matter experts, who can adapt to the changing environment with an absence of centralized control to deliver maximize business value to the customer. Although the self-organizing team can be virtual or distributed, the best answer for this question is a self-organizing team.

Reference: *PMBOK® Guide*, 6th Ed., page 310

9. C. High-variability environments incur more uncertainty and risks. These risks are identified, analyzed, and managed during each iteration of the project through frequent reviews and knowledge sharing using a cross-functional project team. Although the other options may be partially correct, the best answer to this question is "Identifying and addressing risks at the beginning and execution of each iteration."

Reference: *PMBOK® Guide*, 6th Ed., page 400

10. A. As stated in the *PMBOK® Guide*, "agile methods build and review prototypes and release versions in order to refine requirements". The scope is defined and redefined throughout the project to bridge the gap between the real business requirements and the originally stated business requirements. Through the use of prototypes, early feedback on the requirements can be gained from the customer as it serves as a working model of the expected end product.

Reference: *PMBOK® Guide*, 6th Ed., pages 133, 717

11. C. According to the *Agile Practice Guide®*, "the single most important practice is the retrospectives because it allows the team to learn about, improve, and adapt its process." Lessons learned is concerned with overall project performance and in predictive environments. This process has traditionally been executed towards the end of the project. The lessons learned process helps future project performance and not the current project that is in progress. The other two options are not directly relevant to this question.

Reference: *Agile Practice Guide®*, page 50

12. C. The *Agile Manifesto* emphasized the importance of people and their interactions with each other. One of the critical success factors of an agile/adaptive project is its ability to maintain stable, dedicated, self-organizing, and cross-functional teams through the duration of the project. This ensures the productivity of the project is maintained at optimal levels. Therefore, team productivity is directly linked to team composition. If stable, dedicated, cross-functional teams cannot be maintained, it will have a direct impact on the team's overall performance.

Reference: *Agile Practice Guide®*, pages 38, 98

13. A. The backlog is a list of work items that is prepared by the product owner (product manager). Through the life cycle of the agile/adaptive project, according to the business value of the work items (highest priority to lowest priority) the work items in the backlog are refined into more granular detail. This can occur at different intervals during the course of the iteration. As the team is only refining the items just prior to execution, there is very little waste as the team does not spend time refining items that may have fallen to a lower priority during the execution of the project. Therefore, backlog preparation and backlog refinement are two agile/adaptive processes that directly relate to the statement "simplicity—the art of maximizing the amount of work not done is essential" as it drastically reduces the sunk costs of the project.

Reference: *Agile Practice Guide®*, pages 52, 59, 98

14. A. On an agile/adaptive project, the primary measure of progress is "working software". Depending on the type of agile/adaptive project being delivered, the term "working software" can be interchanged with "working product" or "working service". Velocity is the sum of the story points completed for the features in an iteration. Although this choice is closely related to the answer to this question, working software is the best answer based on how the question is stated. The other two responses are not related to this question.

Reference: *Agile Practice Guide®*, pages 9, 25, 64, 66

15. A. According to the *Agile Practice Guide®* "the most efficient and effective method of conveying information to and within a development team is face-to-face conversation." The daily stand-up meetings and the retrospective meetings can be two of the ways in which the team can collaborate face-to-face. In agile/adaptive projects the conversation among team members occurs on an ongoing bases thereby reducing the need for formal weekly project status meetings.

Reference: *Agile Practice Guide®*, pages 9, 98

16. B. Agile and adaptive project management practices advocate the servant leadership approach. A servant leader leads by serving others first. According to the *Agile Practice Guide®*, "the role of the servant leader is to facilitate the team's discovery and definition of agile. Servant leaders practice and radiate agile." Characteristics of a servant leader include: promoting self-awareness; listening; helping people grow; coaching; promoting a safety, respect, and trust; and promoting the energy and intelligence of others. The other leadership styles are not advocated in agile and adaptive practices.

Reference: *Agile Practice Guide®*, pages 33-35

17. C. Following a plan over responding to change is not one of the four values of the *Agile Manifesto*. The four values of the agile manifesto include: 1) individuals and interactions over processes and tools; 2) working software over comprehensive documentation; 3) responding to change over following a plan; 3) Customer collaboration over contract negotiation. According to *Agile Practice Guide®*, "Agile processes harness change for the customer's competitive advantage." As such, changing requirements are welcome even late in development.

Reference: *Agile Practice Guide®*, pages 8-9

18. C. Iterative life cycles allow for feedback to be provided on partially completed or unfinished work so that the product of the project can be improved. In this case the activities are repeated until they are correct/fully accepted. Progressive elaboration is the iterative process of increasing the level of detail in a project management plan as greater amounts of information and more accurate estimates become available. The other two options are incorrect.

Reference: *Agile Practice Guide®*, page 18

19. D. In agile project management, customer value is delivered in increments throughout the life cycle of the project. According to the *Agile Practice Guide®*, "the team gains early feedback and provides customer visibility, confidence, and control of the product. Because the team can release earlier, the project may provide an earlier return on investment because the team delivered the highest value work first." Although speed is important, delivering customer value is one of the key goals in agile project delivery. The other two options primarily pertain to predictive methods of project delivery.

Reference: *Agile Practice Guide®*, page 18

20. A. In iteration-based agile life cycle, iterations are time-boxed to a predefined length of time; in a flow-based agile life cycle the iterations are not time-boxed to a predefined duration. According to the *Agile Practice Guide®*, "iteration- based agile, the team works in iterations (time-boxes of equal duration) to deliver completed features. In flow-based agile, the team pulls features from the backlog based on its capacity to start work rather than on an iteration-based schedule." Both are effective methods of agile/adaptive project delivery.

Reference: *Agile Practice Guide®*, pages 23-25

21. B. The program scenario described is best suited to be delivered using agile development followed by a predictive rollout. Some complex programs require such hybrid approaches in project delivery. According to the *Agile Practice Guide®*, "the early processes utilize an agile development life cycle, which is then followed by a predictive rollout phase. This approach can be used when there is uncertainty, complexity, and risk in the development portion of the project that would benefit from an agile approach, followed by a defined, repeatable rollout phase that is approach to undertake in a predictive way."

Reference: *Agile Practice Guide®*, pages 26-27

22. B. Jane is demonstrating characteristics of servant leadership. According to *Agile Practice Guide®*, "agile approaches emphasize servant leadership as a way to empower team. Servant leadership is the practice of leading through service to the team, by focusing on understanding and addressing the need and development of team member in order to enable the highest possible team performance."

Reference: *Agile Practice Guide®*, pages 34-35

23. D. Agile/adaptive practices focus on building a cross-functional team of generalized specialists. Although each team member brings their own strengths to the project team, the focus of optimizing the flow of value is achieved through the collective ownership of the team rather than individual subject matter expertise. According to *Agile Practice Guide®*, "cross-functional agile teams produce functional product increments frequently. That is because the teams collectively own the work and together have all the necessary skills to deliver completed work."

Reference: *Agile Practice Guide®*, page 39

24. B. The product owner is one of the three common roles within adaptive/agile practices. The product owner is the key interface between the customer and the team. According to *Agile Practice Guide®*, "The product owner works with stakeholders, customers, and the teams to define the product direction. Typically, product owners have a business background and bring deep subject matter expertise to the decisions. In agile, the product owners create the backlog for and with the team. The backlog helps the teams see how to deliver the highest value without creating waste."

Reference: *Agile Practice Guide®*, page 41

25. B. Teams that require flexibility in accepting more work from the product backlog may prefer a flow-based agile lifecycle. According to the *Agile Practice Guide®*, "in flow-based agile, the team pulls features from the backlog based on its capacity to start work rather than on an iteration-based schedule. Each feature may take a different amount of time to finish."

Reference: *Agile Practice Guide®*, page 25

26. C. Agile and adaptive projects advocate a dedicated team structure where 100% of the team's time is allocated to the project. According to the *Agile Practice Guide®*, "people experience productivity losses somewhere between 20% and 40% when task switching. When a person multitasks between two projects, that person is not 50% on each project. Instead, due to the cost of task switching, the person is somewhere between 20% and 40% on each project."

Reference: *Agile Practice Guide®*, pages 44-45

27. A. Although agile and adaptive practices promote co-located teams, at times you will come across teams that are geographically distributed. In order to bridge the gap of physical distance between team members, fishbowl windows technique can be adapted. A fishbowl window involves setting up video conferencing links between a geographically distributed teams; as team members begin their work day they can automatically connect to the "fishbowl". The technique can help reduce the time lags in setting up ad-hoc meetings are effective provided the teams are working in time zones that overlap.

Reference: *Agile Practice Guide®*, page 46

28. A. The project charter is an important document that helps initiate the project. According to the *Agile Practice Guide®*, "the team needs the project vision or purpose and clear set of working agreements." Although the product owner is an important role in an agile project, it is not necessary to identify the product owner in the project charter document.

Reference: *Agile Practice Guide®*, page 49

29. C. Ideally agile teams are co-located within a team space and they are 100% dedicated to the project. As they are a cross-functional and self-organizing team there is no need to "control their work". The team members are given the latitude to achieve the project objectives incrementally working as a self-organizing cross-functional team.

Reference: *Agile Practice Guide®*, pages 39-40

30. B. According to the *Agile Practice Guide®*, the team facilitator or the servant leader "maybe be called the project manager, scrum master, project team lead, tech coach." The role of the product owner is to work with the customer to provide the guidance and direction of the product.

Reference: *Agile Practice Guide®*, page 41

31. B. According to the *Agile Practice Guide*® "the single most important practice is the retrospective because it allows the team to learn about, improve, and adapt its process." The retrospective is typically lead by a facilitator within the team or the role of the servant leader. The product owner may attend the retrospective, however, it is not mandatorily required that they be present at each retrospective.

Reference: *Agile Practice Guide*®, pages 50-51

32. B. In an iteration-based agile project the daily standups are time-boxed to 15 mins each day. In this meeting the team addresses three questions: What did I complete since the last stand-up? What am in planning to complete between now and the next stand-up? What are my impediments (or risks or problems)? According to the *Agile Practice Guide*® "standups are for realizing there are problems-not for solving them." If is far more efficient to release the team back to work after the 15 minutes stand-up meeting and then address the issues one on one or with the relevant parties after the stand-up has concluded.

Reference: *Agile Practice Guide*®, page 53

33. A. In iteration based-agile practices the product owner reviews all product increments created by the team and validates and accepts or declines the increments based on pre-defined acceptance criteria. The interests of the end customer are represented by the role of the product owner. The project sponsor and team facilitator can support this process, however, they are not directly responsible for the acceptance or rejection of product increments. This responsibility solely lies with the role of the product owner.

Reference: *Agile Practice Guide*®, page 55

34. B. When working in an agile/adaptive project, there are many reasons a team can come up with inaccurate estimates. One of the most common reasons for inaccurate estimate is due to the size of the user story. If this problem occurs it is recommended that large user stories be split into several smaller user stories that can be estimated easily. Although getting more senior members and having the product owner provide better descriptions of the user stories can help, this is not the best answer to this question.

Reference: *Agile Practice Guide*®, page 58

35. A. In an iteration-based agile project using a Scrum framework, each iteration is time-boxed to a pre-defined length of time such as two weeks, three weeks, or four weeks. The length of time (duration) for each iteration is kept constant through the life cycle of the project. For example, if the team decides they will work in two week cycles, it is recommended that the duration of the two week cycle be maintained through the course of the project. As a self-organizing team, these decisions are made by the team (not by the product owner, the team facilitator, or the customer) ensuring the team delivers value to the customer through early and continuous delivery of valuable product increments.

Reference: *Agile Practice Guide*®, page 25

36. D. The term life cycle refers to the various stages that a project will go through from start to finish. As stated in the *PMBOK Guide®* "Adaptive life cycles are agile, iterative or incremental." In adaptive, or change driven projects, scope is defined at the beginning of each iteration, which in this case is every month. If the project is following a predictive life cycle, scope, time and cost are approved up front, and any changes are managed through a change approval process. Iterative projects costs and time estimates are managed in increments as the team better understands the product requirements, but typically the scope is defined up at the start. Incremental project lifecycles are similar to iterative, but the deliverables add functionality within a certain time frame.

Reference: *PMBOK® Guide*, 6th Ed., page 19

37. A. In a predictive life cycle approach, project integration management is the responsibility of the project manager, as he/she oversees the project as a whole. In an agile or adaptive environment, the expectations of the project manager remain the same, as he/she is still involved with facilitating and ensuring the right environment for the project team to conduct the detailed planning however the detailed product planning and delivery is delegated to the team.

Reference: *PMBOK® Guide*, 6th Ed., pages 72-74

38. C. The product owner is accountable for the end product that is developed according to the requirements provided by the customer. Therefore, the Product Owner is ultimately responsible for ensuring that maximum business value is derived. The scrum master is responsible for facilitating the Scrum processes and supporting and coaching the team. The development team is responsible for creating the product deliverables and delivering a working product. The project sponsor role is responsible for ensuring budget and resources.

Reference: *Agile Practice Guide®*, page 101

39. A. The four key practice areas (themes) are organizational, technical, planning, and integration as illustrated in table A3-2 of the *Agile Practice Guide®*. Communication and feedback are two of the five core values of XP along with simplicity, courage, and respect.

Reference: *Agile Practice Guide®*, page 102

40. D. Kanban follows many of the agile principles, however the notion of timeboxing is not prescribed as development teams are focused on continuous delivery and flow. According to the *Agile Practice Guide®* "unlike most agile approaches, the Kanban Method does not prescribe the use of timeboxed iterations."

Reference: *Agile Practice Guide®*, page 103

41. C. While all agile methods do implement some sort of feedback loop, and are focused on managing work, it is the Kanban Method which uses kanban boards to demonstrate the flow of work and limit work in progress. As stated in the *Agile Practice Guide®* "in the Kanban Method, it is more important to complete work than it is to start new work."

Reference: *Agile Practice Guide®*, page 105

42. D. Feature Driven Development incorporates the six primary roles listed above and is more conducive to large software development initiatives. FDD is organized around five processes and supports a core set of software engineering best practices.

Reference: *Agile Practice Guide®*, pages 108-109

43. B. The DSDM method adds more rigor than other adaptive methods by setting the constraints of cost, quality and time at the start of the project. Scope is then formally defined based on these constraints, hence the term 'constraint-driven delivery'.

Reference: *Agile Practice Guide®*, page 110

44. B. The SAFe framework does promote taking an economic view, applying systems thinking and visualizing and limiting work in progress by reducing batch sizes and managing queue lengths. However it also promotes *decentralized* decision making as opposed to *centralized* decision making.

Reference: *Agile Practice Guide®*, pages 112-113

45. A. The LeSS framework is used when there are several development teams working towards the same goal. While LeSS does promotes single-team Scrum principles, it extends to accommodate projects when several development teams are working towards the same objective by adding cross-team coordination, refinement, and retrospectives.

Reference: *Agile Practice Guide®*, pages 113

46. C. Plan driven principles are applicable in *predictive* project management approaches. Disciplined Agile aims to be less prescriptive than some other agile approaches by blending and balancing agile techniques according to the principles of people first, collaborative improvement, fit for purpose life cycles, enterprise awareness and scalability.

Reference: *Agile Practice Guide®*, pages 114, 151

47. C. Crystal Methods acknowledges that each project may have unique characteristics or properties, and thus might tailor various methodologies. According to the *Agile Practice Guide®*, "the family of methodologies use different colors based on "weight" to determine which methodology to use." The word 'crystal' is in reference to gemstones which represent the different values and principles.

Reference: *Agile Practice Guide®*, pages 106-107

48. A. The Scrum framework uses the term *'sprints'* in reference to timeboxed development cycles or iterations, so the sprint backlog is an output of sprint planning that produces product increments.

Reference: *Agile Practice Guide®*, page 101

49. A. Because agile projects focus on maximizing business value, payment terms are "value-driven" rather than structuring a contract that is milestone, schedule or budget based. A value driven contract leverages the ability to incorporate feedback and provides motivation to deliver full business value.

Reference: *Agile Practice Guide®*, page 77

50. C. Iteration-based projects need to see how the project is progressing. They frequently use a burndown chart to illustrate how the work planned is moving along in the time frame allocated. Story points are used as a relative measure of work, risk and complexity. Burndown charts show work remaining. Conversely a burnup chart would show the work completed.

Reference: *Agile Practice Guide®*, pages 62-63

51. B. Velocity equals the number of story points completed in an iteration. By looking at their actual previous performance, teams practicing iteration based agile methods can refine and improve their estimation for upcoming iterations. Although the terms throughput and capacity are closely aligned to velocity, the *Agile Practice Guide®* defines the term velocity specifically to describe story points completed in a defined iteration.

Reference: *Agile Practice Guide®*, page 64

52. A. According to the *Agile Practice Guide®* lead time is "the total time it takes to deliver an item, measured from the time it is added to the board to the moment it is completed." Lead time is one of the measurements to track team performance and can include external dependencies that can have an impact on delivery after the development work is complete.

Reference: *Agile Practice Guide®*, page 64

53. B. Backlog refinement occurs when the team works with the product owner during an iteration to further develop the stories for the next iteration. According to the *Agile Practice Guide®*, backlog refinement is "the progressive elaboration of project requirements and/or the ongoing activity in which the team collaboratively reviews, updates, and writes requirements to satisfy the need of the customer request."

Reference: *Agile Practice Guide®*, pages 52, 150

54. B. In a flow-based agile method the focus is on advancing and completing the work as a team. Individual work performance is not considered, rather the team performance is tracked and measured.

Reference: *Agile Practice Guide®*, page 54

55. B. A spike a technical practice that comes from extreme programming and can be very useful when the team needs to learn some additional technical details. A sprint is timeboxed iteration, while smoke testing is used in system level testing to determine the need for integration testing. The other two options do not pertain to this question.

Reference: *Agile Practice Guide®*, pages 56, 154

56. D. The role of the service request manager is most commonly used in Kanban to manage the continuous flow of work and value to the customer. Unlike most other agile approaches, the Kanban Method does not prescribe the use of timeboxed iterations therefore the flow of work needs to be managed. Scrum, DSDM, and XP are iteration based agile methods.

Reference: *Agile Practice Guide®*, pages 103, 154

57. D. Value stream mapping is a lean manufacturing or lean enterprise technique used to document, analyze and improve the flow of information or materials required to produce a product or service for a customer. This is a team exercise that is led by an expert and it includes representatives from all areas of the process being mapped. Value based prioritization, would indicate that work items are prioritized based on business value, while smoke testing involves validating functions under development are working as intended. Continuous integration involves integrating and validating team member's work with one another on a frequent basis.

Reference: *PMBOK® Guide*, 6ᵗʰ Ed., page 9 and *Agile Practice Guide®*, page 155

58. B. Swarming and mobbing are both techniques for team collaboration in an agile environment. Swarming involves the multiple team members collaborating on a specific *impediment*, while mobbing has multiple team members simultaneously contributing to a particular *work item*. Refactoring refers to a product quality technique.

Reference: *Agile Practice Guide®*, pages 39, 154

59. C. Siloed organization structure only manages to contribute to a subset of the aspects required for delivering value to the customer. This type of organization structure can often create impediments for cross-functional teams as the various team members typically report to different managers with different performances measures.

Reference: *Agile Practice Guide®*, pages 47, 154

60. D. Burndown charts, Scrum boards, and kanban boards are all visual displays also commonly known as information radiators that show project progress and communicate issues. A user story is brief description of a deliverable or requirement which is of value to a specific user or a customer representative.

Reference: *Agile Practice Guide®*, pages 103, 105, 152

61. D. Scrumban originated as an approach to help teams transition from Scrum to Kanban. It leverages some aspects of Scrum such as the sprints, and utilizing the kanban board to visualize work in progress. There are no unique or pre-defined roles in Scrumban as the team members retain their current roles.

Reference: *Agile Practice Guide®*, pages 108, 153

62. A. A multi-tiered contract allows for parties to list contract items that could be subject to change, such as service rates or product descriptions in a schedule of services. Fixed-price contracts break down the project scope into smaller, fixed price deliverables limiting financial risk of over-commitment. A master services agreement can define fixed items of a contract, while a time and materials contract is a combination of cost-reimbursable and fixed-price elements.
Reference: *Agile Practice Guide®*, page 77

63. C. Progressing towards organizational agility means that human resources teams will need to employ more team based incentives over individual incentives. Various business units such as finance and procurement may need to alter their interactions and the way in which they perform their responsibilities to be more effective. Internal management processes and policies will need to be reviewed and amended. According to the *Agile Practice Guide®*, "project agility is more effective and sustained as the organization adjusts to support it."

Reference: *Agile Practice Guide®*, pages 71-79

64. B. UX design is an integral process within product development where UX designers work to enhance the user experience by improving the usability and accessibility between the product and the user. User acceptance testing (UAT) occurs when developed product is validated against pre-defined acceptance criteria. Value streaming focuses on the flow of value through the delivery of products or services.

Reference: *Agile Practice Guide®*, pages 44, 155

65. B. Single loop learning is the most basic form of learning where the aim is to solve an organizational problem without attempting to understand the root cause of the problem. Conversely, double loop learning is a process that challenges underlying values and assumptions when trying to understand root cause of issues rather than focusing only on symptoms. Smoke testing is the practice of using a lightweight set of tests in extreme programming, while continuous improvement is looks to identify opportunities to streamline work or drive efficiencies.

Reference: *Agile Practice Guide®,* pages 151, 154

66. A. According to the *Agile Practice Guide®,* value stream mapping is "a lean enterprise technique used to document, analyze, and improve the flow of information or materials required to product a product or service for a customer." Projects resulting from a value stream mapping exercise case be classified as business process improvement projects.

Reference: *PMBOK® Guide*, 6th Ed., page 9 and *Agile Practice Guide®,* page 155

67. B. An impediment is also referred to as a blocker. In agile and adaptive project practices, the role of the servant leader is responsible for removing impediments so that the interruption to the flow of work is minimized. These impediments can be brought forward by the team in standup meetings as well the impediments can be identified using information radiators such as Scrum boards and kanban boards.

Reference: *Agile Practice Guide®,* pages 34, 35, 53, 59, 152

68. C. Organizational culture will always have an influence and impact on the ability to implement agile practices, however organizational bias places more value on exploration, speed, quantity and flexibility over execution, stability, quality, and predictability.

Reference: *Agile Practice Guide®,* pages 75, 152

69. B. Functional specifications provide a software developer a products' intended capabilities such as system or application performance requirements. Although in agile and adaptive project management practices there is less of a focus on detailed documentation, there is always opportunity to create sufficient and valuable documentation that is deemed necessary for successful project outcomes.

Reference: *Agile Practice Guide®,* page 152

70. B. Personas are highly fictional characters that represent the end user or a group of end users. They are used to provide additional clarity and understanding of how the end users will actually use the product of the project. Although user groups, customers, and characters can be synonymous with the term personas, agile and adaptive practices uses the specific term personas to describe these users or user groups.

Reference: *Agile Practice Guide®,* page 153

71. B. Progressive elaboration is an iterative process whereby the level of detail in the project plan/scope becomes increasingly more detailed as more information is available. Progressive elaboration is how the backlog is refined. Rolling wave planning is an iterative planning technique in which the work to be accomplished in the near term is planned in detail. Refactoring refers to a product quality technique.

Reference: *PMBOK® Guide*, 6th Ed., pages 147, 185, 565, 666 and *Agile Practice Guide®*, page 153

72. C. I-shaped people have a deep specialization in a single domain and have no interest or skills in the rest of the domains or expertise required by the project. Conversely, generalist-specialists, also known as T-shaped people have a deep area of specialization in one area, but also have a broad knowledge of the other skills that the team requires for the project.

Reference: *Agile Practice Guide®*, pages 42, 152

73. C. When leaders are rewarded for local efficiencies rather than end-to-end flow of project delivery or optimizing the whole in regard to the organization, these may be roadblocks to achieving the changes associated with organizational agility due to its narrow focus on local efficiencies.

Reference: *Agile Practice Guide®*, page 73

74. C. According to the *Agile Practice Guide®* "only in a safe, honest, and transparent environment can team members and leaders truly reflect on their successes to ensure their projects continue to advance, or apply lessons learned on failed project so they do not fall back into the same pattern." Organizations considering an agile transformation should look to shifting to a more team based performance rewards system rather than an individual performance based rewards and recognition systems.

Reference: *Agile Practice Guide®*, page 75

75. C. Managing a project using an agile or adaptive approach requires the team to adopt an agile mindset. Trying to control the teams' output or delivery does not support an adaptive mindset. Rather, the team should be given the accountability to deliver the efficiency improvements and appropriate support should be provided to the team as required.

Reference: *Agile Practice Guide®*, page 33

76. B. According to the *Agile Practice Guide®*, the most effective agile teams tend to rage in size from three to nine members." Ideally these team members should work in a colocated team space and be 100% dedicated to the project.

Reference: *Agile Practice Guide®*, page 39

77. D. The role of the product owner is responsible for working hand in hand with the team to ensure the user stories are written and the backlog is prepared and constantly refined. Team members often have more information about dependencies, risks or technical impediments, so it is always a good idea for the product owner to include team members in the story writing process. The story creation process should not be delegated to the role of the team facilitator or servant leader. He or she can help support the process but should not be left responsible for solely working with the team.

Reference: *Agile Practice Guide®,* page 53

78. A. Agile principles promote the use of cross-functional team members who work in the same location, allowing for faster feedback. Agile also promotes the principle that dedicated teams are much more effective than non-dedicated teams as they are more likely to make mistakes if multi-tasking. Distributed or dispersed team members (teams or members working in different locations) can work, but is not considered to be ideal.

Reference: *Agile Practice Guide®,* pages 43-45

79. B. According to the *Agile Practice Guide®,* "Acceptance Test-Driven Development (ATDD) is a method of collaboratively creating acceptance test criteria that are used to create acceptance tests before delivery begins." This practice allows the team to write just enough code and automated test to meet the acceptance criteria. Conversely writing automated tests before creating the product increments relates to test-driven development (TDD). ATDD is a collaborative exercise that involves product owners, testers, and developers whereas in TDD the focus is on code quality and low-level functionality and does not consider the aspect of acceptance criteria.

Reference: *Agile Practice Guide®,* page 56

80. C. The role of the team facilitator is integral to help remove and clear obstacles that are impeding the team's progress. When this role is absent or ineffective the team will likely struggle to make progress. The role of the product owner interfaces with the customer whereas the role of the project sponsor is generally accountable for the development and maintenance of the project business case.

Reference: *Agile Practice Guide®,* page 58

81. D. Refactoring, defining done criteria and agile modeling will help reduce technical debt or design debt on an agile project. Refactoring is a product quality technique to improve the design of the code in order to enhance its maintainability. The definition of done refers to the team checklist of the criteria that needs to be met in order for a deliverable to be considered complete. Agile modeling allows for developers to develop customized software development processes that meets their current development needs and is flexible enough to adjust in the future. Swarming is an agile team collaboration technique where the team comes together to resolve a specific impediment and it does not directly relate to reducing or eliminating technical debt.

Reference: *Agile Practice Guide®,* pages 58, 151, 154

82. B. When a team is measuring story points completed, they are measuring team *capacity* as opposed to work finished, which is one of the supporting principles of the Agile Manifesto. However, measuring story points is also important as it allows the team to rate the relative work, risk and complexity of a requirement or a story.

Reference: *Agile Practice Guide®,* pages 9, 66

83. D. "Lightweight" agile practices support the initiation of the project even if detailed requirements or the scope for the project are not fully realized and frequent changes may be required. Fast, high level estimations and forecasts may be suitable for the long range view, while details can be refined over time. Detailed requirements are not required to initiate a "lightweight" agile project.

Reference: *PMBOK® Guide*, 6th Ed., page 234 and *Agile Practice Guide®,* pages 92, 121

84. D. A hybrid approach combines multiple agile and possibly predictive approaches to attain the benefits agile brings to the table such as iterative development and collaboration, but also layers in the necessary rigor that may be necessary in projects where additional safety and conformance considerations need to be addressed.

Reference: *Agile Practice Guide®,* page 122

85. C. A dynamic scope option contract is used when a project is constrained by a fixed budget, and the project may benefit from revisiting the scope at specific points in the project. An early cancellation option limits customer budget exposure by allowing the customer to cancel the contract or remainder of a project for a fee. Team augmentation is a collaborative contracting approach that allows the suppliers services to be embedded directly into the customer organization. Fixed price increments decompose a project scope into fixed price micro-deliverables such as user stories.

Reference: *Agile Practice Guide®,* pages 77-78

86. D. An agile PMO helps to facilitate the enable the goal of ensuring projects deliver value. It chooses to work with only people who are interested in utilizing the PMO's methods and services, rather than mandating an approach that doesn't get buy in or support. An agile PMO is also multi-disciplinary as it needs to support different project needs that require different capabilities.

Reference: *Agile Practice Guide®,* pages 81-82

87. D. Both speed and quality are important aspects of agile project delivery. Delivering an agile project with speed without adherence to quality will result in poor customer satisfaction, rework, and potential product recalls.

Reference: *Agile Practice Guide®,* page 93

88. D. The team facilitator acts as a servant-leader to support the project team remove impediments and bottlenecks and they promote communication and collaboration among team members and stakeholders. The product owner/service request manager is responsible for ensuring the project achieves maximum business value and sets the direction for the project. The project sponsor, executives sponsor, or business owner ensures the resources and funding for the project are secured and are responsible for enabling success.

Reference: *Agile Practice Guide®,* pages 34-35, 41

89. A. Cross functional team members collectively have all of the skills necessary to produce a potentially releasable working product on a regular cadence. A project sponsor/business owner ensures the resources and funding for the project are secured and are responsible for enabling success. The team facilitator acts as a servant-leader to support the project team. The product owner/service request manager is responsible for ensuring the project achieves maximum business value and sets the direction for the project.

Reference: *Agile Practice Guide®,* pages 40-41

90. C. According to the *PMBOK® Guide, 6th Ed.,* "requests for change and defect reports are evaluated by business representatives in consultation with the team for technical input and are prioritized accordingly in the backlog of work." The role of the servant leader can help facilitate this process but he/she is not responsible for evaluating requests for changes or defect reports.

Reference: *PMBOK® Guide, 6th Ed.,* page 671

91. D. Agile, iterative, and adaptive life cycle project employ both senior and junior project team members. Junior project team members may require some coaching before reaching a fully empowered state. Through progressive trials within the confines of short iterations the team can ensure the required skills are acquired for successful project execution.

Reference: *PMBOK® Guide, 6th Ed.,* page 670

92. A. If the closing process group prematurely closes a project or phase, due the nature of iterative, adaptive, and agile projects there is a very high chance that some useful business value will have been realized. Furthermore an iterative, adaptive, or agile project can be closed at any time if it is deemed that the project will not be delivering the intended business value. Doing so will reduce the sunk costs of the project.

Reference: *PMBOK® Guide, 6th Ed.,* page 671

93. B. Mobbing is a technique where multiple team members focus simultaneously and coordinate their contribution on a particular work item where one person is at the keyboard and the remaining team members are providing input. This technique is also sometimes referred to as mob programming. Swarming occurs when the team works collaboratively to resolve a particular impediment.

94. B. In order to bridge any communication gaps between stakeholders and agile project teams, realistic examples are provided illustrating the requirements in a clear and concise manner. This technique is commonly referred to as specification by example. Prototyping is a method of obtaining early feedback on requirements by providing a model of the expected product before actually building it.

Reference: *Agile Practice Guide®,* page 154

95. B. Blended agile combines two or more agile frameworks whereas hybrid approaches combines both predictive, as well as iterative, incremental, and/or agile approaches. There many ways in ways organizations are combining various agile frameworks that best suit the needs of the organization.

Reference: *Agile Practice Guide®,* pages 26, 150

96. C. Agile or adaptive practices promote the active engagement of stakeholders. Anyone on an agile or adaptive project team can engage with stakeholders as appropriate at regular intervals. Although the role of the product owner is responsible for working hand in hand with the customer, at times the development team may also need to work directly with the customer depending on the project requirements.

Reference: *Agile Practice Guide®,* page 95

97. C. Refactoring is a controlled process for improving code without creating new functionality. The process of refactoring transforms sloppy or unclean code into clean code. Having clean code provides many benefits including simplifying the usability of the code by other programmers as well as troubleshooting problems when they occur.

Reference: *Agile Practice Guide®,* page 153

98. B. Story points are a unit-less measures used in relative user story estimating effort. They rate the relative work, risk, and complexity of a requirement or story. When teams measure only story points, they measure capacity, not finished work. Affinity estimation is a technique many agile teams use to quickly and easily estimate a large number of user stories in story points.

Reference: *Agile Practice Guide®*, pages 62, 154

99. A. Collective code ownership occurs when everyone in the team is responsible for all the code and anyone can change any part of it as necessary to either complete a development task, to repair a defect, or improve the code's overall structure. Collective code ownership has its roots in extreme programming.

Reference: *Agile Practice Guide®*, pages 102, 151

100. A. According to the *Agile Practice Guide®*, user story mapping is "a visual practice of organizing work into a useful model to help understand the sets of high-value features to be created over time, identify omissions in the backlog, and effectively plan releases that deliver value to users." Value stream mapping is a lean manufacturing or lean enterprise technique used to document, analyze and improve the flow of information or materials required to produce a product or service for a customer.

Reference: *Agile Practice Guide®*, pages 58, 155

101. C. According to the *PMBOK® Guide, 6th* Ed., "the project charter establishes a partnership between the performing and requesting organizations." It is a formal document that provides the authorization for the project manager to initiate the project. In an adaptive project, the initiating processes are performed regularly to ensure the project is progressing, and the goals reflect the latest information. As a result, the project charter is revisited and revalidated on a frequent basis.

Reference: *PMBOK® Guide, 6th* Ed., pages 77, 669

102. B. A team charter creates a common understanding of the agile team norms and standards that will allow them to work together more effectively. According to the *PMBOK® Guide,* "the [team] chartering process helps the team learn how to work together and coalesce around the project." Typically the role of the servant leader will lead the chartering process. The project vision statement and business case can service an inputs into this process. A collaborative team workspace can be established by the role of the servant leader.

Reference: *PMBOK® Guide, 6th* Ed., page 319 and *Agile Practice Guide®*, page 49

103. C. An agile life cycle approach allows for continuous feedback where the work can be refined and it supports incremental product delivery. This approach focuses less on upfront planning which is more conducive to more traditional and predictive methods of project delivery. An approach that provides finished deliverables that the customer may be able to use immediately supports an incremental life cycle.

Reference: *Agile Practice Guide®*, page 17

104. A. The requirements for both iterative and incremental life cycles are dynamic. When considering the work activities, in an iterative approach the activities are repeated until correct and the focus is on a single delivery whereas when taking an incremental approach the work is performed once for a given increment and output is frequently delivered in in smaller deliveries. An agile life cycle combines both iterative and incremental approaches to refine work items and delivery frequently.

Reference: *Agile Practice Guide®*, pages 17-19

105. D. According to the *PMBOK® Guide* "A hybrid life cycle is a combination of a predictive and an adaptive life cycle. Those elements of the project that are well known or have fixed requirements follow a predictive development life cycle, and those that are still evolving follow an adaptive development life cycle."

Reference: *PMBOK® Guide, 6th* Ed., page 19

106. A. While the role of the project manager doesn't change during project integration management, the control of the detailed product planning and delivery is delegated to the agile team in an adaptive environment. The project manager focuses more on building a collaborative environment, conducive to allowing the team to respond to change.

Reference: *PMBOK® Guide, 6th* Ed., page 74

107. B. A core tenet of the Agile Manifesto is to place more importance on individuals and interactions over processes and tools. To that end, agile promotes "servant leadership" to facilitate team participation and shared responsibility. According to the *Agile Practice Guide®*, "the value of project managers is not in their position, but in their ability to make everyone else better." In the agile environment, the project manager shifts to more of a coach, facilitating collaboration on the team. Team facilitator and project manager are one in the same role in an agile project. The product owner is a very active role in agile projects and responsible for interfacing with the customers and representing their needs back to the team. As agile teams are self-motivated and they track and manage the status of their deliverables in the daily standup and on the burndown/burnup chart.

Reference: *Agile Practice Guide®*, page 34 – 38

108. C. According to *Agile Practice Guide®*, "traditional EVM metrics like schedule performance index (SPI) and cost performance index (CPI) can be easily translated into agile terms." Earned value analysis is a tool that compares the performance measurement baseline to the actual schedule and cost performance. Velocity is the sum of story points for features that are completed in an iteration, while story points remaining can be displayed on an agile burn-up chart to illustrate work not yet complete. Features delivered is also a measure used in agile projects to demonstrate value to customers.

Reference: *Agile Practice Guide®*, pages 61-64, and *PMBOK® Guide, 6th* Ed., page 261

109. B. Rather than waiting until the end of the project to inspect quality, according to the *Agile Practice Guide®*, "recurring retrospectives regularly check on the effectiveness of the quality processes. They look for the root cause of issues then suggest trials of new approaches to improve quality." Because retrospectives occur at the end of each sprint, there is ample opportunity to address processes affecting quality before too much time elapses on the project.

Reference: *Agile Practice Guide®*, page 93

110. A. Dedicated, cross-functional, and self-organizing teams are preferred for optimal agile team productivity. According to the *Agile Practice Guide®* "people experience productivity losses somewhere between 20% and 40% when task switching." When teams can colocate and dedicate their time to the project team, they can continuously collaborate and be more productive and effective.

Reference: *PMBOK® Guide, 6th* Ed., pages 309-311 and *Agile Practice Guide®*, pages 44-45

111. B. The product owner is responsible for defining scope in the form of user stories that describe product features and requirements set forth by the customer. The user stories are maintained in a backlog, which the product owner creates and manages for and with the team. In traditional project management scenarios, developing the charter happens during the project initiation, with the project manager working with the project sponsor to align the business case, project charter and project management plan. A team facilitator may also be called a project manager in an adaptive environment and acts as a servant leader.

Reference: *Agile Practice Guide®*, page 41 and *PMBOK® Guide, 6th* Ed., 278, 674

112. C. To minimize risks within a high variability environment, agile teams review their work frequently to accelerate knowledge sharing and ensure that any identified risks are being managed. According to the *Agile Practice Guide®*, "risk is considered when selecting the content of each iteration, and risks will also be identified, analyzed, and managed during each iteration." A risk mitigation plan is part of a traditional project management plan and will capture and prioritize risks upfront.

Reference: *Agile Practice Guide®*, page 94 and *PMBOK® Guide*, 6th Ed., pages, 400, 405

113. B. Cost performance index (CPI) is a measure of the cost efficiency of budgeted resources usually expressed as a ratio of earn value to actual cost. According to the *Agile Practice Guide®*, "traditional EVM metrics like schedule performance index (SPI) and cost performance index (CPI) can be easily translated into agile terms." CPI is the earned value (completed features value) to date divided by the actual costs to date.

Reference: *PMBOK® Guide, 6th* Ed., page 261-263, and *Agile Practice Guide®*, page 69

114. C. The second principle in the Agile Manifesto states that: "welcome changing requirements, even late in development." Agile practices embrace change for the customer's competitive advantage. If a change is identified mid-sprint, it may be added to the prioritized backlog and be scheduled for an upcoming sprint based on urgency, priority, and many other factors considered by the product owner working in consultation with the customer. In traditional project management, approved change requests are the output of the Perform Integrated Change Control process. A Scope Management Plan would be determined, outlining change procedures and approvals, and would be tracked and managed in a change log by the project manager.

Reference: *Agile Practice Guide®*, pages 7-9 and *PMBOK® Guide, 6th* Ed., page 93, 118-119

115. D. Servant leadership is the practice of leading the team through *serving* them. While servant leadership is not utilized only within agile environments, it is the style conducive to supporting the team and shifting from managing tasks and activities to facilitating collaboration within the team. Laissez-faire is a more hands-off approach, while the transactional leadership is "management by exception" and emphasizes rewards based on accomplishments. Interactional leadership is a combination of transactional, transformational (empowering and inspiring others with encouragement for innovation and individual consideration) and charismatic (high energy, enthusiastic and confident) leadership styles.

Reference *Agile Practice Guide®* p. 34-38, *PMBOK® Guide, 6th* Ed., page 65

116. C. When considering a flow-based agile method such as Kanban, a cumulative flow diagram (CFD) can be used to help visualize the project progress. Ideally as the work in progress should be maintained at a steady flow and the number of completed tasks should start to increase over a period of time.

Reference: *Agile Practice Guide®*, page 94

117. C. The product owner is responsible for the overall guidance and direction of the product as well as creating the prioritized product backlog for the team. Product ownership is critical to the success of any agile project and this function acts as the key interface to the customer. The team facilitator acts as the servant leader to facilitate the needs of the team.

Reference: *Agile Practice Guide®*, page 41

118. C. Planning to the team's actual capacity without inflating or underestimating the work will result in a more even flow of work. Measuring work in progress (WIP) can be useful when the team is doing too much up front work and seeing re-work as the result. Unless iteration durations are extremely lengthy, it is best to keep the iteration durations to the same length of time and plan to meet the team's capacity instead. Clearly defined user stories are always beneficial, but they won't have an impact on the flow of the work.

Reference: *Agile Practice Guide®*, page 59

119. C. According to the *Agile Practice Guide®* "teams use the daily standups to microcommit to each other, uncover problems, and ensure work is flowing smoothly through the team." Any new work that has come in is dealt with by the product owner through the backlog grooming process.

Reference: *Agile Practice Guide®*, page 53

120. A. Velocity refers to the sum of the story point sizes for the features completed in a given iteration. Measuring velocity is an empirical and value-based measurement that allows teams to plan its capacity for upcoming iterations using this valuable historical data. Agile teams typically improve their velocity the more they work together as a team. Cycle time measures the time it takes to complete a task from the time the task was started. Lead time measures the time it took to deliver an item from the time it was added to the board to the time it was completed.

Reference: *Agile Practice Guide®*, pages, 61, 64, 66

121. B. Effective, cross-functional agile teams look for generalist-specialists or T-shaped people. They typically have subject matter expertise or specialized skills in one area and are versatile and collaborative enough to help out in other areas. I-shaped people have domain expertise in a specialized area, while domain experts only possess expertise in a single domain.

Reference: *Agile Practice Guide®*, pages 42, 152, 155

122. B. An iteration burndown chart displays how the team is progressing based on the amount of work that is remaining. If the trend line is above the ideal slope that means the team is having some challenges or perhaps they have overestimated the number of user stories they can complete within the iteration. If the trend line is below the ideal slope that means the team is progressing much faster than anticipated or perhaps they have underestimated the number of user stories they can complete in a given iteration.

Reference: *PMBOK® Guide, 6th* Ed., page 226 and *Agile Practice Guide®*, page 62

123. A. The team is working at 88% of the rate planned. The calculation for SPI is 23/26 which gives you 0.88 which equals 88%. Ideally, the team will improve their SPI rate as they continue working together in the coming sprints.

Reference: *Agile Practice Guide®*, page 69

124. B. Cost performance index is used to calculate the earned value (completed features value) to date divided by the actual costs to date. In this example, you would divide $2.8M/$3.5M to obtain the CPI. 2.8/3.5 = 0.8 which equals 80 cents on the dollar. In this case, you will most likely complete the project under budget as you have completed 90% of the planned work and yet used 80% of the planned budget.

Reference: *Agile Practice Guide®*, page 69

125. A. One of the 12 agile principles that support the Agile Manifesto states that "the sponsors, developers, and users should be able to maintain a constant pace indefinitely." The Agile Manifesto itself finds more value in "working software over comprehensive documentation," and because agile is flexible and responsive to customer needs, project scope is defined through the backlog refinement process.

Reference: *Agile Practice Guide®*, pages 8-9

126. C. A fundamental measure of success in an agile project is delivery of working product. This is demonstrated at the end of an iteration, which allows for greater frequency of feedback. A backlog refinement session is when the product owner in conjunction with the project team prepares user stories for an upcoming iteration while in the midst of a current iteration. A retrospective is considered the most important practice as it helps the team to learn about what worked well and what could be improved in terms of processes. During the project close phase, the project manager should review all prior phase documentation and ensure that all requirements have been completed according to the defined scope, as well as update all project documentation and deliver a final report.

Reference: *PMBOK® Guide, 6th* Ed., pages 127-128 and *Agile Practice Guide®*, pages 50-55

127. B. By releasing small batches of work in frequent increments, the team can quickly identify and resolve issues or improve processes that are driving inconsistencies in the project. Typically when addressing quality issues earlier in the project life cycle the costs of change are also lower.

Reference: *Agile Practice Guide®*, page 93

128. A. While agile methods do look to utilize teams that are cross-functional in terms of skill sets, and you are focused on quicker time to market with working product, the correct answer is that agile methods build and review prototypes in order to refine requirements. The ability to collaborate with the customer and refine the scope as requirements are better defined or new requirements emerge that you may need to respond to is a key benefit of a more agile approach.

Reference: *Agile Practice Guide®*, page 91

129. C. When considering changes in an agile project, the primary driver for evaluating changes is based on delivering business value to the customer. In predictive methods, changes can be evaluated using a variety of criteria and methods. Alternative analysis is a decision-making tool used to evaluate alternatives or more than one option, while multi-criteria decision analysis is a technique that uses a set of predetermined criteria to provide a systematic approach to evaluating change. Cost-benefit analysis helps to determine if the requested change is worth its associated cost.

Reference: *PMBOK® Guide,* 6th Ed., pages 113-119 and *Agile Practice Guide®* pages 8-9

130. C. Retrospectives allow the team the opportunity to learn about, improve, and adapt its processes. This can include both qualitative measures such as people's thoughts and feeling as well as quantitative measures including data and metrics. The key is to identify the root cause of issues and finding ways to mitigate those issues so that the team and continually improve and the project progresses. According to *Agile Practice Guide®*, "trying to improve too many things at once and not finishing any of them is much worse than planning to compete fewer items and successfully completing all of them." The team should rank the items in order of importance, and select how many items they wish to address for the next iteration. The product owner can support this activity but should not be directing the activity. The team should feel a sense of ownership in the process of continuous improvement.

Reference: *Agile Practice Guide®*, page 51

131. B. Every user story has a unique set of acceptance criteria. Acceptance criteria are used in both traditional as well as agile projects. In traditional projects, acceptance criteria are defined during Define Scope. In an iteration based agile environment, the working product produced and validated against acceptance criteria at the end of the iteration. In an agile project, the acceptance criteria are defined by the product owner in consultation with the customer. The "done" criteria is a team's checklist of all the criteria including the best practices required to be met so that the deliverable can be considered ready for use.

Reference: *PMBOK® Guide,* 6th Ed., page 150-154 and *Agile Practice Guide®*, page 151

132. B. Agile projects deliver incremental business value by continuous delivery and by improving the product or result through prototypes or proofs of concept. The delivery of business value is also maximized through greater accountability and productivity of empowered teams, and improved quality from frequent reviews.

Reference: *PMBOK® Guide, 6th* Ed., pages 7, 33, 700 and *Agile Practice Guide®* pages 4, 20, 23, 37

133. D. According to the *Agile Practice Guide®*, "unlike most agile approaches, the Kanban Method does not prescribe the use of timeboxed iterations. Iterations can be used within the Kanban Method, but the principle of pulling single items through the process continuously and limiting work in progress to optimize flow should always remain intact."

Reference: *PMBOK® Guide,* 6th Ed., page 182 and *Agile Practice Guide®* page 103

134. A. The definition of done is a team checklist created by the team that outlines various criteria that need to be met prior to a deliverable being considered as completed. This can be a set of best practices and generally accepted norms. Both acceptance criteria and done criteria need to be met for each deliverable for it to be considered as fully complete prior to the deliverable being shipped to the customer. The definition of ready is a team checklist of for a user-centric requirement that has all the information the team requires to be able to work on the item.

Reference: *Agile Practice Guide®* page 151

135. B. Solution requirements can be broken down into two categories: functional requirements and non-functional requirements. Functional requirements describe the behaviors of the product such as actions, processes, data, and interactions that the product should execute. Business requirements are the higher-level needs of the organization including the reason why a project was undertaken whereas stakeholder requirements describe the needs of the stakeholder groups for a project.

Reference: *PMBOK® Guide*, 6th Ed., page 148 and *Agile Practice Guide®* page 152

136. C. Agile release planning provides the timeline to understand the project schedule better and determines the number of iterations or sprints and the features that will be developed in every release. Iteration planning is a collaborative event in with the team plans the work for the next iteration. Schedule baseline is the approved version of the schedule model that is used as a basis for comparison to actual results. Schedule compression is a technique used when the project schedule needs to be accelerated without reducing the scope of the project.

Reference: *PMBOK® Guide*, 6th Ed., *page* 216

137. C. According to the *PMBOK® Guide, 6th Ed.,* "when work is being contracted, regular and millstone status updates from contractors and suppliers are a means of ensuring the work is progressing as agreed upon to ensure the schedule is under control." It is good practice to schedule status reviews and walkthroughs to ensure the contractor reports are accurate and complete. Although the 3rd party contractors can be included to participate in some of the meetings, is it not always feasible to have them participate in *all* meetings related to the project hence milestone related updates are more suitable.

Reference: *PMBOK® Guide,* 6th Ed., *page* 224

138. A. Retrospectives are recurring scheduled reviews conducted to record the lessons learned. In an agile approach, the team discusses and identifies improvements and corrective action. JAD sessions are joint application design/development session. They are used in the software development industry and they are facilitated sessions that brings subject matter experts together to gather requirements and improve the software development process.

Reference: *PMBOK® Guide,* 6th Ed., page 224

139. B. A burndown chart is one of the data analysis techniques used in the control schedule process to track the work remaining in the iteration. The critical path method is used to estimate the minimum project duration and determine the amount of schedule flexibility on the local network paths within the schedule model. Performance reviews measure, compare, and analyze the schedule performance again the schedule baseline.

Reference: *PMBOK® Guide,* 6th Ed., page 226

140. C. A high-variability agile project with a strict budget will likely not have a fully defined scope in the onset of the project. Such projects cannot benefit from detailed cost calculations due to the degree of variability of the scope. In order to meet the strict budget constraints, as the scope gets defined, the budget constraints will need to be carefully considered. Flexibility in the project scope and schedule will be required in order to meet the cost constraints of the project.

Reference: *PMBOK® Guide,* 6th Ed., page 234

141. B. An agile release plan provides a high-level summary timeline of the release schedule based on the product roadmap and vision for the product's evolution. A release plan is derived from the product roadmap. The project team uses the release plan to determine the number of iterations required to have a releasable product to be customer.

Reference: *PMBOK® Guide,* 6th Ed., page 216

142. B. When considering a project in an adaptive environment where there is a high degree of variability and the scope of the project is not fully defined, according to the *Agile Practice Guide®*, "lightweight estimation methods can be used to generate a fast, high-level forecast of project labor costs, which can then be easily adjusted as changes arise." In this scenarios, detail estimates are typically reserved for short-term planning purposes. Funding limit reconciliation contents with reconciling the expenditure of funds with any limits on the commitment of funds for the project. In cost aggregation deals with summing the lower-level cost estimates associated with the various work packages for a given level within the project's WBS.

Reference: *PMBOK® Guide*, 6th Ed., page 234 and *Agile Practice Guide®*, page 92

143. C. Recurring retrospectives evaluate the root-cause of the issues and suggest trails of new approaches to improve and increase the effectiveness of the quality processes. In adaptive environments work is undertaken in small batches so that inconsistencies or issues can be easily identified.

Reference: *PMBOK® Guide,* 6th Ed., page 276

144. C. The project sponsor and customer representatives are continuously engaged to provide feedback on the deliverables created to ensure the product backlog reflects the business needs. Although the project owner acts as the voice of the customer and represents the interests of the customer, ultimately it is the customer who can validate and control the scope of the project.

Reference: *PMBOK® Guide,* 6th Ed., page 131

145. C. It is getting difficult to define a long-term scope and adapt to the changing needs in this fast-paced and high variability projects. Therefore adaptive planning uses iterative and on-demand scheduling methods for effective schedule management. Iterative scheduling with a backlog if a form of rolling wave planning and on-demand scheduling is used on flow-based adaptive methods such as Kanban.

Reference: *PMBOK® Guide,* 6th Ed., page 177 and *Agile Practice Guide®*, page 32

146. B. In agile release planning typically a duration of 3 to 6 months is considered for a high-level release schedule summary. Based on this release schedule the team is able to determine the number of iterations required and allows the team to decide on the time to develop a releasable product based on the business needs.

Reference: *PMBOK® Guide,* 6th Ed., page 216

147. C. Long-term partnership with suppliers are beneficial to the organization and suppliers to meet the customer needs and expectations, optimize costs and resources and create value to each other. *PMBOK® Guide, 6th Ed.,* "an organization and its suppliers are interdependent. Relationships based on partnership and cooperation with the supplier are more beneficial to the organization and to the suppliers than traditional supplier management."

Reference: *PMBOK® Guide,* 6th Ed., page 275

148. C. When considering project quality management, customer expectations are met through understanding, evaluating, defining, and managing requirements. Stakeholder engagement with the team ensures that the customer expectations are met and satisfaction is maintained throughout the project in agile environment.

Reference: *PMBOK® Guide,* 6th Ed., page 275

149. A. The scope and schedule are often adjusted to stay within cost constraints of projects with high degree of uncertainty as the scope is not yet fully defined and there might be frequent changes. In this case, due to the budget constraints, a minimum viable product can be delivered to ensure basic functionality of this mobile app.

Reference: *PMBOK® Guide,* 6th Ed., page 234 and *Agile Practice Guide®*, page 23

150. D. Agile methods focus on small batches of work throughout the project lifecycle in order to facilitate changes and incremental delivery. According to the *PMBOK® Guide, 6th Ed.,* "in order to navigate changes, agile methods call for frequent quality and review steps build in throughout the project rather than toward the end of the project."

Reference: *PMBOK® Guide,* 6th Ed., page 276

151. C. When working in an agile project, at times, it may make sense to stop and take stock of the work that the team has committed to completing and asking relevant questions rather than simply forging through to complete the committed work. It is important to encourage the team to always to be thinking of the simplest and the most cost-effective way to do something without compromising quality. Although it is important to keep to commitments, if it means that stopping to take a different approach may save time and money, then the teams are encouraged to ask the relevant questions as appropriate.

Reference: *Agile Practice Guide®*, pages 9, 59

152. C. When agile projects are built around motivated individuals, and the team is provided with the appropriate environment to be successful, there is no need to direct and manage the project work. As stated in the *Agile Practice Guide®*, "a core tenet in both the values and principles of the Agile Manifesto is the importance of individuals and interactions." Teams should be encouraged to self-organize the work and openly communicate issues and risks. Colocated team workspaces help promote better communication and collaboration among team members.

Reference: *Agile Practice Guide®*, pages 9, 38-39

153. A. Predictive life cycles allow for the bulk of the planning to occur upfront; then the project is executed using a sequential process in a single pass. According to the *Agile Practice Guide®*, "when a team works on a project where there is little opportunity for interim deliverables or little opportunity for prototyping, the team most likely will use a predictive life cycle to manage it. The team can adapt to what it discovers, but will not be able to use agile approaches to manage the iterative discovery of requirements or incremental deliverables for feedback."

Reference: *Agile Practice Guide®*, page 15-17

154. B. There is a shared heritage between agile and Kanban. According to the *Agile Practice Guide®* "delivering value, respect for people, minimizing waste, being transparent, adapting to change, and continuously improving" are commons across these approaches. Lean attributes are shared by both agile and Kanban Methods. Kanban is less prescriptive than most agile approaches as it uses a flow-based system and you start where you are as opposed to setting a firm timeline or following timeboxes. Kanban is widely incorporated within agile settings.

Reference: *Agile Practice Guide®*, pages 12-13

155. D. Prototypes can be used in both predictive as well as agile methods. They are a means of obtaining early feedback on requirements by providing a working model of the expected product before actually building it.

Reference: *PMBOK® Guide*, Ed., 6th Ed., pages, 147, 717 and *Agile Practice Guide®*, page 21

156. B. According to the *Agile Practice Guide®*, "agile favors empirical and value-based measurements instead of predictive measurements." Often projects that are green turn to red status with virtually no warning as there is no empirical data that supports predictive measurements. Using relative measures allows teams better assess, estimate, and deliver their work.

Reference: *Agile Practice Guide®*, pages 60-61

157. B. Fixed-price increments allow the customer more control over how the money is spent as you do not have to lock down the entire project scope into a single agreement. A multi-tiered structure achieves flexibility by describing different aspects of the project in different documents. Graduated time and materials contract reward the supplier with higher hourly rates if the work is done earlier than contracted and conversely the supplier would suffer the penalties if the deliverables are late. A dynamic scope option provides the customer the option to vary the project scope at specified points in the project.

Reference: *Agile Practice Guide®*, page 77-78

158. A. Agile recommends that a team be dedicated to the project. Working on more than one project can cause several issues. According to the *Agile Practice Guide®*, "people experience productivity losses somewhere between 20% and 40% when task switching. The loss increases exponentially with the number of tasks." Similar issues of productivity losses are also experienced with multitasking.

Reference: *Agile Practice Guide®*, page 45

159. C. The role of the servant leader is vital to the success of the agile transformation and implementation. This role should be not replaced by an agile coach. An external agile coach can help establish the role of a servant leader for an organization that is newly adopting agile practices.

Reference: *Agile Practice Guide®*, page 41

160. B. A team charter can also be referred to as a social contract. It captures the team values and how they wish to work together. Acceptance criteria define how the work product will pass inspection or be accepted, and a resource management plan determines how project resources should be managed, allocated, and released.

Reference: *PMBOK® Guide,* 6th Ed., pages 319-320 and *Agile Practice Guide®*, pages 49-50

161. C. According to the *Agile Practice Guide®*, "in order to accelerate the sharing of information within and across the organization, agile methods promote aggressive transparency." Aggressive transparency can include inviting stakeholders to project meetings, posting project artifacts in public spaces so that everyone can review the status of the project and help support in resolving misalignments, dependencies, and any other issues that may be apparent.

Reference: *Agile Practice Guide®*, page 95

162. D. Iteration based agile team typically work in two week cycles. The demonstration reviews are scheduled at the end of the iteration and not in a predefined window of time. The product owner reviews the completed increments and accepts or rejects the work.

Reference: *Agile Practice Guide®*, page 55

163. C. Introducing agile approaches into an organization does not necessarily displace traditional project management methods, rather the two can complement each other. As stated in *PMBOK® Guide, Ed.*, the "project life cycle needs to be flexible enough to deal with the variety of factors included in the project." The ability to evolve and adapt is more relevant in environments where there is a high degree of change and uncertainty. When moving to an adaptive environment, organizations are also experiencing a high degree of change.

Reference: *PMBOK® Guide,* 6th Ed., pages 19, 665 and *Agile Practice Guide®*, 73-74

164. B. Kanban Method is most suitable for environments when a team or organization is in need of flexibility with a focus on continuous delivery. Kanban does not use time-boxed iterations, as stated in the *Agile Practice Guide®*, "the principle of pulling single items through the process continuously and limiting work in progress to optimize flow should always remain intact."

Reference: *Agile Practice Guide®*, page 103

165. D. Backlog refinement allows the product owner to present the story ideas and then work with the team to ensure they have all the information needed to plan the next iteration. The estimates for the stories are provided by the team and not the product owner.

Reference: *Agile Practice Guide®*, pages 52-53

166. D. Face-to-face communication is the preferred communication mechanism for agile teams as identified in one of the 12 principles that support the Agile Manifesto: "the most efficient and effective method of conveying information to and within a development team is a face-to-face conversation." Push communications involves sending or distributing information directly but does not guarantee that it was received or the message intended was understood. Conversely, pull communications require that the intended audience or recipients to proactively access content or information through vehicles such as websites, knowledge repositories or a lessons learned database.

Reference: *PMBOK® Guide,* 6th Ed., page 374 and *Agile Practice Guide®* page 9

167. D. Resource planning can be challenging in projects with high variability as there is less time in decision making and centralized tasking. As stated in *PMBOK® Guide, 6th Ed.*, "in these environments, agreements for fast supply and lean methods are critical to controlling costs and achieving the schedule."

Reference: *PMBOK® Guide,* 6th Ed., page 312

168. B. The projects with high uncertainty and risk focus on knowledge sharing between the cross-functional teams and frequently review of the deliverables after each iteration to ensure risks are understood, managed and mitigated.

Reference: *PMBOK® Guide,* 6th Ed., page 397-400

169. D. Although it is important to consider the cost of globally distributed teams in comparison to local teams working on an adaptive project, this issue would be considered in project cost management and project resource management as opposed to project communication management.

Reference: *PMBOK® Guide,* 6th Ed., pages 233, 313, 365

170. D. Earned schedule (ES)/actual time (AT) indicates the efficiency with which the work is being accomplished (not planned). According the *PMBOK® Guide, 6th Ed.,* "ES is an extension to the theory and practice of EVM. Earned schedule theory replaces the schedule variance measures used in traditional EVM (earned value – planned value) with ES and actual (AT)."

Reference: *PMBOK® Guide,* 6th Ed., pages 233

171. A. Projects in high-variability environments where the scope has not been fully defined will not benefit from detailed cost estimates. According to the *PMBOK® Guide, 6th Ed.,* "lightweight estimation methods can be used to generate a fast, high-level forecast of project labor costs, which can then be easily adjusted as changes arise." Detailed estimates are typically only done in short-term planning horizons.

Reference: *PMBOK® Guide,* 6th Ed., page 234 and *Agile Practice Guide®* page 92

172. D. A hybrid approach is combining two or more agile and non-agile elements, usually producing a non-agile end result. As the practice of project management evolves, the project life cycles need to remain flexible enough to deal with the various factors that impact a project.

Reference: *PMBOK® Guide,* 6th Ed., pages 19, 73-74, 178, 679 and *Agile Practice Guide®* page 26

173. C. Typically on agile projects the needs, interests, and requirements of the customer and represented by the role of the product owner. Although customer representatives can attend some project meetings, it is not necessary that they be present at all meetings as the role of the product owner represents their needs on the project.

Reference: *Agile Practice Guide®* pages 9, 41

174. A. Adoption of agile practices are increasing at rapid rates. Since the first publication of the agile manifesto in 2001, organizations have been embracing an agile mindset. According to the *Agile Best Practice Guide®*, "adoption and the desire to operate with an agile mindset is no longer limited to a certain sized organization or those specializing only in information technology." Inspection, adaption, and transparency are critical success factors for delivering value using agile practices.

Reference: *Agile Best Practice Guide®*, page 87

175. D. Developing and implementing appropriate communication strategies adds value to projects and promotes effective stakeholder engagement for successful delivery of the project objectives. These strategies can be the inclusion of stakeholders in project reviews and project meetings, the increasing use of social computing, and taking a multifaceted approach to project communication. According to the *PMBOK® Guide, 6th Ed.*, "along with a focus on stakeholders and recognition of the value to projects and organizations of effective stakeholder engagement comes the recognition that developing and implementing appropriate communication strategies is vital to maintaining effective relationships with stakeholders."

Reference: *PMBOK® Guide,* 6th Ed., page 364

176. D. Project managers spend most of their time in communicating with team members and project stakeholders. As the practice of project management evolves, so has the strategies for effective project communications. The inclusion of stakeholders in project meetings and reviews such as daily standups where appropriate will increase awareness to project progress, risks, and issues. Taking a multifaceted approach to communications such as considering cultural issues, language, generation gaps will be vital. The use of social computing and social media has also supported the increase of effective information exchange. Although engaging with stakeholders who are most affected is very important to the success of the project, this aspect is considered in project stakeholder management as opposed to project communication management.

Reference: *PMBOK® Guide,* 6th Ed., *page* 364

177. A. Non-event risks can be categorized as variability risks and ambiguity risks. Examples of variability risks can include errors found during testing or issues related seasonality such as unforeseen weather impacting the delivery of goods. Ambiguity risks can include areas of the project where uncertainties that might happen in the future such as deficient knowledge might affect the project's ability to achieve its objectives. According to the *PMBOK® Guide, 6th Ed.*, "there is an increasing recognition that non-event risks need to be identified and managed." Technical, management, commercial, and external risks are more traditional categories of sources of risks.

Reference: *PMBOK® Guide,* 6th Ed., pages 398, 406

178. D. Emotional intelligence contends with improving inbound and outbound competencies. Inbound competencies include self-management and self-awareness whereas outbound competencies deal with relationship management. According to the *PMBOK® Guide*, "research suggests that project teams that succeed in developing team EI or become an emotionally competent group are more effective." Being politically astute and having the ability to make things happen can be categorized as political intelligence.

Reference: *PMBOK® Guide,* 6th Ed., pages 310, 349

179. B. Due to resource constraints of critical resources, in some industries, several trends have emerged. Embracing lean management concepts such as just-in-time (JIT), Kaizen, total productive maintenance (TPM), and theory of constraints (TOC) can optimize resource utilization and control project costs.

Reference: *PMBOK® Guide,* 6th Ed., page 310 and *Agile Practice Guide®* page 93

180. A. According to the *PMBOK® Guide, Ed., 6th Ed.,* "complexity itself is a perception of an individual based on personal experience, observation, and skill. Rather than being complex, a project is more accurately described as containing complexity." The three dimensions of complexity can be defined as: system behavior which is the interdependencies of components and systems; human behavior which is the interplay between diverse individual and groups; ambiguity which is the uncertainty of emerging issues and lack of understanding or confusion.

Reference: *PMBOK® Guide,* 6th Ed., page 68

181. C. According to the *PMBOK® Guide, 6th Ed.*, "an organization and its suppliers are interdependent. Relationships based on partnership and cooperation with the supplier are more beneficial to the organization and to the suppliers than traditional supplier management." Mutually beneficial partnerships with suppliers will meet and exceed customer needs and expectations, optimize costs and resources and create value for each other.

Reference: *PMBOK® Guide,* 6th Ed., page 275

182. C. Agile projects benefit from project team structure that improves collaboration among team members. In order to achieve the best outcomes for the project, agile advocates the use of "generalist-specialists." These team members have a specialized set of skills in one area and general knowledge in other areas of project requirements. This is especially useful when back-ups are required, and team members need to support each other for the successful delivery of the project.

Reference: *Agile Practice Guide®* page 40

183. D. Aggressive transparency promotes the acceleration of sharing information within and across the organization. This can include but not limited to inviting stakeholders to project meetings and review, posting artifacts in open spaces so that any misalignments, issues, dependencies related to the project can be surfaced as quickly as possible. Depending on the severity and impact of the issue, the information may also be shared with senior and executive management as appropriate.

Reference: *PMBOK® Guide,* 6th Ed., page 506 and *Agile Practice Guide®* page 123

184. A. Many project management frameworks have emerged to cater to a variety of project needs. Some frameworks are more formalized than others. Frameworks can support both predictive and adaptive approaches. Scrum, extreme programming, DSDM, Kanban, and Scrumban are examples of project frameworks. Selecting the most appropriate framework depending on the needs of the project will be vital to the success of the project.

Reference: *PMBOK® Guide,* 6th Ed., pages 19, 548 and *Agile Practice Guide®* page 80

185. A. As stated in the *PMBOK® Guide, 6th Ed.*, "agile release planning provides a high-level summary timeline of the release schedule (typically 3 to 6 months) based on the product roadmap and the product vision for the product's evolution." With inputs from the customer, this high-level timeline is created by the product owner in concert with the team. The high-level release schedule will determine how many sprints the team will need to complete a releasable product.

Reference: *PMBOK® Guide,* 6th Ed., page 216

186. A. An agile practitioner is a broad term that describes those involved in agile practices. This term is not limited to a servant leader, however, a servant leader would be considered an agile practitioner. According to the *Agile Practice Guide®,* an agile practitioner is "a person embracing the agile mindset who collaborates with like-minded colleagues in cross-functional teams." An agile practitioner can also be referred to as an agilest.

Reference: *PMBOK® Guide,* 6th Ed., pages 10, 37, 548 and *Agile Practice Guide®* page 150

187. D. Distributed teams have cross-functional team members, at times in small clusters, working in different locations whereas dispersed teams may have each team member working from a different location. Due to the globalization of projects, it is no longer viable to only consider colocated teams for agile/adaptive projects. Although agile promotes face to face communication, and when possible it is considered the preferred method, more often than not organizations are now having to look to a global workforce. Organizations are also benefiting from being able to garner specialized skills that may not be readily available in a specific geographic area. Provided careful consideration is given to strategies that bridge the gap of physical distance among team members, distributed and dispersed teams can be a viable option for agile and adaptive projects.

Reference: *PMBOK® Guide,* 6th Ed., page 311 and *Agile Practice Guide®* pages 43-45, 122

188. A. A basic system or structure of ideas or facts that support an approach is called a framework. Tailoring is known as using the appropriate combination of processes, inputs, tools, techniques, outputs, and life cycle phases. A standard is a document established by an authority, custom, or general consent as a model for example.

Reference: *PMBOK® Guide, 6th Ed.*, pages 2, 28, 711, 723

189. B. Disciplined Agile blends various agile techniques and follows the principles of putting people first; encourages collaborative improvement; promotes full delivery life cycle; it is goal-driven; it offers guidance at an enterprise level, and it is scalable covering multiple dimensions of program complexity.

Reference: *Agile Practice Guide®* page 114

190. C. Enterprise Scrum can be utilized in various sizes of organizations including small, medium, and large companies. It is viewed as a holistic approach that extends beyond a single project, and its techniques can be generalized and customized to fit the needs of the organization. It can also be scaled as necessary.

Reference: *Agile Practice Guide®* page 114

191. B. A team charter works best when the team prepares it. It provides structure, guidelines, and basic team operating principles and agreements. The team charter can guide how the team will make decisions, conduct meetings, and resolve conflicts. A team charter can be used in both predictive as well as agile and adaptive projects.

Reference: *PMBOK® Guide, Ed.*, pages 318-319, 347, 724 and *Agile Practice Guide®*, page 49

192. C. An agile PMO is multidisciplinary with competencies that extend beyond the discipline of project management. According to the *Agile Practice Guide®*, the role of multi-project management is to "coordinate between agile teams by communicating between projects. Consider sharing items such as progress, issues, and retrospective findings and improvement experiments. Help manage major customer releases at the program level and investment themes at the portfolio level using an appropriate framework." Any decisions related to how best the team should proceed with the project execution is left to the self-organizing and cross-functional team.

Reference: *Agile Practice Guide®*, page 82

193. D. Depending on the size, scale, and capabilities of the organization at times it may be best to outsource the project delivery to a vendor. Agile and adaptive projects can be successfully delivered using vendors provided the risks and issues are carefully considered and managed. Contracts should also be carefully crafted so that equitable financial viability is considered for all parties. In order to help mitigate the loss of product knowledge, staying engaged in agile practices such as retrospectives and other meetings and will ensure knowledge transfer.

Reference: *Agile Practice Guide®*, page 83

194. D. Osmotic communication was first embraced by the founder of crystal methods. It contends with communicating via osmosis where team members can hear conversations and pick up relevant information as necessary. This occurs when the team is working in colocated workspaces.

Reference: *Agile Practice Guide®*, page 107

195. B. Scrum of Scrum also known as "Meta Scrum." It is a scaling technique to coordinate multiple Scrum teams. It can be scaled to support multiple Scrum teams at the project, program, and portfolio levels. According to the *Agile Practice Guide®*, Scrum of Scrum of Scrums can be used on "large projects with several teams may result in conducting a Scrum of Scrum of Scrums, which follows the same pattern as SoS with a representative from each SoS reporting into a larger group of representatives."

Reference: *Agile Practice Guide®*, page 111

196. B. The Kanban Method uses the role of a flow master to manage the flow of work. This role can also be referred to as a service request manager or a team coach. The flow master is focused on helping and supporting the team similar to the scrum master on scum projects.

Reference: *Agile Practice Guide®* pages 12, 151

197. A. According to *PMBOK® Guide,* 6th Ed., "project life cycles can range along a continuum from predictive approaches at one end to adaptive or agile approaches at the other." The series of phases that a project passes through from its inception to completion is called life cycle. Particularly, agile life cycle is an approach that is both iterative and incremental to refine work items and frequent delivery. An incremental life cycle is an approach where finished deliverables can be sent to the customer for immediate use. In predictive life cycles the project scope, time and cost are determined in the early phases of the project.

Reference: *PMBOK® Guide,* 6th Ed., pages 19, 665 and *Agile Practice Guide®*, page 17

198. D. At times it may be necessary to tailor an approach to best suit the needs of the organization. Due to the exploratory nature of this project, both adaptive and predictive methods can be considered. Prior to selecting and potentially tailoring multiple approaches, it is best to learn about agile project management and then craft the best approach that will be most beneficial to the organization. It is not necessary to only take a predictive method.

Reference: *Agile Practice Guide®*, page 32

199. C. The role of a service request manager is used in Kanban to manage the flow of work. A service request manager can be synonymous with the role of the product owner.

Reference: *Agile Practice Guide®* pages 12, 154

200. A. If you are experiencing unexpected and or unforeseen delays you will want to ask the team to check in more frequently, visibly track impediments on an impediment board, and try to visualize the flow of work in progress using a tool such as the kanban board. When dealing with difficult stakeholder demands, you might employ a servant leadership style with either the stakeholder or product owner to facilitate team empowerment. The issue of siloed teams can be managed by asking project members to self-organize as cross-functional teams and articulate why this is beneficial from an agile perspective. Unclear work assignments can be resolved by helping the team to manage their work.

Reference: *Agile Practice Guide®*, page 59

Bonus Questions

201. A. Except for identifying business needs, which is part of the Project Scope Management knowledge area, the other options are considered trends and best practices in Project Integration Management knowledge area.

Reference: *PMBOK® Guide*, 6th Ed., pages 73, 132

202. B. Knowledge and requirements management should be considered when tailoring the application of Project Scope Management processes into a project. The other factors are associated with the Project Integration Management knowledge area.

Reference: *PMBOK® Guide,* 6th Ed., pages 133, 74

203. C. Trends and emerging practices in Project Schedule Management knowledge are comprise of iterative scheduling with a backlog and on-demand scheduling. The othe options are associated with Project Integration Management and Project Cost Management knowledge areas.

Reference: *PMBOK® Guide*, 6th Ed., pages 177, 73, 233

204. D. Some of the general financial management techniques used in Project Cost Management are return on investment, discounted cash flow, and investment payback analysis. The other options are key concepts from Project Integration Management, Project Scope Management, and Project Schedule Management knowledge areas.

Reference: *PMBOK® Guide*, 6th Ed., pages 233, 72, 131, 175

205. A. Trends and emerging practices in Project Quality Management knowledge area comprise of customer satisfaction, continual improvement, management responsibility, and mutually beneficial partnership with suppliers. Emotional intelligence is one of the trends and emerging practices in Project Resource Management knowledge area.

Reference: *PMBOK® Guide*, 6th Ed., pages 275, 310